ETHNOGRAPHY FOR E

DOING QUALITATIVE RESEARCH IN EDUCATIONAL SETTINGS

Series Editor: Pat Sikes

The aim of this series is to provide a range of high-quality introductory research methods texts. Each volume focuses, critically, on one particular methodology enabling a detailed yet accessible discussion. All of the contributing authors are established researchers with substantial practical experience. While every book has its own unique style, each discusses the historical background of the approach, epistemological issues and appropriate uses. They then go on to describe the operationalization of the approach in educational settings, drawing upon specific and vivid examples from the authors' own work. The intention is that readers should come away with a level of understanding that enables them to feel sufficiently confident to undertake their own research as well as to critically evaluate other accounts of research using the approach.

Published and forthcoming titles

ETHNOGRAPHY FOR EDUCATION

Christopher Pole and Marlene Morrison

Open University Press

Open University Press
McGraw-Hill Education
McGraw-Hill House
Shoppenhangers Road
Maidenhead
Berkshire
England
SL6 2QL

email: enquiries@openup.co.uk
world wide web: www.openup.co.uk

First published 2003

A catalogue record of this book is available from the British Library

ISBN 0 335 20600 X (pb)   0 335 20601 8 (hb)

Library of Congress Cataloging-in-Publication Data
CIP data has been applied for

Typeset by RefineCatch Limited, Bungay, Suffolk
Printed in the UK by Bell & Bain Ltd, Glasgow

For Jacqueline, Charlotte and Lizzie (CP)

For Bethan and her future in education (MM)

Contents

Series editor's preface

I had never realized just how fascinating research was in its own right. I was expecting the research methods course to be boring, difficult and all about statistics but I couldn't have been more wrong. There is so much to consider, so many aspects, so many ways of finding out what's going on, and not just one way of representing it too. I have really been surprised.

(Student taking an MA in educational studies)

I never knew that there was so much to research. I thought that you just chose a method, applied it, did your statistical sums and came up with your findings. The reality is more complicated but so much more interesting and meaningful.

(Student taking an MA in educational studies)

The best thing for me was being told that qualitative research is 'proper' research – providing it's done properly of course. What goes on in schools is so complex and involves so many different perspectives that I think you often need a qualitative approach to begin to get some idea of what's going on.

(Student taking an MA in sociology)

I really appreciate hearing about other researchers' experiences of doing research. It was quite a revelation when I first became aware that things don't always go as smoothly as some written accounts seem to suggest. It's really reassuring to hear honest reports: they alert you to pitfalls and problems and things that you might not have thought about.

(Doctoral student)

I am sure that comments such as these will be familiar to anyone who has ever taught or taken a course which aims to introduce the range of research approaches available to social scientists in general and those working in educational settings in particular.

The central message that they convey seems to be that the influence of the positivist scientist paradigm is both strong and pervasive, shaping expectations of what constitutes 'proper', 'valid' and 'worthwhile' research. What Barry Troyna wrote in 1994 continues to be the case, namely that:

> There is a view which is already entrenched and circulating widely in the populist circles ... that qualitative research is subjective, value-laden and, therefore, unscientific and invalid, in contrast to quantitative research, which meets the criteria of being objective, value-free, scientific and therefore valid.
>
> (1994: 9)

Within academic and research circles, though, where the development of postmodernist and poststructuralist ideas have affected both thinking and research practice, it can be easy to forget what the popular perspective is. This is because, in these communities, qualitative researchers from the range of theoretical standpoints utilize a variety of methods, approaches, strategies and techniques in the full confidence that their work is rigorous, legitimate and totally justifiable as research. And the process of peer review serves to confirm that confidence.

Recently, however, for those concerned with and involved in research in educational settings, and especially for those engaged in educational research, it seems that the positivist model, using experimental, scientific, quantitative methods, is definitely in the ascendancy once again. The signs are there to be read in, for example, the types of research that receive financial support, in the curricula that are being specified by funding councils for postgraduate research methods training programmes, and in the way in which those of us working in England and Wales entered the new millennium with the government-endorsed exhortation to produce evidence-based research that,

> [first] demonstrates conclusively that if teachers change their practice from x to y there will be significant and enduring improvement in teaching and learning; and [second] has developed an effective method of convincing teachers of the benefits of, and means to, changing from x to y.
>
> (Hargreaves 1996: 5)

If it is to realize its commendable aims of school effectiveness and school improvement, research as portrayed here demands 'objectivity', experiments and statistical proofs. There is a problem with this requirement, though, and the essence of it is that educational institutions and the individuals who are involved in and with them are a heterogeneous bunch with different attributes, abilities, aptitudes, aims, values, perspectives, needs and so on. Furthermore these institutions and individuals are located within complex social contexts with all the implications and influences that this entails.

On its own, research whose findings can be expressed in mathematical terms is unlikely to be sophisticated enough to sufficiently accommodate and account for the myriad differences that are involved. As one group of prominent educational researchers have noted:

> We will argue that schooling does have its troubles. However, we maintain that the analysis of the nature and location of these troubles by the school effectiveness research literature, and in turn those writing Department for Employment and Education policy off the back of this research, is oversimplified, misleading and thereby educationally and politically dangerous (notwithstanding claims of honourable intent).
>
> (Slee *et al.* 1998: 2–3)

There is a need for rigorous research which does not ignore, but rather addresses, the complexity of the various aspects of schools and schooling: for research which explores and takes account of different objective experiences and subjective perspectives, and which acknowledges that qualitative information is essential, both in its own right and also in order to make full and proper use of quantitative indicators. The Doing Qualitative Research in Educational Settings series of books is based on this fundamental belief. Thus the overall aims of the series are: to illustrate the potential that particular qualitative approaches have for research in educational settings, and to consider some of the practicalities involved and issues that are raised when doing qualitative research, so that readers will feel equipped to embark on research of their own.

At this point it is worth noting that qualitative research is difficult to define as it means different things at different times and in different contexts. Having said this, Denzin and Lincoln's (2000) generic definition offers a useful starting point:

> Qualitative research is a situated activity that locates the observer in the world. It consists of a set of interpretive, material practices that make the world visible. These practices transform the world. They turn the world into a series of representations, including fieldnotes, interviews, conversations, photographs, recordings and memos to the self. At this level, qualitative research involves an interpretive, naturalistic approach to the world. This means that qualitative researchers study things in their natural settings, attempting to make sense of, or interpret, phenomena in terms of the meanings people bring to them. Qualitative research involves the studied use and collection of a variety of empirical materials – case study; personal experience; introspection; life story; interview; artefacts; cultural texts and productions; observational, historical, interactional and visual texts – that describe routine and problematic moments and meanings in individuals' lives. Accordingly, qualitative researchers deploy a wide range

of interconnected methods, hoping always to get a better fix on the subject matter at hand. It is understood, however, that each practice makes the world visible in a different way. Hence there is frequently a commitment to using more than one interpretive practice in any study.

(Denzin and Lincoln 2000: 3–4)

All of the authors contributing to the series are established researchers with a wealth of experience on which to draw and all make use of specific and vivid examples from their own and others' work. A consequence of this use of examples is the way in which writers convey a sense of research being an intensely satisfying and enjoyable activity, in spite of the specific difficulties that are sometimes encountered. This is unequivocally the case with *Ethnography for Education*, where fieldnotes and researcher diaries are used in such a way as to provide a very real sense of what it can be like to be an ethnographer working in a school – Marlene Morrison's notes from a project that investigated primary school libraries are particularly evocative!

While they differ in terms of structure and layout, most of the books in the series deal with:

- The historical background of the approach: how it developed; examples of its use; implications for its use at the present time.
- Epistemological issues: the nature of the data produced; and the roles of the researcher and the researched.
- Appropriate uses: in what research contexts and for which research questions is the approach most appropriate; and where might the research be inappropriate or unlikely to yield the best data.

They also describe and discuss, using the approach in educational settings, looking at such matters as:

- How to do it: designing and setting up the research; planning and preparation; negotiating access; likely problems; technical details; recording of data.
- Ethical considerations: the roles of and the relationship between the researcher and the researched; ownership of data; issues of honesty.
- Data analysis.
- Presentation of findings: issues to do with writing up and presenting findings.

As Christopher Pole and Marlene Morrison note, 'ethnography has become, if not the dominant, then certainly one of the most frequently adopted approaches to educational research in recent years' (this volume, p.1). However, having said this, there is by no means consensus on what constitutes an ethnographic study, and the term 'ethnography' has even been used as a synonym for qualitative research per se. *Ethnography for*

Education sets out to clear up some of the ambiguities and offers a definition that is clear and workable by those who choose to use the approach in educational settings.

Essentially, ethnography seeks to make sense of social settings and social behaviours from inside, privileging the perspectives of the people involved in the situation that is the focus of the investigation. Interview, observation and documentary analysis are, not surprisingly, key research methods within the methodology. Christopher Pole and Marlene Morrison argue for 'inclusive ethnography', that is ethnography which utilizes whatever methods which produce data that shed useful light on the situation. They are, therefore, not opposed to the use of quantitative methods, providing they do not disrupt naturalness.

In arguing a case for ethnography as distinctive research in terms of its scope, the position of the researcher vis-à-vis the researched, the nature of the data it yields and the processes of analysis which those data then undergo, *Ethnography for Education* offers a uniquely thorough, comprehensive, thoughtful and critical text that will be of value to anyone contemplating using the approach.

Final note

It was Barry Troyna who initially came up with the idea for this series. Although his publishing career was extensive, Barry had never been a series editor and, in his inimitable way, was very keen to become one. While he was probably best known for his work in the field of 'race', Barry was getting increasingly interested in issues to do with methodology when he became ill with the cancer which was eventually to kill him. It was during the 12 months of his illness that he and I drew up a proposal and approached potential authors. All of us knew that it was very likely that he would not live to see the series in print but he was adamant that it should go ahead, nonetheless. The series is, therefore, something of a memorial to him and royalties from it will be going to the Radiotherapy Unit at the Walsgrave Hospital in Coventry.

Pat Sikes

Acknowledgements

The idea for this book can be located in our experience as educational researchers and teachers of research methods. We hope to have made good use of the different situations we have encountered as ethnographers working in a wide range of educational institutions and to have succeeded in encouraging others to seek similar experiences.

Our research practices and hence much of the content of this book has benefited from working with supportive colleagues over many years and on different studies. In particular we would like to acknowledge Angela Bolton, Bob Burgess, Sheila Galloway, John Hockey, Phil Mizen, Patrick Roach, David Scott and Rob Watling, as well as many students at the universities of Leicester and Warwick who have helped us to refine our ideas and occasionally bring us back to earth! As usual, none of these people can be held responsible for any of the deficiencies of this book, which are of course our own.

1 | Defining ethnography

Knowing what it is and knowing what it isn't

In choosing to open and read this book about ethnography and education it is probably fairly safe to assume that you, the reader, know something about ethnography and education. We, the authors, might assume that you are required to conduct a piece of research which focuses on some aspect of education and that you have decided to consider ethnography as the most appropriate or the most attractive way of doing the research. Alternatively, it could be that you are considering a range of approaches to research including ethnography, or that you are simply curious about ethnography and education and want to find out more. Whatever the reason, we think it is likely that you know something, perhaps in a very general or vague way, not only about what ethnography is, but also about what it is not. It may be that in seeking to identify appropriate research methodology or methods it is important to know what something isn't as well as what it is.

You probably know something about ethnography for two reasons. First of all because, as Hammersley (1990) said in his book *Reading Ethnographic Research*, there are now many texts about ethnography which introduce students to how to do it, and there have been many more since Hammersley wrote this in 1990. Second and related to Hammersley's point, ethnography has become, if not the dominant, then certainly one of the most frequently adopted approaches to educational research in recent years. At the same time, you probably know something about what ethnography isn't, as in many of the books to which Hammersley refers ethnography is presented as an alternative approach to something like survey-based research. Consequently you may have some idea of what can and cannot be achieved by using ethnography.

The issue of what ethnography is and what ethnography isn't is worth pursuing in these early pages of the book as it relates not only to ethnography as a process, that is, how ethnography is done and the research methods that it may utilize, but also to the kind of knowledge that ethnography might yield, that is, the product of ethnographic research. Having said this, however, identifying what is and what is not ethnography is not straightforward. As Hammersley (1990) says many definitions of ethnography to emerge in recent years have used the term as a synonym for other broadly qualitative approaches to social research such as case study, life history, participant observation and even for qualitative research itself. In addition, more recently, John Brewer (2000) has drawn attention to a dichotomy between method and methodology in the context of ethnography in which he discusses the difference between the characterization of ethnography as a collection of particular research methods and as a theoretical and philosophical orientation towards research. Moreover, to complicate discussion about what is and what isn't ethnography even further, we might also add the fact that the term is frequently used both as a noun and a verb. Researchers talk about doing ethnography as an activity and they also talk about ethnographies as a product of their research, and the field of education has been a particularly fertile ground for ethnography and ethnographies over the last 20 years.

The general point to be made from what might be considered to be these somewhat confusing opening remarks, is that although the term ethnography may to some degree be familiar, its definition is not without ambiguity or complexity. The frequency with which the term is now used in educational and other fields of research may have led to, or at least contributed to, some of the ambiguity which surrounds ethnography, both as a noun and as a verb and may also have resulted in the range of research practice that is now characterized as ethnography. In order to take things further and in an attempt to resolve some of these ambiguities it will be useful to examine some of the characteristics of ethnography, to consider what might be achieved in using or doing ethnography and to offer a definition of ethnography which we will use throughout this book.

Characteristics

Useful insight into the characteristics of ethnography can be gained quite simply by reading many of the published ethnographies that exist. Whether you choose to read ethnographies which focus on educational or other issues it is likely that they will share certain characteristics in terms of the methods that have been used to conduct the research upon which they are based, the scope of the study in relation to its size and the range of issues it seeks to address, and the nature of the findings or the knowledge that the ethnography yields. Having speculated that there will be some common characteristics evident in all ethnographies we do not wish to imply that all ethnographies are the same or that adopting these characteristics as a kind of formula will result in a successful ethnography. Clearly, in reading different ethnographies we soon become aware that each is as individual as the subject matter on which it focuses and that the individuality is in itself a common characteristic of ethnography. However, for the purposes of this discussion we suggest that the principal common characteristics of ethnography are:

1 A focus on a discrete location, event(s) or setting.
2 A concern with the full range of social behaviour within the location, event or setting.
3 The use of a range of different research methods which may combine qualitative and quantitative approaches but where the emphasis is upon understanding social behaviour from inside the discrete location, event or setting.
4 An emphasis on data and analysis which moves from detailed description to the identification of concepts and theories which are grounded in the data collected within the location, event or setting.
5 An emphasis on rigorous or thorough research, where the complexities of the discrete event, location or setting are of greater importance than overarching trends or generalizations.

Having identified these five characteristics, there remains considerable latitude in respect of what constitutes ethnography. While the characteristics are not intended to act as a straitjacket, we do feel that they offer important signals not only as to what constitutes ethnography but also as to what distinguishes it from other forms of research. However, it may be argued that the characteristics are not exclusive to ethnography as they may be applied to other forms of research. This may be the case. Consequently, to add more detail to this attempt to identify and define ethnography it will be useful to consider what researchers expect to achieve by engaging in ethnography and producing ethnographies.

What ethnography achieves

To some extent the identification of common characteristics has already indicated what can be achieved by ethnography. Moreover, as we have already said, given that every ethnography is unique, the precise nature of what may be achieved will vary, in so far as it will reflect the particular circumstances of the discrete location, event or setting within which it is conducted. Nevertheless, in general terms we would hope that ethnography would achieve the following:

• The collection of detailed data, which would facilitate careful analysis of the kind outlined in Chapter 4.

- A comprehensive and contextualized description of the social action within the location, event or setting. Such descriptions are often described as rich, or thick (Geertz 1973).
- The portrayal of an insider's perspective, in which the meaning of the social action for the actors themselves is paramount and takes precedence over, but does not ignore, that of the researcher.
- The construction of an account of the discrete location, event or setting which is grounded in the collected data and which incorporates a conceptual framework that facilitates understanding of social action at both an empirical and theoretical level.

In addition there may be many other things that ethnography achieves concerning, for example, its impact in terms of policy, practice and change or in relation to individual actor's lives or roles within the specific setting. Again, many of these outcomes will be specific to the particular ethnography and therefore difficult to identify in this rather abstract way. Our intention here has been to identify the general features relating to the nature of the outcome of ethnography and what it may achieve in respect of knowledge and understanding of the social world.

Method and methodology

In identifying common characteristics and outcomes we may be seen to relate broadly to what Brewer (2000) refers to as ethnography as method and ethnography as methodology. While we have already said that ethnography's relevance to both of these may contribute to the ambiguity and lack of clarity on what it is in any absolute sense, we would argue that the difference between method and methodology is important not just for ethnography but for research more generally. Moreover, we would also argue that a more complete understanding of ethnography can be achieved only if it is considered in relation to both method and methodology. Brewer outlines the generally accepted view that method refers to the tools that a researcher might use to gather data, for example, questionnaires, interviews, participant observation and so on, and to the techniques by which the collected data are analysed, for example, close reading of text, content analysis, statistical inference and computer aided qualitative data analysis. In both cases, method refers to the rules and procedures that are followed to conduct empirical research consequently as Brewer (2000: 2) states: 'People are not free to design their questionnaire, do their observation or work out correlation coefficients any old way they want; or, at least not if they want their research to be seen as reliable'. In this way, methods can be seen to relate to the tool bag from which the researcher selects the most appropriate instrument with which to gather data and subsequently to analyse those data. Methods also act, therefore, to limit and constrain the data collection process, in the same way that the tools of a plumber or carpenter restrict the work that he or she can do (Pole and Lampard 2002). The common characteristics of ethnography which we identified above may be seen, in general terms, to relate to this notion of method, as these are what shape, limit and define not only what ethnography can do but also how it can be done.

With regard to methodology, Brewer identifies this as 'the broad theoretical and philosophical framework into which these procedural rules fit' (2000: 2). By this he refers to issues of epistemology and the nature of the knowledge that ethnography yields. As we have already said, this equates to our notion of what ethnography can achieve, or perhaps more usefully what we might regard as the outcomes of ethnography. In fairly common sense terms this relates to the accounts of social life studied within the discrete location or setting upon which the ethnography has focused. Again, in equally general and common sense terms we can see from ethnography's concern with everyday events and its emphasis on meaning and action that the accounts that it yields are usually insiders' accounts. That is, they are concerned not with presenting a distanced, scientific and objective account of the social world, but with an account that recognizes the subjective reality of the experiences of those people who constitute and construct the social world. In using the term subjective in this context we do not wish to infer that ethnography can be reduced to mere opinion, dogma or journalism. Our intention is to place ethnography within a theoretical tradition which places a primacy on the importance of situated meaning and contextualized experience as the basis for explaining and understanding social behaviour. Equally, this does not eschew the importance of structure in ethnographic accounts of social action. The concern with contextualized meaning ensures that the structures which shape, limit and in some cases define social action are central to the explanation and understanding of that action.

Similar accounts of the general theoretical and philosophical orientation of ethnography can be found in most of the texts on ethnography to emerge over the past 20 years. While each gives its own slightly different interpretation of the basic epistemological tenets that can be seen to underpin ethnography, the common theme to emerge is that ethnography is located within the approach of naturalism. For example, O'Connell-Davidson and Layder (1994) sate that contemporary ethnography's concern to study people in their natural environments rather than in situations which have been artificially created, as with laboratory or experimentally based research, means that it 'belongs to a tradition of "naturalism" which centralizes the importance of understanding the meanings and cultural practices of people from within the everyday settings in which they take place' (1994: 165).

They go on to locate this approach within the tradition of Verstehen and interpretative analysis. A decade before this, Hammersley and Atkinson

(1983), in what has been one of the most influential and widely read texts in this field, made largely the same point. They drew on Matza's (1969) words to characterize naturalism as 'the philosophical view that remains true to the nature of the phenomenon under study' (1969: 5). This emphasis on naturalism has embedded within it the assumption that human beings, social behaviour and social phenomena are fundamentally different from inanimate physical phenomena in that they are socially shaped and constructed by social actors, human beings rather than the forces of nature. Brewer (2000) locates naturalism with nineteenth century German philosophy of the Geisteswissenschaften tradition, within which human beings are seen to be the creators of their own social worlds rather than mere respondents to external stimuli. However, it is here that confusion can sometimes arise.

Although we locate ethnography within the general approach of naturalism it is not concerned with naturalistic research method. Rather it eschews this as anathema to the epistemological and ontological foundations of ethnography. In an attempt to clarify what is a commonly confused situation, therefore, we can state that naturalism is concerned with the setting and location within which social action is created and experienced. As Hammersley and Atkinson (1983) state, it draws on sociological and philosophical approaches of symbolic interactionism, phenomenology, hermeneutics, linguistic philosophy and ethnomethodology. In sharp contrast naturalistic approaches to research assume that social phenomena, rather like inanimate objects, may be researched by scientific, positivistic methods where concern is more with enumeration, generalization and notions of external, objective realities of the phenomena, rather than its significance and meaning to those involved in its creation.

From this discussion of theoretical and philosophical orientation it is not difficult to identify clear links between methods and methodology in the sense that Brewer (2000) defined them. Where methods are the tools used for data collection and methodology refers to the general theoretical and philosophical underpinnings of the research, then the link exists in the capacity of the method to yield data which will facilitate analysis within a methodology. In this case, that of naturalism. The intention to collect data from 'real life' situations which are as far as possible undistorted by the researcher, in a way which conveys the subjective reality of the interior world of the participants, leads to the identification of particular methods. In short those which do not seek to create artificial situations or require those at the focus of the research to change their behaviour in any significant way. Traditionally, these methods included different forms of observation and participant observation, conversation and listening techniques together with, in some instances written sources of data including a wide range of documents. More recently, technological advances have widened the scope of methods at the disposal of the ethnographer to include photography, video and other visual media. More recently still and continuing to emerge are a range of tools described as virtual methods (Hine 2000) where the internet and other forms of information technology are utilized.

While we will consider specific methods in detail later in the book, the intention here is not only to establish in broad terms the kinds of research tools which may be seen to contribute to a definition of ethnography, but also to demonstrate that important link between method and methodology. Having located ethnography in relation to a particular methodological orientation and subsequently identified particular methods as commensurate with that methodology, the temptation is to suggest a somewhat neat and tidy relationship between the two and in doing so, to have placed limits on the kinds of method open to the ethnographer. In general terms we may be seen to have allied ethnography very firmly to qualitative methods. We would defend this alliance as one which is epistemologically justifiable, as in order for ethnography to have specific meaning we believe it requires some kind of limits or boundaries which distinguish it from other approaches to research, and the methods identified make an important contribution to establishing such boundaries. However, identifying some methods as appropriate by implication means that others are inappropriate. It is here that things become more complex, as to categorically and universally rule some methods out is difficult and may be against the scope of the methodological orientation of ethnography.

While 'pure' forms of ethnography may rely primarily on methods of participant observation and other methods in which there is direct contact between researchers and researched within the specified setting, more inclusive forms have also embraced some quantitative methods based on questionnaire and survey research. If one takes this more inclusive approach, then the inclusion exists not merely with the methods deployed but also with the methodology. In simple terms, while qualitative methods of research may be seen to equate to methodologies based on an epistemological tradition of interpretivism, more quantitative methods may be seen in broad terms to be allied to positivist traditions where concern rests primarily with the external realities of any given social situation, rather than its meaning to and experience by social actors. If a more inclusive approach to ethnography becomes a method and methodology of 'anything goes' and at the same time there is seen to exist this over-simple and indisputable division between on the one hand, positivism and its methods and on the other interpretivism and its methods, then we fear that any claims that ethnography may have to a distinctive approach to social research would be seriously challenged. We are not advocating such an approach.

Inclusive ethnography

In our inclusive characterization of ethnography we wish to argue a case for pluralism of method but not for methodological pluralism. In doing this we wish to challenge some of the over-simple dichotomies that are sometimes seen to characterize the relationship between particular methods and methodologies. For example, quantitative methods are almost invariably allied to positivism while qualitative approaches are seen, often without question, to belong to a methodology based on epistemological tenets of verstehen and interpretivism. As bold generalizations these assertions may be broadly acceptable. However, some recent writing in this area has questioned this one dimensional link between methods and methodology. For example an interpretation of Hammersley's (1995) article, 'Who's afraid of positivism', may suggest that ethnography and qualitative method may itself be allied to a positivist quest of capturing data and seeking to advance the truth about social phenomena based on that captured data. In this way, the objectives and methodology of qualitative and quantitative research methods have much in common. Similarly, Ward-Schofield (1993) has advocated methods to increase the generalizability of qualitative research, while Jayaratne (1993) advocates the greater use of quantitative methods within a feminist paradigm, traditionally associated with qualitative methods, to 'promote feminist theory and goals and to document individual and institutional sexism' (1993: 110). In a similar vein, Bryman (1988) among others has advocated the combination of qualitative and quantitative methods and has rejected charges that such approaches result in an epistemological confusion, to the extent that findings based on combined approaches become a meaningless mixture of method and methodology. The significance of these pieces, which may be seen as criticisms of traditional dichotomized views of research method and methodology, is that they encourage us to think creatively in ways which challenge established boundaries of method and methodology.

In suggesting a more inclusive approach to ethnographic method it is important to keep in mind the characteristics of and the reasons why it would be chosen in preference to others. Here it is instructive to recall the characteristics of ethnography and what it is intended to achieve. In short, this refers to the privileging of a detailed insider's view over that of the outsider and a concern for the significance and meaning of social action for the actors upon whom the research is focused. While this remains the philosophical principle of ethnography and is, therefore, in essence its *raison d'être*, then the kind of inclusive ethnography which we have suggested above is possible. Consequently, we arrive at a position where ethnography, as a process, may make use of a range of different methods as long as they are utilized within the context of the specific methodological and epistemological tenets of ethnography, as product. We would argue, therefore, that it is possible to use quantitative methods alongside qualitative methods in the context of ethnography as long as the quantitative methods adhere to the epistemological principles of naturalism, in seeking to gather data with as little disturbance to the natural, everyday rhythms of the location as possible. In addition, at the stage of analysis, we would argue that the principal role of quantitative data would be in providing a picture of the wider context within which the specific location and the social action therein take place.

Is there an ethnographic method?

Our assertion that ethnography may make legitimate use of qualitative and quantitative methods as part of what we have described as an inclusive approach to research leads us to pose the question, is there an ethnographic method? Similar questions have been posed about case study (Hammersley 1992b; Bassey 1999; Burgess 2000), where the concern has been to identify what it is that makes case study distinctive, either as an approach to research or as a specific research method. Given the not infrequent use of the term case study as a synonym for ethnography, many of the issues raised in these debates will be relevant to our question about a specific ethnographic method. Researchers' claims to be 'doing ethnography' or 'using ethnographic methods' which are frequently made in conference presentations and research seminars, would seem to imply that there is an ethnographic method that can be readily identified and deployed. Their accounts of their research usually reveal the use of a range of qualitative approaches to data collection. From this we may conclude that qualitative method in general is ethnography and that ethnography is qualitative method. However, we have already seen that our inclusive ethnography also 'permits' the use of quantitative methods. This would seem to complicate matters, as, clearly, ethnographic method is not now solely qualitative method.

Perhaps the confusion can be resolved, at least to some degree, with reference to Brewer's (2000) discussion of 'big ethnography' and 'little ethnography', where the former refers to qualitative method as a whole and the latter restricts it to field research. Our reading of Brewer's (2000) distinction is that 'big' ethnography refers to the whole enterprise of ethnography which includes methodology as well as method, and in this sense the notion of 'bigness' is useful. However, like the accounts of ethnographic research to which we refer in the previous paragraph, it does imply that all qualitative research is ethnography. We would agree with Brewer's general argument, but would temper it slightly by saying that all qualitative methods have the capacity to be ethnographic methods only if they are deployed within the framework of ethnographic methodology. In addition, the definition of 'little' ethnography as fieldwork we also find to be useful, as it places the researcher and the methods firmly within the discrete location, event or setting in which the ethnography is to be conducted. However, we would take issue with Brewer by drawing a difference between fieldwork and field research. For us, fieldwork would be characterized by methods and methodology in the form of that discussed by Wolcott (1995) in his important book, *The Art of Fieldwork*, where he says:

> To me, the essence of fieldwork is revealed in the intent behind it, rather than the label itself . . . fieldwork is a form of enquiry in which one is immersed personally in the ongoing activities of some individual or group for the purposes of research. Fieldwork is characterized by personal involvement to achieve some level of understanding that will be shared with others.
>
> (1995: 66)

While we should not fall into the trap of regarding fieldwork as a synonym for ethnography, the importance of fieldwork to ethnography (Brewer 2000) should not be overlooked. Clearly, the key issues for Wolcott are personal involvement and intent, both of which accord to our earlier attempts to characterize ethnography and which also resonate with Brewer's (2000) concept of 'big' ethnography.

Alongside this notion of fieldwork as a form of personal involvement in the discrete location, stands field research as a less specific approach based on the discrete location, but not exclusively inside it. Consequently, quantitative methods may be seen as contributing to field research but not to fieldwork. On their own, therefore, quantitative methods may contribute to Brewer's (2000) definition of 'little' ethnography, but their lack of engagement with the interior world of the actors within the specific location does not qualify them as 'big' ethnography.

To return to our question of whether there is an ethnographic method, these deliberations lead us to adopt a position similar to that of Wolcott (1995) who identifies 'intent' as the crucial factor in his definition of fieldwork. Consequently, we would argue that single methods in the sense of research tools do not constitute ethnographic methods per se. Rather, it is their location within the wider methodology of ethnography or what Brewer (2000) defines as 'big' ethnography that makes a method ethnographic. As a result, it is feasible to regard both qualitative and some quantitative methods of data collection as having the potential to contribute to ethnographic research. Again, we stress it is methodology which underpins the deployment of the methods, which in turn determines whether or not a method is defined as ethnographic. Consequently, a particular method may be defined as ethnographic in some circumstances and not in others.

In answer to our own question, therefore, we would say that methods cannot be described as ethnographic independently of the methodology which provides the context for them. In addition we would clearly include quantitative methods as having the potential for ethnographic status. Furthermore, as a logical extension of this point, we would, therefore, argue that the range of methods which may be deployed in an ethnographic study is considerable. However, to reiterate one of our earlier points, ethnography is not an approach based on a philosophy of 'anything goes'. The importance of methodology over method ensures the maintenance of boundaries which we regard as essential for the definition of ethnography as a distinct approach to research. In short, there can be no meaningful method without methodology.

The roots of ethnography

By this stage in this opening chapter we hope to have conveyed some idea of what ethnography is in relation to its philosophical and theoretical underpinnings and how it is conducted in terms of the kinds of methods upon which it draws. On the basis of this discussion we have suggested an inclusive notion of ethnography which may involve qualitative and quantitative research methods used in tandem or qualitative methods deployed on their own. The crucial thing is the methodological context within which the methods are used, as it is this that adds the ethnography to the method. Our characterization of ethnography is at the same time both specific, in terms of its methodological and epistemological underpinnings, and flexible in terms of the methods upon which it may draw. While for some researchers this may be regarded as a somewhat contradictory position to take, our response would be to encourage them to look at what ethnography attempts to do and at where it attempts to do it. In ethnography's attempt to understand social action within discrete locations or social collectivities, it needs to be in a position to respond to social action as it unfolds, to make sense of its significance and meaning for the actors who create action and to examine the structures within which it unfolds. In this sense, the extent to which the ethnographer can plan ahead, in anything but fairly general terms is limited. In seeking to be part of the social action in a way that does not influence what happens in any overt sense, the ethnographer is essentially reactive rather than proactive.[1] In order to react in a way which does not affect what is the focus of the ethnography, the researcher needs to be able to blend in, to be accepted by the social actors and to be as flexible as the particular situation demands.

This approach to research, which is now common to and accepted within the study of educational institutions and processes and across the social sciences more generally, has its roots in late nineteenth and early twentieth century anthropology. While it can be seen in the work of several of these early social researchers such as Boas, Evans-Pritchard, Haddon, Radcliffe-Brown, Rivers, Seligsman, it is the pioneering work of Malinowski which is credited as having particular influence on the development of ethnography and in shaping it into the approach which is commonly used by researchers 80 years after his death.

For all of these anthropologists research was something that was conducted in exotic places, far away from their homes. Prior to their expeditions little was known about the people of the north-west coast of North America or of the islands of the Torres Strait. Accounts of life in these lands and others which constituted the British Empire came from missionaries and travelers and as Burgess (1982, 1984) states, were concerned largely with the exotic, the unusual and the untoward, rather than with everyday life. For the anthropologists of the new twentieth century the challenge lay in experiencing, documenting and understanding not just the unusual and the exotic but also the mundane and everyday activities that constituted everyday life for the people of these far away places. To do this, Malinowski (1922) set out a series of preconditions for effective ethnography, in his book Argonauts of the Western Pacific. Reflecting what he was keen to convey as his approach to modern anthropology, this publication became a standard text on how to do ethnography and Malinowski remains perhaps the most influential figure in social anthropology, even in spite of doubts about the extent to which his published accounts of his ethnographic method accorded with his own practices. In particular, the publication of his diary (Malinowski 1967) by his widow includes personal accounts of the day to day rigours of ethnography and shows a considerable distance between the great anthropologist and those he was researching, suggesting that the account of ethnography in Argonauts of the Western Pacific should, at best, be seen as an 'ideal type', rather than an accurate reflection of Malinowski's field experiences. Nevertheless, ideal types are useful and Malinowski remains a key figure in the development of modern ethnography.

In addition to anthropologists of the late nineteenth and early twentieth centuries, modern ethnography draws on the tradition of social research established in the 1920s and 1930s by the Chicago School of sociology. Rather than sail away to exotic foreign lands, the Chicago sociologists studied their own city. Their approach was, however, in many ways similar to that taken by Malinowski and the other social anthropologists. The Chicagoans, led by several pioneering and influential social researchers including Albion Small, Robert Park and Ernest Burgess, sought to gather information about the many different aspects of life in Chicago. Adopting what has since been termed a social mosaic approach (Faris 1970; Bulmer 1984), their research was based largely on participation in the rich and varied social life of Chicago. In most cases their background and university positions made the Chicago researchers outsiders in relation to those they sought to study. However, they were outsiders who were attempting to become insiders, seeking first-hand experience and knowledge of the lives of the natives of Chicago in the same way that Malinowski approached the study of the people of New Guinea. Their intention was to participate in the lives of those who were the focus of their studies, within the natural settings where their lives were conducted. For most, this meant adopting social behaviour to blend in with the researched and the research setting in order to observe and experience what those being researched experienced, at first hand. The approach gave rise to the phrase 'participant observation', one which, as we have already seen, is now frequently used as a synonym for ethnography.

The focus of the Chicago studies was largely on deviant groups in what was a turbulent time in the history of Chicago. These included the homeless (Anderson 1923), gangs (Thrasher 1927), prostitutes (Cressey 1932), a Jack Roller or what more recently we have come to know as a mugger (Shaw 1930), life in the ghetto (Wirth 1928) and of crime and vice (Reckless 1933). In addition, there were studies which attempted to look at more prosperous areas of the city located along what was known as the Gold Coast (Zorbaugh 1926), on the shore of Lake Michigan.

The significance of the Chicago School to modern ethnography rests, therefore, in its methodology and in the focus of its research. Its collected work shows very clearly that the value of ethnography is not restricted to the far away, the exotic or the untoward, rather it lends itself to a study of the structures and interactions which shape many locations, communities and social groups. Moreover, while the approach of the Chicago sociologists was largely qualitative, relying on what Park (McKinney 1966) described as getting 'the seat of your pants dirty in real research', they also made good use of statistical method. As Bulmer's (1984) excellent history of the Chicago School reminds us, a range of methods was deployed in order to produce the mosaic of the city. This included using statistical method to trace the extent of crime and violence in the city (Reckless 1933) and the development of quantitative mapping, leading to techniques of social zoning and to concentric zone theory (Burgess and Bogue 1964), which remain key tools in the field of urban sociology and social geography.

The influence of the Chicago School and of Malinowski's anthropology can be seen in the emergence of ethnography as a dominant approach in social scientific research in the latter half of the twentieth century. In the areas of health, industry and work, deviance, social movements and of course education, studies which focused on the researcher(s) as participant(s) within organizations or social groups grew both in number and in respectability as not only the methods which they deployed, but also the methodology upon which the methods drew, became accepted as an epistemologically respectable alternative to more positivistic approaches which had hitherto tended to dominate the study of social life, institutions and processes. This continued growth in ethnographic studies in what were now familiar settings led Burgess (1984) to talk about ethnography coming home 'from coral garden to city street'. The locations may have changed but the principles upon which the study of the locations was based remained essentially the same. By the middle of the twentieth century, ethnography had proved itself to be adaptable, capable of producing detailed accounts of many different aspects of social life in ways which, while grounded in the particular circumstances of the discrete location, event or setting, were nevertheless illustrative of wider social processes. Moreover, analysis of the detailed descriptions produced by ethnographic research yielded conceptually grounded accounts (Glaser and Strauss 1967) of social phenomena which challenged the validity of positivistic research, concerned with cause and effect, widescale generalization and statistical significance, at the expense of depth and detail. Ethnography had not only come home, but it had its feet firmly under the table!

Challenges to ethnography

To this point we have given what might be interpreted as a very positive account of ethnography and what it might achieve. Given that we are writing a book about ethnography and education and that we (the authors) have both engaged in ethnographic research in a variety of educational settings over the past 15 years, this may not seem unusual or unacceptable. However, although we may generally be regarded as supporters of and advocates for ethnographic research, we do not seek to offer an unconditional or uncritical portrayal of ethnography. Rather our approach is one, largely, of pragmatism, but pragmatism based on an acceptance of the epistemological position of naturalism and a recognition of the importance of social construction of reality (Berger and Luckman 1967) and of knowledge about the social world. Consequently our approach to educational and social research is one which emphasizes the importance of insider accounts, of observation and participation in social action to facilitate the collection of primary data at first hand. Having said this, we recognize that not all topics for research in education, or indeed other areas of social life, lend themselves to such an approach. There will be many instances where a more quantitative, widescale, positivistic, external approach to study will be acceptable above that of ethnography. For example, research undertaken on behalf of policy makers, where specific data relating to finances and spending plans allied to a particular educational initiative, may stipulate that quantitative data are collected. Consequently, we would argue that it is not just a question of ethnography not being suitable for some topics, but suitability may also be dependent on the reasons why the research is being undertaken in the first place.

Moreover, as we have also seen, our view of ethnography is one which we have characterized as comprehensive, incorporating quantitative methods where appropriate. Again, this can be seen as evidence of a pragmatic approach to research where the aims, objectives and focus of the specific study are the things that determine the methods to be deployed. Clearly, ethnography cannot be the only approach to educational research and to hold religiously to its use without due attention to the focus or purpose of the research would lead to what Mills (1959) has called 'the fetishism of method' and what Bryman (1988) alludes to as epistemology over technology.

The principal criticisms of ethnography which lead some researchers to question not only whether it is appropriate for their work but also more fundamentally its validity as an approach to research relate to the nature of the knowledge which it yields. In particular, researchers from a more positivist tradition have accused ethnography of imprecision where language used in description has be seen to lack rigour, for example, the tendency to describe and characterize events rather than quantify them. In addition, ethnography has been accused of subjectivity, where its findings have been seen as particular interpretations of specific social action by the researchers concerned, amounting to little more than anecdote and mere opinions presented in a style that perhaps has more in common with journalism than science. Allied to such accusations have been others which draw attention to ethnography's inability to generalize. Consequently, its concentration on the discrete location or social action is seen to have little to contribute to understandings of wider social issues, being both time and space bound.

Such criticisms challenge the methodological legitimacy of ethnography, rather than the methods that it might employ, as methods can clearly be deployed in a range of different contexts, underpinned by different epistemologies. The challenges are at one level difficult to counter, as it seems to us that they are not without foundation. However, the fact that they tend to emanate from researchers often more closely associated with quantitative methods and the positivist tradition in social research, means that they need to be viewed not as technical criticisms or challenges to what ethnography is able to achieve, but as epistemological challenges about the nature of the knowledge which ethnography yields. In short, we would agree with these and other similar challenges. Moreover, we do not see the need to counter them by arguing that the findings from ethnographic research are precise or objective or generalizable. To do so would be to fall into a technical trap of judging ethnography by characteristics to which it does not aspire. Ethnography does not set out to do or be any of these things and in its more general defense we would argue that as long as ethnographers do not claim that their research can meet what are essentially positivistic characteristics, then such challenges are largely irrelevant. Furthermore, the converse of those and similar criticisms can often be leveled at non-ethnographic methods in that they are over precise, not allowing for the uncertainty of social life, lacking detail and depth in the accounts of social action that they advance and failing to acknowledge the role of researcher–researched interaction in the production of social knowledge.

Summary

In this opening chapter we have set out to present a clear picture of what ethnography is and what it can achieve in educational and other fields of social research. We have argued that more than simply the deployment of particular qualitative methods, ethnography relates to a distinctive methodology based on naturalism and the Weberian notion, verstehen. Like many other approaches to social research, ethnography does not lend itself to short pithy definitions. However, in an attempt at least to be relatively brief and accessible, we can define ethnography as:

> An approach to social research based on the first-hand experience of social action within a discrete location, in which the objective is to collect data which will convey the subjective reality of the lived experience of those who inhabit that location.

Our discussion of ethnography thus far, leading to this definition, has been fairly theoretical. We have taken this approach out of a belief that it is important to understand the theory of the approach before drawing on examples in any abstract sense. However, now that we have a definition to work with and hopefully an understanding of the principles which underpin that definition, the remainder of this book will make extensive use of examples drawn from our own and other researchers' experience of ethnography in a range of educational settings. In particular, this is the approach we will take to Chapters 2 and 3, which focus on the methods involved in doing ethnography.

Note

1 We do recognize there may be occasions when ethnographers wish to take a more proactive approach, perhaps initiating a specific course of action in order to observe its impact on and the reactions of those at the focus of the research. However, while this may be a legitimate approach to take in particular circumstances, we would urge that such interventions are taken only after careful consideration of their likely consequences for the research setting and its participants, which, of course, may not be fully appreciated before such action is taken.

2 | Doing ethnography: researching first-hand experience

Thinking about your research topic and doing ethnography

In Chapter 1 we looked at what ethnography is and what it isn't. Key terms in our opening definition focused upon ethnography's core tasks to *research social action* within a *discrete location* from *first-hand experience*. Doing educational ethnography has, therefore, a primary objective to collect data that conveys the subjective reality of the lived experience of those who inhabit 'educational' locations and for various purposes.

We know that reading, writing and curiosity are essential aspects of doing ethnography. Whether this is more or less the case for all research, we leave for others to debate. Meanwhile, as Delamont (1992: 10) declares: 'If you do not like reading, hate writing, and lack curiosity, you should not choose ethnographic research. Do a survey, where the results, presented in tables, are much easier to write about.'

Ethnography lends itself to a variety of data collection methods. These methods or tools are the subject of this chapter and Chapter 3. New forms of ethnographic representation will also be part of our discussion of the changing uses and usefulness of ethnography in Chapter 5. Here, we focus upon methods that prioritize the collection of face to face, or primary data. The chapter has a key practical purpose, especially for researchers who are using ethnographic approaches for the first time, and Delamont's advice is apt. Our interest in ethnographic practice does not preclude critical evaluation of key aspects. We include examples from research practice since the focus is not only about research tools in abstract, but also upon the ways in which the use of particular research tools is linked to distinctive theoretical perspectives.

As readers you may have already formulated a topic for research investigation and begun to think about ethnography as a possible investigative approach. This link between *thinking about* a research topic and *doing* ethnography is hardly accidental. In *Ethnography for Education*, the researcher's topic is always framed by a key interest in addressing a particular *kind* of research question namely, 'what is going on here?' (Agar 1986; Geertz 1988; Wolcott 1990). Our curiosity might relate to a school, college, university, department, classroom, lesson, teacher or pupil career. The form of enquiry supersedes or even replaces questions that might otherwise be associated with educational research such as 'what's my hypothesis?' or 'how can I measure ... school effectiveness ... teacher motivation ... research outputs from education departments in Higher Education ...?

So, 'what is going on here?' requires researchers to get up close in order to describe and interpret meanings, behaviours, events, institutions and locations. Getting up close has specific implications for the ethnographer. These include particular types of association between researcher and research informant, and data collection methods that prioritize 'rich' and 'deep' understandings of, and immersion in, the educational 'field' or setting that is the topic of interest. Observation, interviews, focus groups, life histories, as well as drama and fictionalized accounts are prominent among face to face data collection methods. In combination, they involve a detailed interrogation of 'talk, text, and interaction' (Silverman 2001), and it is the *multiplicity* of methods and its triangulation that has been described as a routine hallmark of ethnography (Denzen 1970; Brewer 2000).

Data collection involves many personal and professional challenges for the first-time ethnographer, not least of which is the accumulation of vast amounts of data for translation into coherent analysis. Not that 'writing like crazy', in Erickson's (1986) terms, necessarily implies that the study is qualitative or interpretive. 'What makes such work interpretive ... is a matter of *substantive focus and intent*' (1986: 119, our emphasis). Moreover, there are ethical issues in getting up close that may have implications (and repercussions) for the researcher, research informants, locations and reported outcomes. A few weeks, even days, into ethnographic fieldwork may leave some ethnographers running for the sanctuary of the office or study, and the quiet of the library! What the Chicagoan researchers described as 'getting the seat of your pants dirty' requires skill, a presence of mind described by Fielding (1993) as 'rolling with the punches', and 'effort to "think" oneself into the perspective of the members [or informants] – the introspective, empathetic process Weber called "verstehen" ' (1993: 157). Such mental and physical agility also requires a presentation of self to others – a 'stance', or what Fielding describes as a 'front' or 'impression management' (1993: 158). Therefore, before researchers embark on ethnographic research it will be important to ask:

- Am I able to do this?
- Is my entry into this field feasible and do-able?
- Which 'self' will I present?

- How will my 'self' affect and be affected by the research topic and the people, events, situation, and actions in which I participate?
- How much and what will I be able/permitted to write, and for whom and which purposes?
- How will I make my exit from the field?

Morrison still recalls vividly an encounter during the latter phases of an ethnographic study of food and eating in school (Burgess and Morrison 1995), when one school-based feedback meeting to teachers and parents degenerated into accusations of the ethnographer being part of a 'politically correct thought police' sent by 'so-called' nutrition 'experts', and intent upon denigrating teachers about their own and children's eating habits. This session culminated in an angry teacher impressing the remains of an almost cold bag of chips into the ethnographer's increasingly red and ultimately greasy face. (Such outcomes pale into insignificance when considered in relation to ethnographies in which risks to personal safety might be one outcome arising from the full disclosure of the researcher 'self' – see, for example, Fielding's (1981) work on the National Front.) Thankfully in the UK, such risks are rare in ethnographic research about education. Instead, consider Delamont's (1992) comment that the key focus of 'good ethnographic work is on what the educator *takes for granted* . . . and is hard work – exhaustingly hard work – but enormous fun' (pp.7, 9). Nonetheless, the main challenges (and strains) in doing ethnography in educational settings is that the doer is at the core of the research; what he or she sees, hears and participates in are central to data collection and analysis. Nowhere is this more apparent than in *participant observation*, a research method sometimes used synonymously with ethnography, as we noted in Chapter 1.

Observation and participant observation

Most people know intuitively what observation is. A recurrent daily activity, all research applies observation in some form. According to Hitchcock and Hughes (1995), teacher-ethnographers:

> look, listen, ask questions, take part, learn the language, learn and record any specialised kind of language or argot, make inferences from what people say, locate informants, develop relationships, become friends, and experience different ways of life.
>
> (p.120)

A formidable list! But is this what distinguishes educational ethnography from the observational accounts of, say, an educational journalist for a national newspaper or an Ofsted inspector? One response is to distinguish between what 'watchers' observe every day, and what ethnographers do, as a 'terminological' difference:

> Social scientists do something extra with their data; they write ethnographies. *Ethnography* puts together two different words: 'ethno' means 'folk' while 'graph' derives from 'writing'. Ethnography refers, then, to social scientific writing about 'folks'.
>
> (Silverman 2001: 45)

In our case, the 'folks' in which we find interest are many and varied: educators, educational researchers, parents, heads, teachers, students, classroom assistants, dinner ladies and support staff, among others, and the ethnographer is the writer about such 'folks', *par excellence*. Not that all educational ethnographies focus solely on direct observation, as later sections of this chapter, and the next chapter indicate. Ethnographers often work with transcriptions of what teachers or pupils (or other researchers), for example, say and write that they do, and with documents about what educational institutions profess to be and enact. Here, we focus upon observation as the ethnographer's opportunity to listen, watch, record (and subsequently share with informants) what they say and do in specific educational settings and time frames.

Being a participant

Ethnography takes observation a step further since an essential aspect of the ethnographers' role is *participation* in the setting observed. This has key implications: the observer-cum-ethnographer's account includes *auto-biographical* elements, in which researchers are the main research instruments. Among the 'folks' of interest, then, are ourselves. And while the degree of participation may vary, all ethnographies involve participant observation in the sense that it constitutes 'a mode of being-in-the-world characteristic of researchers' (Hammersley and Atkinson 1983: 249), in which key aspects are seeing 'through the eyes of informants', and attention to the 'every day routines' and processes of educational experience, as well as dramatic, atypical events.

So, a challenging feature of 'taking a part' and 'being there' is the extent to which the ethnographer writes her- or himself 'in' to the text. In the following example, Morrison was a participant observer/evaluator on a two-day in-service course in music for primary school teachers organized by a local education authority (LEA). In the findings, which were part of an evaluation of an LEA's in-service programme, she reports:

> All participants indicated that they found it exhilarating and exhausting. The process of concentrated learning was considered to

be the exhausting part; working with fellow professionals in a different environment was also contributory. Towards the end of the day Terry Jones, a teacher participant commented: 'Its exhausting isn't it. Not just thinking about new ideas but being with different people'.

Caron Foley another participant commented: 'Yes, being with children is tiring enough. We're used to that, its just concentrating so hard'.

There were also lighter moments which emphasised the effort that the group, including myself were making. During attempts at music composition, Caron turned to me, having noted the exertion involved in my blowing down a long, cardboard tube, to produce a particular sound: 'Social Science won't be the same after all this, will it!' [laughter]

(Morrison 1990: 64–65, original emphasis)

Later Morrison uses notes from her fieldwork diary to report on the 'atmosphere of the day'. This included: 'At lunchtime in the pub the CT [curriculum trainer] was still very much on duty holding *us* together as a group until conversation developed spontaneously' (Morrison 1990: 66, our emphasis).

Thus, concerns with what passes as the routine and taken for granted, as well as the dramatic or atypical, together with a positioning of the researcher in the field, is one aspect of what distinguishes the ethnographer from the educational journalist, but there is more. Ethnographers adopt specific approaches to seeing educational phenomena that include a particular kind of *theoretical* focus upon people, events and actions. Silverman (2001) describes this as the critical interweaving of 'observational research, data collection, hypothesis construction, and theory building' (p.70). Hammersley and Atkinson (1983) use the analogy of a 'funnel' where there is a progressive focusing of observations in which:

over time its scope is clarified and delimited and its internal structure explored. In this sense, it is frequently only over the course of the research that one discovers what the research is all 'about', and it is not uncommon for it to turn out to be something quite remote from initially foreshadowed problems.

(p.175)

Not surprisingly, this can engender uncertainty and insecurity, not only among first-time ethnographers but also among some less experienced supervisors of research students in education who might look for clearly defined stages from their students in the earliest days of research, rather than a clearly defined question that is, 'what do I want to know?' Notwithstanding such insecurities, observational processes mirror Glaser and Strauss's (1967) account of grounded theory in the sense that *categories* generated in the early stages of observation are 'saturated' through more observation and/or triangulation with multiple methods in order to provide analytical frameworks that have relevance beyond the specific teacher, classroom, curriculum intervention or school investigated.

Similarities and distinctions between ethnographic observation and Ofsted inspections, for example, are both more and less obvious. The Ofsted observer 'witnesses' educational phenomena that are presented as 'routine' but, as far as possible (and knowingly by all parties), are stage managed in order to present a view of a 'normal' week in the life of a school, a textual version of which will become available for purposes of public scrutiny, accountability and school improvement. Ethnography, on the other hand, claims (sometimes with exaggeration) to cause minimum disturbance to the event, situation or person being observed, with different degrees of success that relate to the research problem, the circumstance and temporal issues. Ofsted inspectors claim to use both qualitative and quantitative evidence; in this sense, inspections *do* share at least one common feature with short-term ethnographic observations, namely, the status of '*blitzkrieg*' or 'smash and grab' ethnographies conducted within very limited timescales. Here, ethnographers mine 'the field' of observation as quickly as possible, in sharp contrast to the in-depth and painstaking day by day studies of the 'ordinary' as well as 'extraordinary' things that people are observed doing in educational settings. Purists like Brewer (2000) denounce such brief sojourns in the field as 'worthless' (p.61) ethnography; nonetheless, in climates of limited and short-term funding for applied educational projects, and an increasing penchant for mix-and-match methodologies, 'smash and grab' ethnography is less unusual than in the past.

Levels of participation

As a key tool in the ethnographer's kit, participant observation raises a number of issues. At one level, ethnographers 'get up close' to educational phenomena that everyone in the developed world lays claim to have experience and knowledge of by virtue of having passed through a recognized education system as student or pupil. At another level, researchers work in educational settings with which they have different degrees of familiarity, and this may call for different levels of participation. A range of observational typologies has been described elsewhere (for example, Gold 1958). In educational research, the categories identified by Denscombe (1998) encapsulate the main possibilities:

> *Total participation*, where the researcher's role is kept secret . . . [this can pose ethical issues].
>
> *Participation in the normal setting*, where the researcher's role may be known to certain 'gatekeepers', but may be hidden from most

of those in the setting. The role adopted in this type of participant observation is chosen deliberately to permit observation without affecting the naturalness of the setting, but also allows the researcher to keep a distance from the group under study. The role might be warranted on the grounds of propriety, or the researcher lacks the personal credentials to take on the role in question.

Participation as observer, where the researcher's identity as a researcher is openly recognized – thus having the advantages of gaining informed consent from those involved – and takes the form of 'shadowing' a person or group through normal life, witnessing first hand and in intimate detail the culture/events of interest.

(Denscombe 1998: 150)

Most ethnographies in educational settings adhere to versions of the second and third categories. One example of the third category occurred in a project on supply teaching in English schools by Galloway and Morrison (1993), aspects of which are documented by Morrison and Galloway (1996). This study used multiple methods of qualitative research, which, in the following extract, combines the use of a self-report diary by a supply teacher called Guy Symonds (a pseudonym) with a classroom observation by the researcher (Morrison). The example provides a glimpse into issues that relate to multiple perceptions for recording day to day experiences of research informants. Guy Symonds completed a five-day diary schedule as part of a summer term spent in a boys'secondary school. On the third day he was observed by the researcher. An extract from the supply teacher's diary records the following:

Hours	Main activity	Other
14.15	Science lesson similar to previous one with yr.10 but including more troublesome pupils with lower attention span.	
15.15	Pupils become pests at 15.15 approx.	

Later:
'What was the most demanding task or situation you had to deal with today . . . Any additional comments?'
Dealing with [pupil] in the last double, without telling him where to go. Today's activities were actually fairly straightforward.

Morrison's fieldnotes for the same period read:

2.15pm Yr. 10 dribble in over the next 10 minutes. GS [teacher] aims to repeat lesson given to another Yr. 10 group in the morning. One pupil dribbles football up and down the side of lab. Other boys at window observing fight below. Loud descriptions given. GS moves between lab. and back office. Returns from office with textbooks.

2.25 Pupil [X] enters. Informs GS he can be excused lesson to do English project in the library. No slip to confirm. Boys use loud expletives to deny the truth of X's claim. GS moves to office again to 'phone English Dept' re X's claim. Says 'there's no answer' and writes X a slip to be excused. X exits.

2.30 Voice from the back: 'Are we going to get a lesson or aren't we?' GS writes instructions on board and repeats them verbally. Gives title of book and author – writes – *You should have finished Qs 1–5 on p.37 and Qs1–3 on p.35. If not, then finish. If you have then copy Fig.1 on p.32. Answer Qs 1–3 on p.33.* Boys who are standing or moving are told to sit. One boy distributes books by throwing them to individual pupils. Noisy. Difficult to record everything. One pupil runs tap at bench, soaks his companion's file. He'll 'get the bastard later'. GS moves round class – answers queries – some genuine, some spurious? One pupil drinking from Coke can loudly. Told to remove to bin. Continues drinking – once finished throws can into bin. Boys are then told not to touch equipment or run water.

2.46 X returns. Has been 'thrown out' of the library. GS issues him with paper. Sits down at lab. bench with 4 pupils.

3.00 Ducks fly past window. One boy shouts 'ducks'. Except for 2 pupils at front bench, all rush to the window. 2 pupils at front work quietly; finish exercises. When finished, 1 goes to the toilet. On his return, both put their heads down on the bench until the end of the lesson.

3.10 6 boys (half class) put their coats on, and sit by window. GS hopes they have finished work, will be examining exercise books. Football dribbling recommences.

3.20 All boys close books of own volition. General talk.

3.25 GS switches lights off.

3.30 Bell. 6 boys kept behind. Not X. GS informs them of his disappointment at behaviour. Expects it of X, he says, but not of them. Future visit to D/Head is threatened sanction. Boys exit. GS talks to me briefly about pupil 'backgrounds'.

(Morrison and Galloway 1996: 42–3)

What is going on here? How does the researcher's observation contribute to the research informant's description of events that afternoon? The supply teacher's schedule describes a 'fairly straightforward' day marred by a few 'troublesome pests', especially pupil X. In the absence of observation, the researcher would be obliged to assess notions of 'straightforwardness' in relation to other research findings about supply *and* regular teaching experiences. As Morrison and Galloway (1996) report: 'this teacher's language is linked to what he views as success, in containing classes without outside interference/help, avoiding a major confrontation with one pupil, and keeping a group on task till 15.15 hours' (p.43). The observation adds rather than detracts from the research informant's description of the day as 'fairly straightforward' while simultaneously providing a perspective on a classroom as an 'arena of struggle' (Woods 1990a), and where some contestation over the meaning of learning, as understood by the supply teacher, the researcher and the pupils is apparent. Here, Guy Symonds places his own image of a supply teacher at work, developed from previous experiences of supply and 'regular' work, alongside the researcher's observations. Research informants like Guy are often vulnerable in the sense that they work in unfamiliar contexts, where they might (and often do) feel particularly exposed because their professional skills are very much on trial, not infrequently by 'permanent' teacher colleagues. Observation, in combination with diaries, thus offered the opportunity for *both* the researcher and research informant to present this varied experience qualitatively by 'getting up close'. 'In place of statistically representative information, [observation and diaries] offer glimpses of the infinite variety of life as a "stop-gap" teacher' (Morrison and Galloway 1996: 45).

'Insider' observation

Those who embark on ethnographic research in educational settings face the access and role maintenance and management problems that all social science researchers face. But educators investigating their own institutions confront these issues in particular forms. First, there is a need to make a very familiar or 'normal' setting unfamiliar, as might be the case when a researcher works in his or her own school or classroom. Second, this requirement persists even when the researcher works in a setting that has similar general features to those with which the researcher is familiar, for example, classrooms in another school, but has specific features when observed 'up close'. Third, while much participant observation will be *overt*, there will be times when it will be less obvious to the research informants that the educator-as-ethnographer has stepped (and remains) outside his or her role as 'educator' in the setting being explored. In this sense, ethnographic observation can take on more *covert* characteristics, and this delicate interpenetration of roles remains a key aspect of the balancing act between observation that precludes 'interference' in the action being observed, and the maintenance of relations that requires both ethically informed consent and the need to maintain distance from informants. Research with pupils, for example, poses specific issues that are currently being explored more fully in the education literature (see MacNaughton *et al.* 2001, for example, and the later section on focus groups).

Access and identity

Gaining access in order to conduct participant observation is not just about 'getting in', or even about finding a 'gatekeeper' to ease the passage of your entry (important though the gatekeeper(s) may be in making the surroundings and context visible and understandable, and by introducing the researcher to a range of possible informants). It is also about locating a role and managing entry and exit strategies from the educational setting. Management strategies may not always work as smoothly as the ethnographer would like, as the earlier, rather rueful example from Morrison suggests. In combination, such procedures and issues demand much from the researcher as a person and as a professional. In education, the 'role' taken has not infrequently been one of teacher or classroom assistant. As indicated above, 'outsiders' and 'insiders' face different kinds of problems but in both cases it is likely that as a method, participant observation is likely to place greater demands on the researcher than most other methods. As Denscombe (1998) reminds us, this is likely to involve 'commitment in terms of researcher's time and the degree to which the act of research invades the routine life of the researcher' (p.153). Hammersley and Atkinson (1983: 249) summarize four aspects of fieldwork identity:

1 Whether the researcher is known to be a researcher by all of those being studied, or only by some, or by none.
2 How much and what is known about the research, by whom.
3 What sorts of activities are and are not engaged in by the researcher in the field, and how this locates her or him in relation to the various conceptions of category and group membership used by participants.
4 What the orientation of the researcher is, and how completely he or she consciously adopts the orientation of insider or outsider.

Observing and taking fieldnotes

Fieldnotes are key elements of participant observation and while it is rare to record *too much*, the importance of storing and organizing the writing as you proceed can never be underestimated (a point made cogently by Delamont 1992: 119). Fieldnotes are also intensely temporal, or what Denscombe (1998: 151) calls 'urgent business'. Because memories are 'selective' and 'frail' (Denscombe 1998) there is a need to make notes where possible *in* the field as well as making further notes *outside* the field as soon as possible after the observation, preferably at the end of each day or half day. For ethnographic observation in educational contexts, we do, at least, have the advantage of working in settings where 'writing' is an unremarkable activity, if more so in classrooms than staffrooms.

But what should fieldnotes contain? A glib response would be to argue that it depends upon the research topic. We might also return to the term 'funnel'. So, in the early stages of observation, the ethnographer is striving to gain a broad idea about 'what is going on here'. The period of early 'scanning' (Delamont 1992: 112) demands much in terms of writing notes that are legible (later), coherent and potentially insightful. This is followed by a much more detailed focus upon specific phenomena. If we return to the extract from Morrison's participation in an inservice course in music for primary teachers, for example, this was followed by detailed shadowing of several but by no means all of the teachers who had attended that course. Observers cannot be everywhere, and small scale researchers, in particular, can only be somewhere for some of the time. In the example from Morrison (1990), she observed teacher Linda Brown who worked in an inner city primary school. In her work, she was encouraged by the curriculum trainer to use environments which were familiar to the children both inside and outside school, to develop themes explored on the course. This would involve relating sounds to environment, to produce a musical project about 'living in our area'. The playground, streets and local shops were used as arenas to coordinate words, activities and sounds. The teacher and trainer had four groups of children working in different parts of the school. In the following extract, Linda Brown was being observed in the classroom developing themes that she had learnt on the course:

> I [Morrison] joined one group. The children were able to articulate their learning to the researcher –
>
> I sat on the window ledge in the corner of an activity area . . . Colin, one of five children in the group said:
>
> Have you come to see what we're doing with Miss Brown and Miss [ ]?
>
> MM: Yes, you carry on
> Shane: Well, we're making sounds using words from out there [points to window and playground]
> Colin: what we do in the playground. Like running, walking, talking
> Darren: [very loudly] and SHOUT . . . INGGGG
> Shane: Come on let's practice. We'll show you. [to me] [Physically pushes the group members into a kind of presentational order] We're making sounds like the words.
>
> This would be the arrangement in which they would present their efforts to the class, a few minutes later. Using the playground words they performed a set of sounds by expressing the words at different speeds and tones to create a pattern of sounds. Then the groups combined and . . .
>
> (Morrison 1990: 67–8)

Wolcott's (1981) advocacy of four staged strategies for participant observation remains pertinent – observation by broad sweep; observation of nothing in particular (especially in the early stages); searching for paradoxes; and searching for problems facing the group being observed. There are many examples of 'paradoxes' sought and found in the literature of educational ethnography.

For example, Morrison (1996) reports on an ethnography of food and eating in a secondary school in which science teachers discussed the importance of nutritious diets, geography teachers discussed the effect of 'burger' empires upon cattle grazed lands of the USA, and art teachers encouraged children to produce practical designs for fast food bars. Beyond the classroom, pupils were encouraged to 'eat up' fast during lunch breaks of 25 minutes daily, and children's use of vending machines provided a vehicle for school fund-raising. Where teachers remained unaware of what their colleagues 'did' in relation to food focused education, and pupil practices beyond the classroom were in marked contrast to what was being advocated within, ethnography provided an important vehicle for revealing the contradictions and paradoxes inherent in teaching and learning about food in school. Another favourite illustration comes from the ORACLE educational research project (Galton and Delamont 1985) in which Delamont subsequently records: 'During the ORACLE project, we found that children drew more in ordinary lessons than they did in art, and moved more in ordinary classes than they did in PE' (Delamont 1992: 115).

What participant observation can and cannot do

Especially for the single-handed researcher, participant observation cannot constitute all there is to know either about ethnography or the topic under investigation. Claiming more from the analysis of participant observation than the data actually suggest is always a challenge for the lone ethnographer in an educational setting for limited periods. While, to a degree, this is so for all data collection methods, the participant observer is, perhaps, especially vulnerable to issues of personal perspective drawn from one set of senses rather than those of multiple observers, and of the tendency to observe the 'exciting' or 'dramatic'. Readers might wish to refer back to Morrison's account of an afternoon in the life of Guy Symonds, the supply teacher. Did she select the dramatic events of a lesson? Should she have done? What do you think?

In participant observation, as for all the methods upon which an ethnographer may draw, *reflexivity*, discussed specifically in Chapter 4, is critically important. Such extracts remind us that ethnographers *always* impact upon their chosen fields of study whether this relates to our being active in what is going on in the classroom, school hall, or management meeting, or by virtue of being there at a specific time and location. Moreover, this means that not only do we inevitably influence the fields we observe but we may also 'change ourselves' as observation causes us to reconsider, rethink and reflect upon our actions and attitudes as we collect and analyse observational data. This form of observation reminds us that participant observation is especially demanding, and for these and other reasons, is rarely used alone but more often in tandem with other methods like interviewing.

Interviewing

Much has been written already about how to interview in educational settings (Powney and Watts 1987; Hitchcock and Hughes 1995). This section intends to discuss issues most pertinent to interviews in ethnographic contexts, frequently in conjunction with observation. So, our focus turns to what research informants *tell us* they think, say and do, and how we, as ethnographers, interpret that 'telling'. We will consider types of interview commonly used in ethnography, like focus groups and life history, but leave the nuts and bolts of interviewing techniques to burgeoning guides for small scale researchers (for example, Denscombe 1998, chap. 7 in particular). Interviews have been given many labels in accordance with the nature of the questions asked, the relationship between the interviewer and the interviewee, and the number and kinds of people involved.

All interviews focus upon a verbal stimulus to elicit a verbal response. This offers a starting point (Brewer 2000; Silverman 2001) but does not take us very far. It is when we question attempts 'to treat interview questions and answers as passive filters towards some truths about people's identities' (Silverman 2001, following Baker 1982), that we begin to see interviews as *constructions* by interviewer and interviewee of 'some version of the world appropriate to what we take to be self-evident about the person to whom we are speaking and the context of the question' (Silverman 2001: 86). Ethnographic interviewing is usually (but not always) positioned towards one end of the continuum of quantitative–qualitative approaches to interviewing. At the 'standardized' end are highly structured interviews in which the interviewer attempts to control and 'teach' (May 1993) interviewees 'to reply in accordance with interview schedules' (p.93). Ethnographic interviewing is more often (but not always) located at the other end of the continuum where 'the respondent is encouraged to answer a question in her or his own terms' (May 1993), and, indeed, pose questions to the ethnographer as part of the verbal exchange.

Perspectives on ethnographic interviewing

Silverman (2001) examines interviews from various perspectives:

> According to *positivism*, interview data give us facts about the social world. The primary issue is to generate data which are valid and

reliable, independent of the research setting. The main ways to achieve this are the random selection of the interview sample and the administration of standardized questions with multiple choice answers which can be readily tabulated.

According to *emotionalism*, interviewees are viewed as experiencing subjects who actively construct their social worlds. The primary issue here is to generate data which give an authentic insight into other people's experiences. The main ways to achieve this are unstructured, open-ended interviews usually based upon prior, in-depth participant observation.

According to *constructionism*, interviewers and interviewees are always engaged in constructing meaning. Rather than treat this as standing in the way of accurate descriptions of 'facts' or experiences, how meaning is constructed becomes part of the researcher's topic . . . A particular focus is on how interviewees construct narratives of events . . . and people and the turn-by-turn construction of meaning.

(p.87)

While ethnographers might differ in the extent to which they apply (or, perhaps, admit to applying) standardization in interview procedures, much of what is described as ethnographic interviewing resembles the second and third categories identified above. These, in turn, have become associated with unstructured and, to a lesser extent, semi-structured interviews, both of which have become almost commonplace in educational ethnography. If the term 'unstructured' is synonymous with ethnographic interviewing, it is, of course, a misnomer; ethnographic interviews are structured in accordance with a systematic research design. However, the interviewer has greater scope in asking questions, and the interviewees in answering questions (and raising others) than might occur, for example, in structured interviewing. And if 'unstructured' is a misnomer, then semi-structured has become a kind of 'catch-all' half-way house between structured and unstructured interviewing, that commonly allows the interviewer greater flexibility to introduce 'probes' for expanding, developing and clarifying informants' responses.

Unstructured interviewing has become a powerful tool in the ethnographers' kit, not surprisingly because it adheres closely to ethnography's main claims to explore the educational worlds of actors *from their own perspectives*. Morrison (1995) in her thesis on 'Supply Teachers' Work and Lives' used an unstructured interview approach, in association with observation, in order to explore pupils' understandings of what happened on those occasions when pupils in school were taught by teachers who were not their regular teachers. That is, she described this as unstructured, and used an opening focused 'issue' as a format to provide a gateway into conversations with pupils, and then three further prompting themes as an initial framework for those conversations as follows:

Interviews with pupils

Summary: General interest in the ways pupils and teachers experience learning in schools. Specific interest in pupils' learning experiences which might be irregular, different, unusual in relation to their regular timetables with designated teachers.

Areas of interest
1. *Gateway*: Focus on a recent occasion during the last week when learning situation was different, irregular, unusual ... what happened ...
2. Pupil awareness
   - changes in routine
   - advance notice
3. Classroom strategies
   - work set   Continuity, new work
               Support from other teaching staff
               Pupil expectations
               Follow-up by pupils, 'regular teacher(s)'
4. Other comments

(Morrison 1995: 264)

The difference between types of interview can also be one of degree and interpretation. Morrison (1995), for example, applied a 25-item teacher interview schedule in her interviews with supply teachers. The difference between the supply teacher schedule (semi-structured) and a structured interview lay in its *relative* open-endedness, both in terms of the ordering of the questions and the flexibility given to informants to elicit responses, and the use of probes. This contrasts with the standardization of questions and the potential for fixed, multiple choice answers that is more a feature of structured interviews. Elsewhere, Hitchcock and Hughes (1995) introduce other 'fuzzy' overlaps, this time between 'conversations' and 'interviews' as researchers apply 'a method to the madness' (Schwarz and Jacobs 1979) of research into routine and not so routine aspects of educational experience:

It [the unstructured interview] has distinct advantages for the researcher working within a known culture with fellow professionals ... Indeed, the teacher-researcher using unstructured interviews will quickly see how these merge into a conversation. Conversations are, of course, a major element in any kind of ethnographic field research. Conversations not only constitute an important source of data but might also be regarded as a method of research in their own right. Once this happens, it is transparent that elements of everyday life will be incorporated into the unstructured interview.

(p.163)

Such 'conversations' demand proficiency and insight on the part of the ethnographer: 'it is always a controlled conversation which he [sic] [the interviewer] guides and bends to the service of his [sic] research interest' (Palmer 1928: 171).

Let us return for a moment to the categories of emotionalism and constructionism identified by Silverman (2001). At one level, Morrison's (1995) thesis into the lives and work of supply teachers is not atypical of ethnographies that draw upon interview data (as well as observations and diaries) from a range of educational actors, in this case, supply teachers, regular teachers and pupils. The analysis of interview data strives to make visible those aspects of educational experience, which, in England at least, have remained largely marginalized, peripheral and even denied, except during periods of major teacher crises, such as teacher shortages. In this sense, part of the appeal of the thesis is its intersubjectivity – an appeal to the authenticity of the, as yet, unheard voices and experiences that are then reported and interpreted by the researcher. Viewed in this light, such accounts might be considered under Silverman's category of 'emotionalism', or what Brewer (2000) calls *humanistic ethnography*.

At another level, however, there is an understanding that the interview data are constructed accounts. Of particular interest to the researcher were interview data from regular teachers. Here, regular teachers presented images of themselves which strove to maintain a distance between themselves (as regular teachers) and others (supply teachers) who were not considered 'real' or 'good' teachers (in contrast with their 'good' selves), but simultaneously evoked reluctant admiration from interviewees who declared those 'others' to be like 'gold dust', colleagues who tolerated regimes and experiences that they – the 'committed' – could not imagine tolerating. In this sense, their constructions of supply teachers juxtaposed worthiness as a scarce commodity, with unworthiness as 'the uncommitted'. Supply teachers, on the other hand, provided their own situated and often dramatic and dramatized accounts; the interview data is peppered with stories of survival against the odds of negative experiences in classrooms and staff rooms. In combination, such situated and constructed interview accounts (Silverman's third category) support the researcher's subsequent interpretations of the data which focus upon the status and identity of a kind of educational super hero(ine) – the feisty temp in educational settings. Accounts are not seen as oppositional. They are mutually supportive rather than competitive; the 'facts' of supply teachers' lives and work are seen both in relation to the data collected during interviews and the account constructed and negotiated by interviewer and interviewees.

If intersubjectivity and mutual rapport are keys to 'ethnography for education', are there drawbacks to prioritizing the informant's 'voice'? Silverman (2001) highlights three challenges. First, ethnographic interviewing places a potentially heavy burden on interviewees 'to talk' (regardless of whether, in hindsight, they might have spoken less rather than more if dir-ected to do so). Second, the assumption that in-depth interviews necessarily yield 'unique' rather than predictable insights into individual experiences needs at least to be questioned. Third, the status of the interview as a socially constructed 'game', rather than a 'telling it as it is', raises questions about its 'naturalness' and its capacity to capture authentic data. The counterpoint to the first challenge may be for ethnographers to establish clear and unambiguous parameters agreed by as many parties as possible. The second and third challenges remind us that interviews, like all data collec-tion methods, do not and could not constitute the entire 'reality' of the educational setting, and that multiple methods and triangulation are critical elements in arguing for the plausibility and credibility of our work.

Interview encounters

Previous research has demonstrated quite clearly that research informants will respond differently depending upon how they perceive the person asking the question and/or the intent behind the question. While not wishing to exaggerate this effect, the issue is especially pertinent in the case of ethno-graphic interviewing where the interviewer may already have become a familiar 'sight' in the research setting and where some, if not all, potential informants will have an impression about 'who the person is' and 'what the researcher is like', even if, on some occasions, the researcher's justification for being in the setting may have been embellished or mythologized by other potential informants. In such ways, the researcher's identity and personality can have specific impacts upon the opportunity to develop rapport and trust between interviewer and interviewee.

Following a research study entitled *Public Libraries, Ethnic Diversity and Citizenship* (Roach and Morrison 1998), for example, we note how Morrison (1999) reflects upon the processes of research conducted by two researchers – a white female and a black male – each located in two different research centres of the same university. In one example Morrison recalls that:

> While working in Midcentre City Library, contact was made with community members who . . . gave their time generously to the writer in order to support this research but within an overall framework where interviewees expressed views on both consultation overload and underload. This co-existed with perceptions that they were, on occasions, marginalised in the discussion of 'important' information, and that consultations were part of a stage-managed *fait accompli* in which their influence upon practice was minimal. Not surprisingly then, my role as researcher was construed, on at least two occasions, as a role of a member of that City elite seeking yet more information

about the quality of 'their' life experiences, this time in the guise of interests in public libraries. As an interviewee from one organisation – focused upon the interests of one ethnic group – said to me at the start of the interview: 'what could you possibly know to write down that would express my experiences?' and 'why didn't the Council employ someone who is [the same ethnic origin category as me i.e. the interviewee]?'

(Morrison 1999: 79)

Morrison goes on to discuss how the final account was written in order to represent and interpret views as carefully and insightfully as possible. Is this 'mission impossible' for the ethnographic researcher? Denscombe (1998) offers sensible advice:

> We bring to interviews certain personal attributes that are 'givens' and which cannot be altered at whim to suit the needs of the research interview. Our sex, our age, our ethnic origin, our accent, even our occupational status, are all aspects of our 'self' which, for practical purposes, cannot be changed. We can make efforts to be polite and punctual, receptive and neutral, in order to encourage the right climate for an interviewee to feel comfortable and provide honest answers. What we cannot do is change our personal attributes.

(p.117)

Aspects of this apparently straightforward advice may need even more unpacking. Remaining neutral or detached is not a pathway to successful outcomes that is advocated by all ethnographers. Feminist interviewers, for example, aim to empower and help research informants rather than remain dispassionate or distanced from them. Here, the key word is *partnership*, and a key concern is how the term is understood. Accordingly, women interviewing women are mutually engaged in capturing women's stories and experiences (including the interviewer's) in a manner that as far as possible encapsulates the 'conversation' referred to earlier (see also Oakley 1981; Roberts 1981; Smith 1987; Reinharz 1992). Whether the outcomes of such mutual engagement are equally empowering has been contested (Hammersley 1992a) and responses made (Ramazanoglu 1992). Moreover, whether such interviewing 'works' with women who are hostile to feminism remains questionable, a point highlighted by Brewer (2000: 69, following Luff 1999). Meanwhile, the ethic of empowerment and commitment is one shared by other advocates of critical ethnographic research in education, for example, in some areas of race and ethnicity (Connolly 1998).

The pros and cons of interviewing

All this suggests that ethnographic interviews provide rich sources of in-depth data, and can lead to important critical insights, especially about informants' understandings and priorities. Interview data also provide powerful and provocative images and examples, as we note from recent work by Osler and Morrison (2000) when they report on interviews with senior HMI and Ofsted management teams members, that shed previously unreported light into perspectives on race equality and school inspection (pp.39–68).

Interviews can be enjoyable and therapeutic for one or both parties. Skilfully done, interviews offer the flexibility not only to explore and recognize issues but, just as importantly, to develop new insight into themes emerging during interviews. Data can also be checked with informants for accuracy and comment. So far, so positive. However, ethnographic interviewing presents other challenges. Interviewing that is like a conversation highlights practical and ethical issues about what is *for, on,* or *off* the record. Moreover, interviews can be daunting, tiring or onerous for participants, and, at worst, seen as a 'waste of time'. Non-standard responses yield large amounts of data, not all of which are relevant and which, more importantly, may not be seen as relevant *at the time of interview*. This reinforces the need for the systematic collection and organizing of data, regular reviews and ongoing memo writing, coding and cross-checking between this and other data, as part of the iterative process of collection and analysis (see Chapter 4). The mechanics of data collection are also important, and the issue of whether interview notes and audio recording, or interview notes only, are deployed needs to be considered carefully not only as a research design issue but also whether data variously collected constitutes the same kind of commitment to 'telling it as it is'.

As long as the strengths and limitations of interview data are appreciated – that interviews focus upon what people *say* they say, write and do *rather* than what they do say, write and do – it is possible to celebrate the use of interviews as important tools in the ethnographer's kit. Meanwhile, interviews demand much of the ethnographer in terms of sensitivity and ethical awareness, that, on occasions, demands that 'the listening ear' also 'bites his or her lip'. Some kinds of interview make specific demands, and it is to several of these that our attention now turns.

Life history interviews

Life history interviews provide opportunities for detailed understandings of individuals, usually in terms of constructed narratives of events, episodes and contexts that underpin 'lives' within and beyond education. As Coffey (1999) points out, research informants portray, and researchers interpret, 'lives' as 'sequences, consequences, time, causality, structure and agency' (p.128). It is not difficult to see why life history has such an appeal for educational ethnographers; a specific focus upon teachers' and pupils' life histories, for example, not only facilitates linkage between individuals and classrooms, schools, and the wider public and policy communities, but also illustrates how individual perceptions of education pattern and influence informants' involvement in it (Goodson 1990; Woods 1993; Goodson and Sikes 2001).

The disciplinary heartland of life history, as for many forms of ethnography, is anthropology. Our interest lies in how the 'folks' encountered in educational settings 'cope with' the educational experiences they encounter, rather than upon the way that educational systems and structures 'cope with' the stream of individuals who pass through them (Mandelbaum 1982). Redfield's (1955) early anthropological description of life history as 'a succession of added comprehensions' (pp.56–65) is apt here. From the perspective of educational research, life history interviews allow researchers to consider what informants *think* is happening in education, what they *expect/have expected* to happen, what they *make happen* and what *has happened* to them and others as a consequence of schooling and/or educational experiences.

Life histories have biological, cultural and social dimensions and patterns. Earlier advocates, like Mandelbaum, argue for an emphasis upon 'principle *turnings*' or changing points in individuals' lives, and how individuals *adapt* to the experiences that affect their lives, as a means of making sense of lives and careers (Mandelbaum 1982: 148). So, in educational research life histories are used to link teachers' and pupils' histories with school histories and patterns of educational innovations and curriculum development (see, for example, Goodson 1983, 1990; Hitchcock and Hughes 1995; Goodson and Sikes 2001). Moreover, with increased emphasis upon an advocacy of reflexive and reflective practitioner practice among teachers and teacher-researchers (discussed, for example, by Skilbeck 1983; Elliott 1990), there has been a resurgence of the genre that foregrounds autobiographical and, on occasion, intensely personal, sensitive and provocative aspects of teacher, pupil and researcher experience.

All this suggests that the use of life history interviews is not for the faint-hearted, a point well made in Goodson and Sikes' (2001) book on *Life History Research in Educational Settings*. Here, the authors explore not only the popularity of researching educators' perceptions of curriculum and subject development, pedagogical practice, as well as managerial concerns, but also examine, in depth, questions of ethics and power as they emerge from the detailed storylines and scripts that constitute life history data. Considerable skills are required by researchers who probe the lives of participants who are seen as 'active doers and seekers' rather than 'passive research participants' in educational activity (Mandelbaum 1982: 150). It should also be apparent that life history interviews are usually multiple and time-consuming and demand prolonged commitment to people and situations.[1] Life histories bring into sharp focus research skills in *getting in*, *getting on* and *getting out* of research situations and relationships. For example, one of the present authors (Pole 1999, 2001) conducted life histories with 20 teachers of black and Asian origin in which he was able to locate their teaching careers within wider life experience. Working across four generations of black and Asian teachers which included those in training to become teachers, those at different stages in their careers and retired teachers, Pole's interviews lasted between 8 and 20 hours. Clearly, interviews of such length are not conducted at one 'sitting' but take place over several months. By the end of the interviews, Pole felt that not only had he come to know the teachers very well but they had also come to know him. He had become part of their lives.

Taking a chronological approach to start with, he knew the details of their ancestors, their early lives and education, their relationships, where they had lived, their tastes in music and literature, how they like to spend their spare time, their views on politics and religion, as well as the whole gamut of their experiences as teachers. This enabled a holistic picture of the teacher to be constructed and the teaching career to be viewed not in isolation but as a part of that whole life experience.

Conducting life histories takes patience, inquisitiveness and empathy on the part of the interviewer. For the interviewee it demands a willingness to be open and ideally to be analytical, often confronting issues in their own lives in ways which they may not have been confronted previously. In the case of Pole's research a further dimension was added to the life history experience which was central to much of the substantive content of the study, namely that of ethnicity. As a white researcher, Pole was attempting to understand the experiences of black teachers. While he felt that this difference inevitably cast him as an ethnic outsider, Pole at the same time felt that it enabled him to pose questions which would not have been posed by someone of the same ethnicity as the interviewee. He felt that the absence of any shared experience in this respect meant that he did not take things for granted or at face value. He questioned and asked for clarification, pushing the interviewee for more information, more analysis and greater depth to their life stories. While Pole was very pleased with the interviews, on some occasions he was also aware that interviewees may have held things back for fear of offending him. For example, his interview with Carol Chambers, a black deputy headteacher, whom he interviewed for approximately 16 hours across five separate meetings, revealed some reticence on her part in this respect, as the following excerpt from the life history illustrates. This exchange follows comments Carol had made about her suspicions of many white people:

Carol Chambers: I feel bad though, talking like this, because we're going into a place . . . we're going into an area now where I feel bad talking to you.

Chris Pole: Why?
Carol Chambers: Well partly because you're white.
Chris Pole: Well, that's what it's all about isn't it?
Carol Chambers: I know but it's . . . I don't know.
Chris Pole: I mean, I would be surprised if you didn't have those kinds of feelings if you've lived a life where you felt that you've been on the outside. Where you've been discriminated against. I won't be offended.
Carol Chambers: Well I hope not. Please, please don't. I really feel bad.

The fact that this exchange occurred well into the life history interview and there was a very good rapport between the participants meant that they could be open and honest with each other, not only about the content of the interview but also about how it was progressing. However, this was a situation which was reached only as a result of time and considerable effort on the part the participants, both of whom saw value in the research and wanted it to succeed. The fact that it did succeed is evident in the comments made by the participants as they ended the life history interview, approaching 16 hours of conversation.

Chris Pole: OK. I can't think of anything else at the moment, but I'll be in touch again after this has been typed up and you've had a chance to read through the whole thing. Bedtime reading.
Carol Chambers: All right. OK.
Chris Pole: Is there anything you thought that maybe I should have asked you about, or you were expecting me to, or that we haven't talked about?
Carol Chambers: I don't really know. You've come across as a very competent interviewer, because it doesn't feel like an interview and you do seem to have covered things and you have remembered things. And when I go off, you pull me back on.
Chris Pole: I have found it very easy to talk to you.
Carol Chambers: Oh good.
Chris Pole: And I have enjoyed talking to you. It's been a privilege for you to tell me all these things and I know you had concerns the second time we met, you know [referring to Carol's suspicion of some white people, reported above].
Carol Chambers: Yes I know. [Dramatic voice] Why am I here? Why am I doing this? [Laughter]
Chris Pole: OK. Well, thank you so much.
Carol Chambers: OK. Well, thank you.

Although these closing remarks may appear to suggest something of a mutual appreciation society, they need to be regarded in the context of the 16 hours of conversation that preceded them. Delamont's (1992) characterization of research as a golden journey, 'a similar exercise to going on a voyage of discovery' (Delamont 1992: vii) seems highly appropriate in this context. Like most life history interviews, this was a journey not just through Carol Chambers' life and career in a linear, chronological sense, but it was also through her philosophies and beliefs, emotions, prejudices, aspirations, hopes, expectations and fears. In this sense, the interviewer's comment that it had been a privilege to share that personal journey, which was at times difficult, cathartic and self-revealing, not just for the interviewee but also for the interviewer, was surely not hyperbolic.

Explanations and justifications

The rationale for life history is that it offers special and unique insights into individuals' lives. Its specificity can raise methodological concerns about research that is based on single instances. Moreover, the editing and analyses of life history data raises issues that are often addressed about in-depth interviews in general, or what Stronach and Maclure (1997) describe as the 'storying' of the dialogue (p.34). For these writers, the 'telling it as it is' becomes a process of 'subduing' and ordering the data of life history in order to produce a coherent narrative. Not all ethnographers, and especially those with postmodern tendencies, view this as entirely unproblematic, arguing that 'narratives that promote coherence, singularity, and closure, and which aim to set up a close camaraderie with the reader are ultimately conservative' (Stronach and Maclure 1997: 57).

None of the above suggests an abandonment of life history. Rather that we continue to scrutinize the 'tell it like it is' conventions of early ethnography and provide further encouragement for ethnographers to look towards a range of tools to represent educational activity and experience. Among these are focus groups and, more recently, other forms of ethnography like fiction and drama, and these are introduced as the final tools discussed in this chapter. First, to focus groups.

Focus groups

It is clear that not all ethnography is primarily focused upon individual biographies or, indeed, upon the minutiae of deeply personal moments. Rather, some ethnographers are choosing to use focus groups in order to explore specific sets of issues in educational settings. For proponents like Kitzinger (1994), focus groups are useful in examining 'how knowledge, and more importantly, ideas, both develop, and operate within a given cultural context' (p.116). The term 'focus group' has also been used interchangeably with group interviews. But two features, in particular, can be used to distinguish focus groups from other kinds of interaction that involve face to face interaction with more than one informant simultaneously. First, focus groups are focused in the sense that they usually involve *collective activity(ies)* to provide the framework for the interaction. In educational settings, for example, this might be a video or audio recording, photographs, charts, diagrams, short readings or word prompts for teacher, pupil or parent groups. Second, the core purpose of focus groups is to collect and analyse data that are primarily concerned with the *interaction* among members of the group (Kitzinger 1994; Catterall and Maclaran 1997). This is not to argue that focus groups might, and frequently do, provide ethnographically insightful data about individual group members, but rather that their primary purpose is linked to furthering researchers' understandings about group processes and norms, and how these develop.

Moreover, as Morgan has suggested (1988, 1993), focus groups are especially useful in helping to investigate why people hold the views they do, precisely because a key aspect of group participation is the need for members to explain opinions and attitudes, especially when challenged by others, when asked to respond to a question, or to provide further justification for what they have done or said during the group encounter.

Kitzinger (1994) highlights nine advantages of focus groups as a means to:

1 highlight informants' attitudes, priorities, language and frames of reference;
2 facilitate a wide range of communication;
3 identify group norms;
4 gain insight into social processes;
5 encourage conversation about 'embarrassing' or sensitive subjects, and to allow researchers to:
   • explore differences in the group;
   • use conflict to clarify why people do what they do;
   • explore arguments to see how participants change their minds;
   • investigate the ways in which some forms of speech affect group participation.

Challenges: an example

Unlike the use of focus groups with school pupils in class time where members are, in a specific sense, a 'captive audience', Roach and Morrison (1998) used focus groups as part of a research study designed to investigate young people's use of public libraries and for which purposes. The first challenge was in accessing informants and deciding upon location, size and number. (In other contexts, Oates (2000) reports on similar challenges.)

Repeated advertising and promises of free refreshments and library advice, did result in three groups of eight participants. A comfortable location in the centre of a municipal library that provided a safe, rather than isolated, space for discussion proved helpful. The focus group leaders applied vignettes of library experience, real and imagined, and books, as props to promote discussion. The task was complex and the researchers took a twin pronged approach, one researcher acting as discussion 'moderator' and the other as 'reticent discussant', taking careful note of group dynamics, movement and body language. Both roles were demanding and required skills of moderation, listening, as well as targeted observation. The focus groups presented different challenges that were linked to the varying dynamics of the groups. The use of a tape recorder with a conference microphone attached was not without problems; some voices were hardly audible and transcription was a lengthy, sometimes frustrating process of discerning between voices, people and language.

But the advantages outweighed the disadvantages. Used in conjunction with document analysis and interview data, they provided data from 24 participants that would otherwise have been impractical on a one to one basis. The groups allowed the researchers to interact directly with partici-pants who had hitherto been unknown to them, and, in several cases, to one another. Participation evolved as informants were gradually able to build upon one another's comments through proactive and reactive verbal and non-verbal interaction. Young people appeared to like this form of engage-ment. This supports other accounts of focus groups as appropriate for research with children and young people (Stewart and Shamdasani 1990; O'Kane 2000).[2]

While the focus group data were challenging in terms of analysis and interpretation, they gave the researchers access to a wide range of issues concerning young people's understandings and views about what library use meant for them, and gave the researchers new insights into young people's perceptions of what constituted 'safe' or 'risky' environments in which to work, learn, rest and socialize. In the triangulation of different methods, it was, therefore, possible to compare and contrast the different kinds of data collection that took place in the relatively 'private' and 'public' arenas of individual interview and focus groups encounters. While you might be cautious about using focus groups as a first stage strategy, readers may be drawn towards this approach at later stages in ethnographies, and there are precedents in published research that readers may find helpful.[3]

Drama and fiction

In recent years, differing forms of telling education as it is have emerged. In part, this reflects a loss of innocence about and challenge to 'thick description' as privileged, exhaustive and/or neutral 'mechanisms of representation' (Atkinson 1992: 38), and where the certainty and authority of texts might be considered to have become even more exaggerated by recent use of computer assisted analytical models and typologies. The intellectual currents of poststructuralism and postmodernism have also renewed debates about both the writing and reading of ethnography as active constructions. Still, the 'root metaphor' (Atkinson 1992) for ethnography has, until recently, remained unchallenged: 'the silent and unknown is given voice by the ethnographer who speaks for the other' (p.39).

Different forms of parody and pastiche have emerged to become parts of the scholarly writing up of ethnographic 'doings' and also core to the research design (see below). Moreover, literary metaphors have been used increasingly in ethnography to examine critically ethnographic data that apply conceptual descriptors grounded in the work of specific authors. For example, we note Schockley Lee's (Schockley Lee and Lee 1998) extensive ethnography about Alvin Haines, an elementary school principal in the US, dubbed 'the White Knight', that is a critical examination of his role through a conceptual framework grounded in the work of Foucault. This is reported by Fazzaro (1998) who examines principalship from the perspective of institutional discourses that constitute social relations in school. 'This form of power operates by "constructing" the character and disposition of those subject to institutional practices' (p.1). So, in this fascinating ethnography, a Foucauldian framework is used to represent a 'White Knight' principal who is simultaneously represented as an oppressor of pupils, parents and teachers, and also as oppressed by the structures, principles and values within and beyond education that had 'constructed' him.

Rationales that underpin representational experimentation have been practical and ethical as well as intellectual. Bassey's (1999) reporting of a research study focused on 'what it is like to be a student on final teaching practice' is represented as a series of fictionalized 'Dear Emma' letters, as a playlet in two acts and as diary extracts. Very practical justifications are provided for this fictionalized form of representation that allowed:

> several accounts to be condensed into one; it permitted potentially defamatory statements to be delocalized, and, it was hoped, grasped the reader's attention. It also enabled us, in the four letters to Emma, to change cross-sectional data from three different generations of student teachers, into a simulated longitudinal account of one person's experience.
>
> (Bassey 1999: 160)

For some researchers, fiction or drama is used from early stages in the research process, and may be especially relevant for practitioner-ethnographers who are reflecting upon their own practices as well as those of colleagues in specific educational settings (often their own). Indeed, the 'story' has an established provenance in research into teaching and with teachers, with prominent advocates among action researchers like Carter (1990, 1993). Underpinning research of this genre is the promotion of 'event-structured knowledge' (Carter 1993: 7) acquired through the accumulation of shared teacher stories to enable teachers to enhance their understanding of professional and pedagogical beliefs and practices. Similarly, action researcher Evans (1998), reports on a similar approach used in a research project. This centred on developing her role as an effective secondary school teacher and also in developing:

> opportunities for teachers to take time out of every day 'busyness' in order to reflect upon and improve pedagogical practices . . . As part of the methodology [teachers] used 'story' to help come to a focus, to put their thoughts in order, to clarify what they were thinking and to move forward their professional development.
>
> (p.493)

Evans' story is one which will be familiar to many senior teachers and lecturers who have responsibilities for the continuing professional development (CPD) of staff in the schools, colleges and/or universities in which they work, and where there is an interest in developing, through research, a more reflexive culture rooted in professional practice. She uses fictionalized story telling first, to present the dilemmas that underpinned the focus of her research, namely: how best to structure CPD sessions organized and delivered by heads of year and heads of department in a secondary school, and second, to use story as a means of exploring those heads' perspectives on how to promote effective CPD practices.

A brief extract from the fictionalized account of the 'dilemmas' is illustrative. Here, Adele, CPD team leader, is engaged in conversation with Vera, a member of the same team, and Joseph, the leader of another CPD team. Liz is Adele's deputy team leader:

Just Tell Me What to Do!
One day Adele worked with Liz to set up an activity which they both thought would be directly useful in the classroom. Vera didn't want to take part.

'I've got books to mark' she said. 'You don't need me do you?'

'Yes' replied Adele, surprised and somewhat dismayed by the question. 'I want all the team to have experienced this activity before planning their year 8 lessons.'

'Well' said Vera, 'I can't understand why you don't just tell me what you want me to do and I'll do it. After all that's your job – and if you can't tell me just send me on a course so that someone else can! Look at the amount of time we waste trying to work things out for ourselves – surely someone somewhere must have the answers.' . . . Adele wasn't happy with this turn in events, as up till now, Vera had – more or less – kept her disgruntlement to herself . . . She decided to talk to a colleague about it, and outlined the problem to Joseph. What did he think? How did he use his INSET time?

'Well' said Joseph, 'There isn't enough time in the day to gain commitment. I'd just tell them – do this, do that – then they can go off and get on with something else. After all, they're not going to do what you dream up for INSET in their own classrooms are they? So they might as well get on with their marking'.

(Evans 1998: 496–7)

In practitioner ethnography, then, fictionalized accounts or stories have been used to discover and explore personal meanings in ambiguous and problematic situations; to distance research participants from situations, and open up conversations and group interviews without embarrassment; to express feelings and values in a fictional setting; and, perhaps most importantly, to locate the activities and perspectives of practitioners and practitioner researchers as part of their own biographies in order to make sense of them (Evans 1998: 503).

Allied to an intellectual critique of ethnography has been the fragmentation of ethnographic texts in a variety of forms. Among these is the use of dialogue, for example, between ethnographer and informants, advocated by earlier users of such representational forms (like anthropologist Dwyer (1982)). Atkinson (1992) records that Dwyer's ethnography comprised an ongoing dialogue between himself and a research informant to provide a counterpoint to the ethnographer's authorial and authoritative voice. The extent to which such an approach is either novel or, in effect, successful in removing the supremacy of the ethnographer's voice (even if we were to agree that this was desirable and from whose perspective) seems questionable. As Atkinson (1992) comments:

It is indeed ironic to reflect that the interrogative strategies employed in Dwyer's interviews with a Faqir [in Morocco], and celebrated by him for their revelatory power, would in other contexts be treated quite differently. The question-and-answer sequences, when translated into other contexts such as . . . the school classroom, would normally be found to be enactments of domination and control [which Dwyer was trying to resist].

(p.44)

In other educational contexts, dialogic engagement, whether face to face or through correspondence, has been used to progress, report, evaluate and reflect upon research that has involved school teachers and external researchers. In a collaborative project that included a media, mathematics and environment workshop in a rural primary school, Watling *et al.* (2000)

use written correspondence between themselves to write their reflections about the project. This provides a powerful mechanism for considering what happened during the study and the bases upon which reflection occurred. For example, in written response to the question posed by teachers Carole Hignett and Alison Moore which was, 'in what ways were your expectations altered by the children's input?' researchers Cotton and Watling reply (Watling *et al.* 2000: 424–8):

Tony C: The power of video – this seems to give children the freedom to be involved in their work. The video was a powerful tool in terms of developing the pupils' own reflective practice. I was surprised and a little alarmed at the difficulty they found in describing the mathematics they were involved in. This emphasised for me the importance of mathematical archaeology, that is constantly pointing out how mathematics underpins much of the day to day decisions we make . . .

Rob W: I have known this school, the teachers, and many of these children for five years. In fact I have done similar work with some members of these classes when they were in their Nursery and Infant School. What impressed me then, and what seems to have disappeared, is their ability to plan, work and reflect on things together . . . But something has changed. My inclination is to look to the curriculum, the greater amounts of time pre-allocated to particular tasks, the targets, the tests, and the standardisation of the day. All of this has removed or reduced the autonomy of the teacher who is now being told what to teach and how to teach. De-skilled rather than re-skilled. In turn the children are being told what to learn and how to learn. Denied the practice in making choices, they are losing their vital ability to work together. A little emptier than last year, it seems to me – a reversal of the process we call education.

The project could, therefore, be seen as aspects of 'critical collaborative action research' (Elliott 1991) into which ethnographic approaches and the use of 'written conversations' were embedded.

Summary

In each of the methods discussed in this chapter, our intention has been to provide not only a critical introduction but also to convey a sense of the excitement, tension and diversity in the collection of data referred to here as 'primary', and by Pole and Lampard (2002) as 'active' rather than 'passive' data. In 2003, 'systematic ethnography' may have lost some of its earlier 'naivety' (Brewer 2000: 142) but none of its potent appeal to research first hand experience.

In its latest forms, we may need to find effective counterpoints to balance the potential danger of fictional and dialogic excesses prevalent in some forms of educational ethnography so that it does not lose its core reference to the educational settings and people in which we are interested and committed – the problem of researchers becoming 'overwhelmingly self-referential' (Atkinson 1992: 50), tensions to which we return in later chapters of this book.

Meanwhile, ethnography may or may not be 'fun' or 'easy' to begin, but, as a complex activity, it continues to raise multiple issues of methodology and epistemology. In the next chapter, our focus turns to the collection of data which already exist 'out there', secondary data sources which, in combination with primary data, are part of the holistic enterprise that is educational ethnography.

Notes

1 While we would argue that most life history studies have involved multiple interviews, Plummer (2001) distinguishes between long and short life histories where the latter may involve only one interview.
2 Readers thinking about using focus groups with children rather than young people would find O'Kane's (2000) recent account of using participatory techniques, like focus groups, in facilitating views about decisions which affect children, as expressed by 'looked after' children by local authorities in England and Wales, especially insightful. For O'Kane and others, focus groups provide a method 'to break down the power imbalance between adults and children, and . . . to create space which enables children to speak up and be heard' (pp.136–7).
3 For example, when Janesick (1998) studied deaf culture in Washington, DC, and addressed the question 'How do some deaf adults manage to succeed academically and in the work place given the stigma of deafness in this society?' she used individual interviews and observations first. This was followed by focus groups and life history approaches once she had come to learn more about perspectives on deafness among the 12 participants in her study.

3 | Doing ethnography: secondary sources of ethnographic data

Introduction

In the opening chapter to this book we characterized ethnography as an inclusive approach to research in which a wide range of research methods could be deployed in the study of social action within a discrete location. We included within this wide range both qualitative and quantitative methods. In taking this position, which not all exponents of ethnography would accept, we sought to emphasize that by including a diverse range of methods within the ambit of ethnography we were not advocating an 'anything goes' approach to research, far from it. Our intention was to emphasize that ethnography is a holistic approach to research, rather than a research method in itself. We also stressed that the macro-perspective within which ethnography is generally located, that is one based on verstehen (Weber 1949), allows it to deploy a range of research strategies and methods in its pursuit of the perspective of the insider.

While ethnography is often concerned with explaining and understanding social interaction, it also seeks to locate that interaction within a wider context which takes account not only of individual agency but also of social structures. The data collected as part of an ethnographic study, therefore, may perform different roles in the pursuit of this holistic picture. As we have already seen, different kinds of data may be characterized in different ways. For example, Chapter 2 dealt principally with what are often described as primary sources of data. In these instances, data are collected on the basis of face to face contact between the researcher and those who are being researched. These data can be contrasted with those discussed in this chapter, which may be designated as being from secondary sources, where there may not be that immediacy of contact between researcher and researched. The data may already exist and the researcher is, therefore, merely putting them to a use which is different from the one for which they were originally created. Or perhaps more graphically, Mason (1996) distinguishes between data generation and data collection. Mason sees qualitative data largely in terms of the former. Although secondary data sources such as diaries, photographs, maps, timetables and works of art are not created for the purposes of a specific research project, they have the capacity to tell a researcher a great deal not only about those who created them but also about the context and the social world in which they were created. Consequently, when a researcher makes use of such data he or she may be seen as merely collecting what already exists. In this respect, Pole and Lampard (2002) draw a distinction between passive and active data. However, Mason (1996) believes that characterization of data in terms of such opposing concepts fails to recognize that even with so-called secondary or passive sources of data a process of generation occurs as the researcher interacts with the data, interrogating them for relevance to the focus of his or her specific research project. Mason states:

> In this sense, your data sources are those places or phenomena from or through which you believe data can be generated (ask yourself, potentially, could I generate data from this source?); your data generation methods are the techniques and strategies which you use to do this.
>
> (1996: 36)

Mason's position, while perhaps not shared by all researchers, is one which places a primacy on the role of the researcher in the research process by stressing that this can never be passive as he or she seeks an understanding of the ways in which social life is constructed and experienced. In our view, even Lee's (2000) interesting insight into what he, drawing on Webb *et al.* (1966), calls unobtrusive measures emphasizes that although data may be, in his terms, found, captured or retrieved, their significance and relevance to the research being undertaken depend not only on the nature of their interpretation by the researcher, but also on their recognition as data by the researcher in the first place.

While at one level this discussion may be reduced to a question of semantics, and some would argue that it matters little what label we give to different kinds of data, so long as they continue to inform the research, at another level the discussion draws attention to important issues relating to the centrality of data analysis to ethnography. It emphasizes that on their own, data are of little use to the research process. To be meaningful and hence useful, the researcher must work with them in a thorough, systematic yet creative way in order that they might yield insight into aspects of social life.

Having noted these interesting and important debates about generation and collection, secondary and primary, active and passive data, we agree with but wish to develop a little further, Mason's position that all data is in a sense generated. In our view, data from these various sources are not merely generated in a mechanistic, objectified fashion which would imply that all researchers would produce the same findings from the same data in a positivistic sense, akin to laboratory based experiments which may be repeated time after time in order to check reliability. Our notion of data generation is one which is closer to a social constructionist perspective, in that the process of generation together with the information which that process yields is dependent on the researcher responsible for the generation. The position is one which may be seen to ally us with a relativist or even a postmodern position (Scheurich 1997; Stronach and MacLure 1997). If this is the case, it is not our intention to in any way call into question the value of empirical research or to suggest a highly structured, statistically rigid methodology as an alternative. It is our intention to emphasize that in generating, collecting or constructing data, researchers have choices. These relate to what is identified as legitimate data, how much data should be collected how and to what depth of theoretical exhaustion (Glaser and Strauss 1967; Strauss and Corbin 1990, 1997) data should be subjected, what issues to pursue and to emphasize when writing from the data and how to present an authoritative account of the research (Atkinson 1990). All of these aspects of what might be termed the research endeavour are mediated through the researcher.

Our stance in this chapter which deals with secondary sources of data which ethnographic research might employ, and in the previous chapter which focused on primary sources, therefore, is that the data and in turn the knowledge that different methods yield will depend as much on the researcher as on the methods themselves. We draw this conclusion in respect of all research methods and methodology whether they are characterized as primary or secondary, active or passive and whether the data are regarded as generated or collected.

Having said this, we do nevertheless recognize a difference between methods relating to the proximity of the researcher to the collection or generation of the data both in spatial and temporal terms. The presence of the researcher, the notion of being there (Geertz 1988) we feel is significant not only in respect of the capacity of the researcher to affect the data that are collected, but also in respect of his or her capacity to witness at first hand the context in which the data are collected or generated. We suggest, if a little tentatively, that a close temporal and spatial relationship between researcher and the generated or collected data has the capacity to facilitate a fuller, more holistic account of social action or a discrete location. For this reason we have divided our consideration of methods which might be used by the ethnographer into these two chapters. This chapter deals with those methods where there is a greater temporal and spatial distance between the researcher and the collected or generated data. It considers surveys and official statistics, diaries, photography, art and other sources of visual data, the Internet and finally what we have termed other documentary sources.

We also recognize, however, that there may be many other forms of data which fall into this category which is based upon spatial and temporal distance. Perhaps there are sources of data which we have yet to recognize as valuable to ethnography, the potential of which to inform us about the social world may only fully emerge as the primary reasons for the existence of those sources themselves begin to develop. A good example of such a development in recent years would be the Internet. Only now as the massive implications of the rapid growth of the World Wide Web become apparent has this become acknowledged as an important source of data (Lee 2000).

In considering these different sources of data we wish to stress that it is not our intention to provide a 'how to do it' guide to their effective use in ethnography. There are already many textbooks which offer the intending researcher advice and detailed guidance of this nature. It is our concern, however, to provide a discussion of these various data sources in the context of ethnography. Heeding Mills' (1959) warning to avoid falling towards a form of abstracted empiricism, our prime intention is to provide a methodological account of these sources, where many other books have been concerned principally with method.

Surveys

We have already argued that quantitative data can have a legitimate role in ethnographic research. At the same time, we feel it is also fair to say that surveys and other methods which yield quantitative data cannot, on their own, constitute ethnographic research. However, we might also make the same statement in relation to many methods which yield qualitative data. Our interpretation of the role of surveys and official statistics as part of ethnography, therefore, is that they offer an important source of supporting and contextualizing data against which the more qualitative data may be viewed.

While the textbooks to which we alluded earlier discuss many different forms of survey research and engage with their individual nuances, we will restrict our discussion to the questionnaire and include here both self-completed questionnaires, frequently sent to potential respondents through the post, and verbal questionnaires, where a researcher reads out particular questions to a respondent in a particular order and often provides pre-specified answers to those questions, from which the respondent has to choose. In many instances, verbal questionnaires like this are referred to as interviews. While this may be strictly true, if one defines an interview simply as the imparting of verbal information from one party to another, this method does not capture the essence of or the complexity of a more open-ended and discursive interview, such as the kinds discussed in the previous chapter. As such we feel that this may be a misleading use of the term interview. We see the nature of the data collected from verbal exchanges between interviewer and interviewee as very different from that collected via a more highly structured survey.

Our concern here is with the form of survey which collects only data of a quantitative form and during which there is little or no affective interaction between researcher and respondent. Perhaps the best way of characterizing the survey is to use Marsh's (1982: 7) frequently cited definition. She states that a survey takes place when:

1 systematic measurements are made of the same set of properties, or variables, for each of a number of cases;
2 the resulting data can be laid out in the form of a rectangle, or matrix, in which the rows correspond to the cases and the columns correspond to the properties or variables;
3 the intention is to look at patterns in the variables by aggregating information from the different cases.

Marsh's definition is useful because it places considerable emphasis on the way in which survey data are displayed and analysed, emphasizing aggregation and patterns. The definition is compatible, therefore, with our identification of survey data as supporting or contextualizing data in respect of ethnography as we can see it as providing the backcloth against which more detailed, action orientated data could be placed.

In its reference to systematic measurement, Marsh's definition also evokes something of the process by which survey data are collected. In order to facilitate systematic measurement, the survey requires precision in the collection of data, while the identification of patterns from aggregated cases requires a structured approach which is applied in the same way to all such cases. The structured questionnaire is the obvious and most frequently used example of such a research tool in social and educational research. An example (see Figure 3.1) taken from a study conducted by the National Foundation for Educational Research, one of the principal exponents of survey research in education in the UK, which evaluated the government's Beacon School initiative (Rudd *et al.* 2002) illustrates clearly the approach taken to the collection of systematic data.

The example shows clearly not only the kinds of questions posed to facilitate the collection of precise, systematic data but it also illustrates the degree of uniformity required in the collection of such data. Respondents are told explicitly how they should answer the questions by ticking boxes or placing a numerical score in the appropriate place indicated on the pro-forma. From this it is easy to see how a high level of uniformity could be achieved across the completed questionnaires facilitating the aggregation of cases and the production of matrices to reveal patterns in the data leading to generalizable findings. In turn, such findings could be subjected to a range of statistical tests, designed to demonstrate the reliability of the findings. The

Figure 3.1 An example of approach taken to collection of systematic data

C5 Do you in any way restrict the amount or frequency of Beacon activity your school undertakes? (Please tick one box)

                      Yes ☐   Please answer question **C6** below.

                      No ☐   Please answer question **D1**.

C6 Have you had to decline any requests for Beacon activity from another school/institution? (Please tick one box)

                      Yes ☐   Please answer question **C7** below.

                      No ☐   Please answer question **D1**.

C7 If yes, how many schools?   ☐☐
(**Note**: '1' should be written as 01)

C8 Why did you feel unable to offer assistance to the school/schools in question? (Please tick all boxes that apply)

Too busy   ☐

Lack relevant expertise   ☐

Over subscription for activities   ☐

Other (please specify)   ☐

....

C9 Were you able to refer the school/schools to an alternative source of expertise? (Please tick one box)

                      Yes ☐   Please answer question **C10** below.

                      No ☐   Please answer question **D1**.

Source: Rudd *et al.* (2002: xxii)

questions posed are unambiguous, requiring short, precise, easily recorded answers. The questionnaire is laid out in a clear and attractive fashion and respondents are guided through it with detailed instructions, which ensure they are answering the questions appropriate to their particular circumstances. Many of the responses to questions can be easily converted from the questionnaire by means of optical reading technology or, where an open-ended question has asked the respondent to express an opinion, by manual coding techniques to a computer program designed for the analysis of statistical data.[1] The result of all this will be a series of charts, tables and statistics which offer an insight into trends in social behaviour across a given population. In addition, the data also lend themselves to a wide range of statistical techniques which will allow different characteristics of the population to be analyzed and for the comparison of different variables identified in the questionnaire.

In addition, the strengths of surveys are seen to lie in the belief that they can provide findings which can be related to entire populations, that the validity of findings can be calculated in terms of degrees of significance and error and that findings are as free as possible from the impact of the researcher. In addition, surveys are often quicker and cheaper to conduct than research, which relies on the collection of very detailed qualitative data. However, many of these qualities of the social survey and the data which it yields contrast markedly with those of other methods used by the ethnographer, and the nature of the data which they might yield. Where the social survey looks for generalizable data across a population or populations, many other forms of ethnographic data are particularistic, looking to explain social action from within a precise location or population. Moreover, the goal of and belief in objectivity which are usually pursued by the survey researcher, who also attempts to minimize his or her own impact on the collected data and who usually has little contact with those who provide it, are not usually the goal of the ethnographer. This is not to imply that ethnographers or qualitative researchers more generally aim for subjective research which is little more than a product of their own prejudice. Rather that the epistemological starting points of the two approaches are different. Where the survey looks for the overview, seeking out general trends in the data as far as possible untainted by the researcher, the more qualitatively orientated data collection methods attempt to capture the essence of a particular situation from the inside. In using such methods the researcher recognizes that his or her presence inevitably impacts upon the social action therein and consequently upon the data that are collected.

However, as Bryman (1988) has stated, epistemological differences between qualitative and quantitative research methods are often over-stated and it is frequently the more technical concerns of cost and time which determine the methods that the researcher chooses to use. In the case of ethnographic research we believe it is better to see qualitative and quantitative research as complementary in respect of producing the holistic picture of whatever is being researched. The generalizable, quantitative data generated by the survey can thus provide the context against which to view the detailed qualitative data. In attributing survey research and quantitative data a role in ethnography in this way we are not, however, arguing that surveys or statistical data can, in and of themselves, be regarded as ethnographic data. The role which we have attributed to them is one which supports the qualitative data. It is, therefore, a limited role which surveys play in ethnography but, nevertheless, is one which can make an important contribution to providing as complete a picture as possible of the discrete location or interaction upon which the ethnography focuses. Having said this, we would not wish to imply that an ethnographic study would be incomplete without such a quantitative element. Clearly, there are many ethnographies where quantitative contextual data are not provided and where the ethnography offers a detailed study of a particular situation limited by that situation itself. To conclude this brief discussion of the place of surveys in ethnographic research we would argue that they should be regarded as part of the toolbox of methods from which the ethnographer is able to draw. As with any other method, there will be occasions when it is appropriate to use survey methods and others when it is not. The point serves to emphasize that ethnographic data collection methods per se do not exist. Methods become ethnographic when they are used in a particular context and when the data that they yield are analysed in ways which are commonly seen to lend themselves to an ethnographic approach. In this sense, successful ethnography requires the ethnographer to discriminate between methods not only in relation to the data which they will yield individually, but also in terms of the extent to which these will complement those collected by other means.

Official statistics

In many ways official statistics may perform a similar role within ethnography to data collected by means of social surveys, in that they offer a context against which to view more detailed qualitative data. Collected centrally by government departments or other agencies of government their focus is usually on a national level, as they seek to document trends in aspects of social life which can facilitate comparisons across time. *The Oxford Dictionary of Sociology* defines official statistics in the following way:

> Statistical information produced, collated and disseminated by national governments, their agencies, and the international bodies which link them. These data are almost invariably nationally representative, because they are obtained from complete censuses or very large-scale national sample surveys, and they usually seek to present definitive information conforming to international definitions and classifications or other well-established conventions.
>
> (Marshall 1998: 463)

The areas of social life about which official statistics are compiled continue to grow and now include those of health, education, employment and unemployment, crime, work, spending, births, marriage and deaths, demographic trends, housing and many other areas. In addition, each of these areas can be sub-divided to reveal quite detailed information relating to particular issues. In the field of education, for example, official statistics are gathered in relation to school attendance and truancy, examination entries and pass rates, drop out rates from universities and the number of school exclusions, to name but a few of the many areas. A principal source in which to locate official statistics is the huge range of publications made publicly available by Her Majesty's Stationery Office (HMSO). In the field of education it is currently the Department for Education and Skills which is responsible for collecting and disseminating official statistics via HMSO. However, in recent years the development of electronic means of recording, storing and disseminating data have made the Internet an important and useful location for official statistics.

The abundance of official statistics and the relative ease by which they can now be accessed by the general public can make them a useful starting point for ethnographers, helping them to identify a field in which to conduct their research and also highlighting issues of interest and importance within a general field. In addition, like data generated and collected by social surveys, they can act as a useful contextual backcloth against which to view an ethnographic study which has focused on a particular location or set of circumstances. However, as with social surveys, a gap exists between the researcher and the information conveyed by official statistics. As official statistics are gathered by government departments, via the civil service and other officially sanctioned research organizations such as the Office for National Statistics (ONS), the number of researchers directly involved in their collection is actually quite small. Moreover, those researchers who are involved, by and large, tend to be involved only in their collection, analysis and a fairly standardized form of reporting, based on the statistics. They do not tend to be the same researchers who would be involved in ethnography. In fact, most users of official statistics tend to be just that, users rather than collectors or creators of the data.

While this degree of distance may also be the case with many other forms of secondary data, the official status of official statistics, in many ways differentiates them from most other sources of secondary data. Moreover, it is also seen as the source or reason for limitations associated not only with their use, but also with their identification and collection. For example, O'Connell-Davidson and Layder (1994), Reiner (1996) and Levitas (1996) refer to rape, crime and unemployment statistics respectively to draw attention to the way in which official statistics can be important in defining behaviour and social trends simply by deciding what should count as rape, crime or unemployment. As Pole and Lampard (2002) illustrate, between 1979 and 1989, 30 changes were made to the way in which unemployment was counted, including the decision to include only those in receipt of benefit, rather than those registered for work. This shift and many others of a similar nature not only resulted in a change to the numbers recorded as unemployed but also to the definition of unemployment. Against the background of industrial decline characteristic of the late Thatcher era, it is difficult not to see such changes as politically motivated. The government of the day was responsible, via the Department for Employment, for the collection of unemployment figures, consequently there existed an opportunity to legitimately massage the figures by changing the way in which unemployment was defined. Similar claims could be made about the annual collection and publication of crime figures by the Home Office, or indeed many other collections of official statistics which relate to politically sensitive issues. The point we wish to make from these examples is that despite their 'official' tag, which suggests a degree of reliability and encourages confidence in them, official statistics may be seen as a social construction, in their reflection of the definitions given to particular forms of social behaviour by those responsible for their collection. In addition, as Coleman and Moynihan (1996) have shown in their discussion of the 'dark' figure in crime statistics, official statistics can only reflect what information is available to those responsible for their compilation. In the case of crime, therefore, only crimes reported to the police will appear in official crime statistics. Failure to report a crime effectively removes any chance that it would be included in the annual analysis of crime and offences in the UK. Similarly, to highlight an example specifically from the field of education, the absence of information relating to ethnic origin of teachers in official statistics on the teaching profession, compiled by the government department responsible for education in England and Wales, could be seen as contributing not only to their 'invisibility' of black teachers within the profession but also to a form of institutional racism.

Having raised these various concerns about serious flaws and shortcomings inherent to official statistics, one might understandably ask why they might be considered useful to ethnographic research. The answer to this question draws on both the negative aspects of official statistics which we have discussed above, and also to what some see as their positive attributes. For example, Bulmer (1980) draws attention to the fact that official statistics are based on very large sample sizes and data sets. In the case of the national ten year census, information about the entire population is collected. Bulmer's argument is that only national governments have the resources to collect data of this magnitude and while he recognizes some of their shortcomings he believes that these are largely out-weighed by the scope of the data, which are available to the social researcher at virtually no expense. Moreover, he argues that the serious concern that has been expressed about official statistics in recent years has made those responsible for their collection sensitive to their inherent problems and concerned to address them. Meanwhile, by identifying the negative aspects of official statistics, their shortcomings can be used to foster a more critical perspective on educational and other social issues as researchers become alerted to issues raised by the way in which the statistics are compiled. For example, O'Connell-Davidson and Layder (1994) say that the failure of official rape statistics to reflect the actual number of women (and men) who experience rape encourages closer scrutiny by researchers of police and court procedures. It says much about the cultural norms and values of a society and the ways in which it defines and categorizes rape and also leads researchers to pose questions about why victims fail to report rapes to the authorities. They state:

Considered phenomenologically, we can see that official rape statistics do not provide 'numerical facts' on the subject of rape. They are not an objective measure of the incidence of rape, but rather reflect a series of interpretations and actions by different social actors (the rapist, the victim, the victim's friends and relatives, the police surgeon, police officers, solicitors, barristers, judges, and jurists), which are critically shaped by those social actor's ideas, values and beliefs.

(O'Connell-Davidson and Layder 1994: 76)

In the field of education, the absence of statistics on the ethnic origin of teachers may be seen to have contributed to the 'invisibility' of black and Asian teachers. In turn, this absence of information can be argued to have contributed to an inaccurate characterization of the teaching profession in terms of race and ethnicity (Pole 1999) which provided part of the motivation for studies into the experiences of ethnic minority teachers such as those conducted by Benn (1998), Osler (1997) and Pole (1998). Interestingly, the ethnographic approach of these studies goes a considerable way to compensating for the gap in information on ethnicity and teaching left by the paucity of official statistics in this area.

In our view, what the educational ethnographer can take from this discussion of pros and cons of official statistics is a healthy scepticism about their capacity to provide reliable data. While accepting much of Bulmer's (1980) argument about their positive aspects, we also appreciate the reservation which O'Connell-Davidson and Layder (1994) express. Official statistics may contribute to the contextual background against which ethnographic research is conducted in the field of education. They may, for example, help to see characteristics of individual schools against the national picture, acting as a form of triangulation. In addition, they may also encourage the ethnographer to consider the conceptual framework; the definition and selection procedures which contribute to the creation and collection of official statistics. This itself may contribute to the quest of the holistic picture, which we identified as an objective of ethnography in the opening chapter and may result in the conduct of more ethnographic work which fills the gaps or corrects the perceptions left by official statistics.

Like data generated by social surveys, official statistics do not, on their own, constitute ethnography. However, their use in conjunction with other methods, together with recognition of their limitations, may make them useful contributors to an ethnographic database.

Diaries

In many ways, the use of diaries in ethnography contrasts markedly with the use of official statistics. The degree of certainty which researchers seek through the use of official statistics together with their capacity to provide national and international perspectives on social and educational trends is not a possibility for research which utilizes diaries. Like many of the tools that the educational ethnographer makes use of, the diary provides access to particular, parochial and time bound data. In doing so, however, it often provides a level of personal detail not available through other methods. At the same time, it may also offer a degree of reflexivity on the part of those responsible for writing the diary, which is also rare in other methods.

Diary research may be divided into two main types based on the purpose for which the diary entries were made and consequently on their intended audiences. In short, there are diaries that, although they may yield interesting and useful ethnographic data, were not written for this purpose and whose intended audience is usually the diarist himself or herself. There are also those diaries that are written specifically for research purposes, where the audience is the researcher. Although there may be similarities in these different types of diary of the nature we suggested above, in that they are time bound, parochial and often very personal, there are also many differences. For example, diaries which are written specifically for research purposes will usually be focused towards particular activities or occurrences and will usually involve the diarist writing within guidance given by the researcher. Diaries which are written for reasons other than research, most usually for consumption by the diarist himself or herself will tend to be more wide ranging and discursive. They may be factual, recording particular events and activities, but they may also be more personal, recording the diarist's views, opinions and feelings about a particular topic. With the diary designed and written for research purposes, it is hoped that the great majority that is written will be targeted at the research topic and, therefore, of use to the researcher. Meanwhile, the researcher who seeks to make use of the more discursive, 'naturally occurring' diary may find that they are faced with large amounts of material that is of little or no relevance to the specific topic of their research.

An example of the diary which is deliberately constructed under the guidance of researchers, specifically for research purposes can be seen in the work of Mizen *et al.* (1999) in their research into working children. As part of their study into the work and economic lives of young people Mizen *et al.* tracked working children over the course of a full school year. In addition to individual interviews, focus groups and photography, the researchers asked the children to complete several diaries throughout the year. These were carefully designed and addressed specific issues relating to their experience of work. At approximately two month intervals the children were asked to complete a diary which covered their activities over a full week. To provide a focus for the diaries, which also engaged with findings emerging from other aspects of the research, they were asked to write about topics such as spending, health and safety, the relationship between school and work, the experience of work, and relationships at work. Figures 3.2 and 3.3 show the instructions that the children were given about completing the diary and a completed diary.

The information provided is detailed and targeted and although it does

Figure 3.2

Example X

> For each day starting the Friday of the week when you get the diary, please keep a record at the end of the day of anything that you did in your spare time even if it's just 'visited a friend' 'watched tv', hanging around the park/shops etc/ and everything you spent. Even if you don't do much, you might spend money, it might be bus fare 40p, bag of crisps 27p, magazine £1.80, you get the idea? Please try and be as accurate as you can, and as honest as you can, we're not going to make any moral judgements about what you spend money on, that's a promise. If you don't spend anything on a date please say so.
>
> Example XX
> Friday: Did anyone give you any extra money today, for bus fares, school expenditure etc.
>
> Yes ☑ No ☐   If yes, how much £50p.
>
> | Spending (amount and what on) | Leisure activities |
> |---|---|
> | At school i spent £1.00 on food and i brought 10 fags. At £1.76 | Me and my best friend went UP the comp. to meet our boyfriends, i lent him £10.00 |
>
> Total £12.76
>
> Saturday: Did anyone give you any extra money today, for bus fares etc.
>
> Yes ☐ No ☑   If yes, how much £..........
>
> | Spending (amount and what on) | Leisure (what do you do, where, who with?) |
> |---|---|
> | On saturday i brought a magazine which cost me £1.75 I also brought some Tampax at £3.15 10 fags £1.76 | I went on the waltzers at the fair 3 times which cost me £3.00 I am now saving up for my Holiday. |
>
> Total £9.76.

Figure 3.3

Example X

Has anything changed about the way other people spend money on you since you have had a job, or when you have had a job in the past? For example, do you buy things for yourself now that other people used to pay for or buy for you?

Example XX

Now i have started working again i can buy my own fags where as my mum was paying for them for me. I now have paid all the money back to her though, and i braght her some fag's for a change. Since i started work again i have started to go out more as i have money to spend on thing's. Now i am working again my friends who don't have job's are being really nice so i will lend them money. So i tell then to get off there fat Arse's and get themselve's job's.

Has your work affected your leisure time, could you tell us how? For example, the time available to do your own thing or see friends, the things that you do, who you see, where you go?

My boyfriend is getting upset with me as i only see him three time's a week as i work weekend's and some nights a week, plus i have homework.

I don't see my friends very often either as i don't have the time. My mum also get's upset as sometime she only see's me in the morning when i get up to go to school or to go to work.

That's life and if you don't work for what you want you don't get it.

not offer precision in respect of exact times it does, nevertheless, offer an overview of a young person's spending pattern over the period of a week. In addition to the factual information relating to what her wages were spent on, the diarist also reveals information about her home circumstances, about family relationships and a broader pattern of activities than just those that are suggested by what she chooses to spend her money on. In this instance, the directions given by the researchers structure the diary entries. However, they do allow the researcher to conduct analysis in accordance with concepts which may have been highlighted in data collected by other means or, indeed, in relation to key social variables which shape the young person's experience of work and spending. Morrison and Galloway (1996) also adopt this approach in their research into supply teaching. The detail of the information provided by the diarists which focused on their experience as supply teachers, allowed the researchers to analyse at the level of gender as a first order concept. Their claim being that the diary operated as an effective substitute for observation. They state:

'Diary accounts confirmed the predominance, but not exclusivity, of women in supply work for a multiplicity of reasons. This research drew upon and added to, the contribution of gender studies in making women's work visible' (1996: 46).

Galloway and Morrison's claim that the diary made women's work visible is interesting, in that in a literal sense, the diary is clearly not able to do this as it is a means of data collection usually conducted away from the action with which the researchers are concerned and is a solitary activity involving only the diarist. Nevertheless, Galloway and Morrison's findings show quite clearly the capacity of the diary to shed light on issues of gender in the context of supply teaching in particular and more generally in the context of work. Their use of the diary in this way illustrates its capacity to yield data at different levels. For example, there are those which are conveyed by the factual and descriptive elements of the data which give an account of the action in any given situation. At the same time, at a more analytical and grounded level (Glaser and Strauss 1967) there are those data which facilitate the identification of key concepts such as gender, social class, ethnicity and age which allow a more structural account of social action.

In this sense, the deliberately constructed diary created for research purposes can be a particularly valuable source of different kinds of data. However, its creation may not be without difficulty. In particular the problem of attrition often means that diaries of this nature are incomplete, as those completing them loose interest or fail to find the time to make entries conscientiously. Offering some form of incentive may be helpful. Mizen *et al.* (1999) paid their diarists £10 for each completed diary, giving the children an opportunity to earn £60 over the course of the school year. However, while this resulted in a high rate of completion, the researchers could never be certain whether diary entries were made hurriedly in advance of meeting with the researcher and the chance to receive another payment of £10, or whether they had been made throughout the week as directed by the researchers. In some respects this may not matter. What may be more important is the extent to which the diaries actually conveyed a true account of activities in which the children engaged during the week in question. Certainly, the opportunity for fabrication of data existed. However, one might also argue that diaries are not alone among research methods in presenting such opportunities. Moreover, the interviews which Mizen *et al.* (1999) conducted, based on the children's diary entries were intended to highlight any such instances.

Diaries written for reasons other than research, also offer the ethnographer a rich source of information. However, the style of such diaries and the reasons why they are written mean that the data they convey are rarely as specific and targeted as those contained in diaries which are deliberately constructed. The information in diaries such as these, although valuable to the ethnographer, may be much more discursive, it may relate more to inner feelings and reflections than to events, social structures or organizations. It may also be highly selective, reflecting what the diarist felt to be important to record from his or her perspective rather than a more rounded account of events. Nevertheless, despite what some might regard as the shortcomings of this nature of diary, the personal diary can offer a mine of information for the ethnographer, allowing access to personal reflection unavailable via any other means. Having said this, examples of such diaries being used in research are difficult to find, not least because they are often regarded as private documents for personal consumption which may only come to light after a person's death. At this point they may be destroyed or closely guarded by relatives. However, an example of such a diary is that written by Malinowski (1967) the influential anthropologist to whom we, in part, attributed the development of modern ethnography in the opening chapter of this book. His diary, published posthumously by his widow, offered very different insights into the man and his work, some of which were far from flattering. For example, Malinowski's reflections of fieldwork with natives of the Trobriand Islands suggest a man who was bored by his work, having little patience with those he was researching and indeed the language of the diary, although translated from Polish, reveals a racist and sexist aspect to his personality. The diary presents a picture of Malinowski which forms a sharp contrast to that which emerges from his academic writing (Malinowski 1922, 1935) and from secondary accounts of his work (Firth 1957).

The case of Malinowski's diary raises an interesting question of ethics, which to a greater or lesser extent is relevant to all research based on diaries of this nature. In this case there remains uncertainty as to whether Malinowski intended his private diary to be published or indeed read by anyone other than himself. That it was published posthumously, when clearly Malinowski was unable to object, adds to the uncertainty. The issue of intent and audience underpins the question of ethics here and in other cases where diaries are used without the explicit permission of the author. While we may justify their use by referring to the time elapsed between their writing and publication, and their value for research purposes, or by characterizing the author as typical of many people of similar circumstances, the fact remains that the diary, which is usually a highly personal document, is being used for purposes for which it may not have been intended. Set alongside this, however, is the fact that such diaries may yield rich and detailed information for the ethnographer, not available by any other means.

Photographs

Photographs and photography offer the ethnographer a source and a form of data which is in many ways very different from those of most of the methods we have considered so far. While the objective of all of the collection methods which we discuss is to convey as detailed an account of the reality upon which they focus as possible, most rely of the representation of that reality via oral and written means. Even observation and participant observation, which rely on the researcher seeing and participating in the social action, tend to be written up in the form of fieldnotes or a research journal in which a detailed account of what is seen and experienced is given. Photography offers the ethnographer a different medium with which to represent social reality. In quite a literal sense, it seeks simply to represent what it sees without interpretation or mediation via the words or impressions of the researcher. It is an approach to data collection which stresses the importance of the here and now, captured at the precise moment at which the camera shutter closed. Clichés such as 'the camera never lies' suggest a passive role for the photographer who with his or her equipment becomes merely a technical conduit for the image at which the camera is pointed. In the context of research, therefore, we might attribute photography to a somewhat positivistic approach to data collection, which sees the images it conveys as a form of pure data untainted by the interpretation of the researcher. Indeed, this may be the objective of the best forms of photojournalism, where the photographer seeks not to interpret or to theorize, but merely to convey.

In identifying photography as appropriate for inclusion in the tool bag of ethnography, we inevitably move beyond simplistic, technicist conceptions of image creation and of the role of the photographer-ethnographer in the research process. To see photography in positivistic terms of literal representation is to over simplify the medium by looking at the photograph merely as an artefact and to ignore the role of the photographer and the process by which the photograph comes to be taken. Our approach to photographs and photography as data collection methods for ethnography is, in most respects the same as our approach to other methods which the ethnographer might use for educational or other research. As with interviews, observation, documentary and survey research, we see photographs and photography as a means of representing the researcher's interpretation of the research setting or focus. As with these other methods, the researcher decides which data are important to report or to record and what emphasis to place on them in the process of data analysis. For the photographer-researcher the same decisions and choices pertain. For example, while we may look to the camera as a means of capturing the image before it, the researcher must decide just what to put before it, where the lens should be pointed and when the shutter should fall to capture the image. What appears on the photographic print is not arbitrary. As with the interview or the observation note, the photograph represents a selection from a wide range of different data available. While for the interviewer, the selection comes in the kinds of questions that are posed, the line of the conversation that the researcher decides to pursue and the emphasis given to the answers, for the photographer selection comes in what to place inside the frame and what to leave out, when to take the photograph, how many photographs to take and from what vantage point. In the context of photography many of these decisions may have a literal manifestation. The photographer has to stand somewhere and at some point must press the button to close the shutter, but they also embody theoretical and epistemological issues which inform not merely the image that is captured, but also the knowledge of the social interaction which that image seeks to convey. In short, different kinds of photographs convey different kinds of knowledge.

Scott (1990) draws on the work of Mussello (1979) to identify three types of photograph each of which reveals something different about its subject matter. For example, in what Scott describes as the sub-genre of *idealization* there is an emphasis on formal posing such as may occur at weddings and other formal gatherings. In photography described as *natural portrayal*, Scott says although there may be a degree to which the event is actually reconstructed for the camera, there is the intention to record events as they actually happened. Finally, he identifies the *demystification* sub-genre. Here, the photographer deliberately seeks to create what Scott calls 'an alternative image' of a person 'through candid photography in situations which do not figure in the other two sub-genres – while sleeping, partially dressed, or in other embarrassing situations' (1990: 195).

While Mussello's (1979) typology is applied to what Scott (1990) calls 'home mode' photography and the examples used for illustration are drawn from family occasions such as weddings, holidays and Christmas celebrations and so on, it also serves as a useful tool in the context of educational research. Think, for example, of the formal photographs which record the whole class, some standing, some seated with teacher and perhaps headteacher strategically placed in the centre of the front row, or perhaps, less common, the annual whole school photograph typical of public or Grammar schools with ascending rows of pupils starting with the youngest classes seated on the floor, up to the eldest on the back row, high up on scaffolding of some description, and somewhere towards the centre of the structure a row of staff, perhaps in gowns. Such photographs show the school or the class, not as one might find it on walking round the school, but on *idealized* best behaviour, portraying a sense of the school unit, the human collectivity, which is usually only present through the personification of the school name. Alternatively, the photographs taken on sports' day of children completing the 100 metres relay race, or of the action from a year 6 football match, may be taken as examples of *natural* portrayal, the school going about its usual business. Finally, the *demystification* label may be applied to photographs of staff members captured in unfamiliar circum-stances, for example, taking a part in a school play or caught off guard during a sixth form field trip. Each of the different types of photographs reveals a different aspect of school life, and there may be many more categories to which we might wish to attribute photographs: collectively, they add to a mosaic of the school and of school life.

In the context of ethnographic research, perhaps more significantly than providing such a picture, the typology allows us to get beneath the photo-graph as artefact, and to look beyond or behind the image. By classifying photographs in this way we are able to ask questions about the school, for example, what kinds of activities go on in and out of school? How does it portray itself to the outside world? What are the differences between public and private presentation of the school? The photographs, therefore, become heuristic devices which the ethnographer can use not only to pose more questions about the school, but also as a valuable resource in and of them-selves. A distinction can be drawn here between what Bolton *et al.* (2001) refer to as visual sociology and Visual Sociology, where the former plays a supportive, illustrative role alongside other data and where the latter is a form of data in its own right which can be read and analysed in the same way as textual data. In both ways, we wish to argue that photography has the capacity to make a significant contribution to ethnography.

Nevertheless, despite its capacity to yield data of a different nature, perhaps somewhat surprisingly, photography has not been used a great deal within ethnographic research. This may be due in part to the cultural emphases which place a primacy on written or verbal information in the research context, to which we alluded earlier. Alternatively it may relate to technical issues associated with the availability and affordability of equip-ment and processing, and to the suitability or possibility of using the medium in specific contexts. Interestingly, using a camera may sometimes be deemed unacceptable or overly intrusive while other methods of recording what is happening in a particular situation, such as detailed note-taking, may not. Making a visual representation of social settings which includes individuals may sometimes be seen as unacceptable by those whose image appears in the photograph as they can be identified with a degree of certainty which is perhaps not present in ethnographic fieldnotes. No matter how detailed these are, they are rarely as 'real' as a photograph.

Paradoxically, however, despite the capacity of photographs to convey a true visual likeness of people and places, their relative absence from social research may be associated with concerns about the authenticity and reliability of photographic data. For example, collections of photographs, perhaps found in an attic or at the back of a cupboard when sorting through the belongings of deceased relative, may raise more questions about family history than they answer. The appearance of people on photographs who are unknown to surviving family members may prove intriguing if not a little frustrating or even perhaps worrying. The significance of the mystery person may be lost forever with the death of whoever took the photograph or of those who also appear in it. Similarly, the significance and even the bare facts surrounding occasions or locations depicted in photographs may also be lost over time unless there has been a systematic attempt to catalogue and record basic details alongside the photograph. However, in recent years the relative affordability of photography means that many of us now take many more photographs than ever before. As a consequence, the chances of systematic records being maintained for all but a few highly significant photographs, such as those relating to weddings, christenings, graduation ceremonies and other similar events, seems remote.

One of the problems associated with photography as a source of secondary data is that it often tells an incomplete story and is reliant, therefore, on the existence of an additional script, either that of memory or that of a written record, for the realization of its social significance. The reliability of the photograph may also be compromised by concerns about its authenticity. This may be an issue which relates both to archive photographs that are found or acquired as historical documents on social life, and to those that are created specifically for research purposes. At the heart of this issue is the question: can we believe what we see? The camera may never lie but it can only convey the images that it is 'told' to convey. What is placed in front of the camera is usually at the discretion of the photographer. In addition to blatant manipulation of images in the dark room and, as is becoming increasingly common, by digital means, the photographer has the capacity to 'fix' the information conveyed by a photograph in a variety of ways. These may include asking the subjects to strike particular poses or to adopt certain kinds of behaviour, requiring certain combinations of participants to pose for the camera together, including particular objects in the photograph; or setting the photograph against a particular background. The photographer may deploy some of these tactics deliberately to achieve a desired image and other tactics may reflect the cultural norms of the era and context in which the photograph was taken. For example, as Scott (1990) points out, typical wedding photographs bring together the two sides of the supposedly united family standing beside the bride and groom, while Victorian studio portraiture often placed subjects against fairly ostentatious backdrops similar to stage scenery, which included plush furnishings, panelled rooms and large windows. In each case the intention was to fix the photograph in a way which ensured certain images were being conveyed. In the case of the wedding, themes of unity and family harmony are to the fore and with Victorian portrait photography the intention was often to demonstrate wealth and good living. At a more mundane level, the idea of wearing best or good clothes and perhaps particular items of jewellery for formal portraits may also be seen as an attempt to convey a sense of respectability and a level of wealth in what may be a subtle yet very deliberate way via the medium of photography. Again, the way in which school photographs are often posed may be relevant here. For example, the class teacher or headteacher insisting that full uniform be worn on the day of the school photograph may say more about the desire to convey a particular image of the school than it does about a concern to capture reality! In all of these examples the issue is not one of deliberately attempting to deceive those who see the photograph. It is more a case of putting forward an image which is perhaps a little flattering of those who appear in it, or in keeping with the cultural values of respectability dominant at the time at which the photograph was taken. The resulting photograph may not, therefore, be strictly authentic in its portrayal of the natural or usual circumstances of its subject. It has been constructed by the photographer and the subject with the intention of conveying a particular image.

Bryman (2001) addresses issues of selection in photography and the value of photographs to social research. His discussion also relates to questions of authenticity. Drawing on Sutton's (1992) work on Disneyland his claim is that a process of selection occurs as we take photographs and as we show them to other people. In the context of a visit to Disneyland, the selection takes place in the context of the construction of a good time. People visit Disney's Magic Kingdoms to have a good and, if possible, a magical time. The photographs we choose to take, therefore, should reflect the magic and the good time. Consequently we avoid taking photographs of the long queues which often build up around entry to particular rides, and we do not take photographs of moody children having been denied an expensive Mickey Mouse sweatshirt or baseball cap by a weary parent. Sutton argues that the photographs we choose to take and show to those not with us at Disneyland, are those which construct an image of a great time being had by all. In this respect they may be far from authentic representations of the Disneyland experience. Rather, they are a collusion between those visiting the park, which includes the photographer(s), and the Disney organization in the construction and perpetuation of the Magic Kingdom.

There will of course be many other examples of this nature, where a preferred version of social reality has been constructed and perpetuated, which we will all be able to think of from our own experiences that are represented in our personal collections of photographs. The examples serve to demonstrate that although the camera never lies, it does not necessarily tell the whole truth and that it is certainly capable of telling multiple truths. While the issues raised here may be seen to call into question the capacity of photography to provide useful data for ethnography, we would argue that in no way do they totally discredit it. Moreover, issues of authenticity, representation and selection are present in every data collection method not merely those which rely on visual representation. The issues do raise some important questions about the value of photographic research which suggest that we should analyse and interrogate visual data with the same degree of detail as we would any other data. However, we believe that photographs, both those that are 'found' and those that are created specifically for the purpose of research can add a perspective on social life not available via other means. They can prompt us to ask questions of the research partici-pants and, as in the Disney example, they may reveal the ways in which we all construct our own social realities.

Art and artefacts

We referred above to Lee's (2000) interesting book on unobtrusive research in which he revives a tradition which, among other things, involves realizing the potential of a wide variety of everyday objects to reveal patterns of human behaviour. For example, drawing on the work of Webb *et al.* (1966), Lee refers to the classic example of measuring the wear on floor tiles as a means of assessing the level of human traffic in a particular part of a building, or taking account of the number of fingermarks on a museum display case to assess the popularity of a particular exhibit. The information yielded by such techniques may be limited to fairly crude measurements of use or observation and tell us nothing of the nature of that use or of the people who constitute that traffic or look at the display. They do, neverthe-less, provide one very general indicator of human behaviour specific to a particular location.

The examples that Lee cites raise the wider possibility of using a range of artefacts as indicators of social behaviour. We may include here works of art of various kinds which may have the capacity to tell us something not only of the subject of say the painting or the sculpture, but also of those who created them and the time and context in which they were created. For example, sixteenth century portraiture may be useful not merely in its depiction of the physical likeness of members of the aristocracy but also for providing clues about social mores, albeit limited, of the day and also as a means of recording something of the property and possessions that they owned. On another level, the paintings of this period are also of interest for what they fail to include. As portraiture was the prerogative of the wealthy, we learn little of the lives and circumstances of those without the financial means of commissioning such work. The picture of social life in the sixteenth century which can be gleaned from an examination of artwork of this time is, therefore, limited largely to depictions of the wealthy, their homes and their possessions. To obtain a fuller picture of social life of this period, therefore, the limited content of its artwork tells us that we must look beyond this medium to other documentary sources which offer an alternative perspective on society.

In a similar yet much more recent way, studio photographs which recently arrived immigrants to the UK had taken to send back to their relatives in the West Indies, India, Pakistan and so on in the early 1960s, often included household items such as radios and other electrical goods. These were deliberately positioned to suggest a certain level of material wealth and hence achievement. Similarly, the whole family was usually dressed in their best clothes, which may have been bought especially for the photograph. In the context of long distance emigration, motivated by economic need, these seemingly ordinary, everyday objects took on a symbolic significance in which they were used to justify the move to the UK to those back home. The use of artefacts in this way reveals much not only about the significance of material possessions but also about the difference of cultures experienced at the time by those arriving in the UK.

The significance of artefacts to social life and culture is both responsible for and, at the same time, a response to much of the industry which now surrounds the marketing of goods and services. The segmentation of markets (Dibb *et al.* 1997) to enable particular kinds of goods to be targeted at particular kinds of people, and the creation of lifestyle, leads to a commonsense assumption that the possession of certain kinds of artefacts is indicative of certain kinds of behaviour. Logically it would seem to follow, therefore, that knowledge about possession of certain kinds of artefacts is knowledge about participation in certain kinds of activities. Owning certain kinds of equipment, for example, sports equipment, hi-fi equipment or tools would, in the main, suggest that the person who owns them engages in activities associated with them. Consequently, it may be that knowing about the things that a person posseses means that we also know a good deal about that person. Not just in literal terms, for example, that he plays golf or that she enjoys listening to Frank Sinatra, but also figuratively, in that the possession of artefacts of a particular quality or style, for example, shirts made by Yves St Laurent, the novels of Kafka or Le Cruset kitchenware, may suggest a certain level of income, a particular level of education and a belief in purchasing things that will last a long time. They may also suggest a middle-class lifestyle that values goods deemed to be of high quality which is reflected in their price. At an institutional level of the school, the possession of certain types of equipment, say for PE or science, the state of the decor and furnishings might indicate something about the availability of financial resources in the school in an absolute sense, or about the priorities given to particular activities in the school by those who make decisions about spending priorities. In addition, the physical positioning of particular arte-facts, for example, the prominent display of the school emblem, its motto, religious iconography, examples of its artwork or its sports trophy cabinet may indicate something of the nature of the school in terms of those activities that are particularly valued by those responsible for promoting the public image of the school. It may be indicative of the kind of ethos that the headteacher and the governors wish to convey to prospective pupils and parents and to the world beyond the school in general.

An example of the use of artefacts as indicators of ethos and the nature of the school can be seen in Pole's (1991) study of the introduction of records of achievement in a prestigious boys' grammar school. Fieldnotes for this case study of the way in which a traditional, academically orientated institution attempted to introduce a new form of assessing and recording pupil progress reveals how the presence of particular artefacts encountered during the researcher's first visit to the school left him in no doubt about the kind of school to which he was seeking access. For example, the notes record 'the oak panelling' of the school lobby where the researcher was asked to wait before being shown by the school secretary to the headmaster's (sic) study. The fieldnotes record that hanging on the walls were:

> the plaques which carry the names, in what looks like gold leaf, of the boys who gained places at Oxford or Cambridge Universities, the earliest date being 1901. More plaques record the winners of the annual Governors Award, given to the winners of the house Rugby tournament, dates for this award go back to 1947.

As the researcher is taken from the lobby to the head's study the notes detail more 'dark oak panelling' inside the heads' study and a: 'large heavy desk in the centre of a large room with a high ceiling, two sash windows looking out over a quad, a rather well worn Persian style rug over wooden floor boards and two leather chairs placed in front of the head's desk'. On the panelling at the back of the head's desk was 'a painting of King's College Cambridge' and behind the door, which led to the head's 'private toilet', hung 'an academic gown'. The 'two book cases' which stood either side of the windows were also of a solid 'dark oak' construction and held a 'collection of classic English literature texts together with volumes which offered commentaries on these texts'.

The notes are rich in their attention to particular artefacts. That things like the academic gown and the painting of King's College Cambridge are evident in this location contributes to an academic ambience or ethos about the school. The iconography of success represented by the gold leaf names of the boys who gained places at Oxford or Cambridge and the importance of rugby football represented by the record of the winners of the Governor's Award all serve to establish, to those waiting in the lobby that this is a school which recognizes traditional scholarly and sporting values. The messages that the artefacts send out are clear from the moment anyone sets foot inside the school. They form part of the school's identity as the leading academic establishment in the area, and as any educational ethnographer who spends time in a range of different kinds of schools would quickly appreciate, they contrast with the artefacts evident in other schools where they may have worked.

Clearly, reading artefacts as text (Grint and Woolgar 1997) is about interpretation and, as with any sources of data, there is no absolute certainty that the interpretation given to the possession or use of artefacts is the correct one. As there may be different readings of an interview transcript or of a set of photographs, then there may be different 'readings' attributable to artefacts. Furthermore, as with many secondary sources of data, artefacts can only ever tell a partial story and may perhaps be most valuable when used as part of multiple strategy (Burgess 1984) research design. However, from the content of someone's dustbin to the type of car that they drive and the books on their bookshelves, we would argue that it is possible to infer something about them and their social lives. Furthermore, at the level of the institution or the organization, artefacts can provide an insight into ethos, values, priorities and identity. To this end, artefacts offer another possibility to the educational ethnographer.

Summary

What we hope to have shown in these two chapters is that the range of research methods available to the ethnographer is wide and varied. Our approach to ethnography is eclectic and this is reflected through the different kinds of data that we believe ethnographers can legitimately and usefully collect and call upon. We have not identified any single method as an ethnographic method per se, but have taken the view that many methods have the capacity to yield data which may contribute to the creation of ethnography. In adopting this approach it is important to recognize that the methods that an ethnographer might deploy are not used in isolation, but form part of a research process. In the context of ethnography, the research process is defined by a particular kind of research design, a particular approach to data analysis and to representing the data and writing based upon it. In short, we might conclude that it isn't the data on their own that make a piece of research ethnographic, but it is their contribution to a wider research process which includes particular approaches to analysis and issues relating to representation, as we discuss later in this volume. However, in claiming this, we do not suggest that the ethnographer can use any old method that comes to mind in the hope that it will contribute to a wider research process. What we hope to have established in Chapters 2 and 3, and also in Chapter 4, is that ethnography is a distinctive approach to research which requires careful planning and execution, and that to really understand the place of data in ethnographic research it is necessary to understand their relationship to the other constituents of the ethnographic research process.

Note

1 In most cases, survey data in educational and social research is analysed by means of the Statistical Package for Social Sciences (SPSS) software (see Pole and Lampard 2002 for detailed examples of the use of this package), now available for use on most personal computers.

4 | Analysing ethnographic data

Introduction

The focus of this chapter is upon the analysis of ethnographic data. We try to do two things: first, to separate out for readers those various elements that comprise the processes engaged in by ethnographers when they attempt to understand and interpret the data they collect, and second to describe and explain what happens when those elements coalesce. Analysis involves exciting, laborious, painstaking and complex activities that, in combination, are rarely unsystematic. We like Watling's recent (2002b: 262) definition of analysis as: 'the researcher's equivalent of alchemy – the elusive process by which you hope you can turn your raw data into nuggets of pure gold. And like alchemy, such magic calls for science and art in equal measures'. In ethnography, terms like 'messy' and 'continuous' (Bryman and Burgess 1994) may not have always encouraged systematic attention to this 'magical' process. Yet analysis takes us to the heart of ethnography and, therefore, its epistemological and technical challenges. Part of the technical challenge is the sheer volume of data collected and produced as ethnography, mostly in textual forms; part of the epistemological challenge is the range of approaches available to represent the meanings and interpretations that can be applied to ethnographic analysis.

The ethnographer is centrally implicated in both 'challenges'. While recognizing the importance of computer-assisted data analysis (a theme discussed here and revisited in Chapter 6), our task in this chapter is to take critical account of a range of analytical approaches without constraining them into a straitjacket of one procedural route. Some of the challenges in having the analytical 'nerve' *and* will to explore the data for recurring themes and patterns will be outlined, and these are supported with reference to examples from educational ethnography, some of which involved a lot of, and some less, prior instrumentation. But instrumentation nonetheless.

When to begin

At which point in ethnographic research doec data analysis begin? Research literature confirms that analysis is not a distinct phase but occurs simultaneously and continuously as a key aspect of research design and process (Becker 1966; Burgess 1984). While the iterative link between data collection and analysis is a key feature of all qualitative research, this may be of small comfort for the newcomer to ethnographic research in education. Moreover, it seems unlikely that answers to the question posed could be written on a postcard! Published accounts make it clear that ethnographers vary considerably in their explication of the point at which they claim to begin the 'explicit' process of analysis. As Bryman and Burgess (1994) point out, 'sometimes, analysis seems to begin more or less immediately upon entering the field . . . whereas others appear to delay analysis pending the accumulation of a substantial body of data' (p.218).

Because educational ethnography often starts from particular conceptual frameworks that are then 'tested', refined or qualified in the field, then it is also possible to argue that the earliest stages of analysis come *before* fieldwork begins. Hammersley (1990) discusses, for example, the contributions made by the early ethnographic studies of Hargreaves (1967), Lacey (1970) and Ball (1981) in

> developing and testing pupil experiences of schooling in terms of differentiation-polarisation theory in [school] settings that both vary the level of differentiation and control some of the other relevant variables. In this way they complement one another in a way that few other ethnographic studies have achieved.
>
> (Hammersley 1980: 116)

The extent to which these writers would agree or disagree with a notion of complementary frameworks that *preceded* data collection is not certain. However, Bogden and Biklen (1982) draw a distinction between analysis that begins in the field, and analysis that occurs after data collection. And Miles and Huberman (1994: 10,12) describe this pre-fieldwork component as 'anticipatory data reduction', that is, the first aspect of the first component of analysis – *data reduction*. This is followed by, and overlaps with *data display*, and *conclusion drawing/verification*. All components form part of an interactive process: 'Even before the data are actually collected, anticipatory data reduction is occurring as the researcher decides (often without full awareness) which conceptual framework, which research questions, and which data collection approaches to choose.' (p.10)

For ethnographers working increasingly in tightly framed *applied* frameworks of educational policy and practice, 'anticipatory data reduction' may take on a special nuance, although the processes involved preclude neither novel nor emergent concepts or outcomes. We draw upon an example of research by Roach and Morrison (1998) entitled *Public Libraries, Ethnic Diversity and Citizenship* as a case in point. The study illustrates the inter-relationship between 'novel' (in public library circles at least) conceptual frameworks, data collection and analysis. The study focused primarily on the relationship between public library services and diverse ethnic communities. Extended case studies took place in four local public library service areas and examined, in detail, a range of issues that related to the provision of library services in ethnically diverse settings. In each of the authorities a predominantly ethnographic approach to fieldwork was used, combining documentation, interviews, surveys and observation analysis. In important respects, the study provided a departure from, as well as some continuity with, library-focused research that has frequently been funded from within, rather than from outside the academic and practitioner library communities. This is most apparent with regard to the conceptual frameworks used to inform the research design. The study did not begin with a conceptual 'blank sheet' or a 'traditional' library focus, but remained open to conceptual development and (re)orientation as the research progressed. Morrison (1999) explains this by describing the study as:

> a social scientific exploration of the public library as a model of public service . . . Because ethnic minorities ha[d] been regarded as a 'problem' for library service providers – requiring the deployment of specialist consultants and new funding formulas – the relationship between public libraries and ethnic diversity had not been explored previously. In this sense, the research presented a challenge to those who had assumed that the traditional paternalism of the local state was the appropriate base on which to define public policy.
>
> (1999: 80–1)

This conceptual framework was reflected in the 'big' research issues posed and in the framing of the sub-issues and processes embedded as part of the research that first:

> posed the fundamental question: to what extent is the public library service open and accountable to ethnic minority citizens? In problematising the public library service rather than its users, basic questions were also raised about citizen empowerment. [The research then probed] the significance of libraries at the interface between the micro-levels of practice and wider, social, historical, and political structures.
>
> (1999: 82)

This meant that: 'When the [research] team asked how citizens saw themselves in relation to the public library, we raised issues of citizenship, of community, and individual rights and responsibilities, as well as what is meant by "public" each of which in sum, or in part, is undergoing trans-formation' (Morrison 1999). In such ways: 'Starting points focused upon new sets of library-focused questions; in doing so, a re-examination of terms like ethnicity, inequality, and disadvantage was also critical' (Morrison 1999). And at the micro-level:

> the research team . . . sought answers . . . to whether in relation to its 'grand' claims as central to democracy and citizenship, the public library service might be expected to exemplify pro-active, anti-racist approaches rather than mirror activities in other institutionalised forms.
>
> (Morrison 1999: 82)

The extracts highlighted above provide initial insight into the ideas and concepts that underpinned Roach and Morrison's (1998) approach at the start of their research. Conceptual perspectives were open but neither 'blank' nor 'empty', and developed gradually and through regular discussion between the two researchers. First principles allowed the researchers to develop a strategic framework for the research overall, even though some emphases were specific to the interests of each case study. The researchers wrote every day and compared writing at regular intervals. Interim analysis for sponsors revealed some of the complexities in writing qualitatively with several agendas and user groups in mind. Yet overall, there is an attempt to address the kinds of questions posed by Lofland (1974: 308) when, in relation to data analysis, he asks:

> How did the leading ideas that organized your present analysis evolve? A sudden flash? Slowly? Other?
> What kinds of models are you using to organize the materials? What were their sources? To what degree did you organize your analysis before writing it out in text, versus writing it and then seeing what you had?
> Did you write a little every day, around the clock in bursts, or some other way? In general what were the most important difficulties?

Which story and who is the storyteller?

Brewer (2000) is among the few recent writers to flag the importance of the relationship between analysis and the 'type of ethnography' being produced. Referring to 'positivist ethnography', he comments:

> Data analysis within positivist ethnography remedies the weaknesses of ethnographic compared to numerate data by constructing objective indicators of insiders' understandings and expressing them in a formal

language, almost as a kind of measurement, such as the development
of codes, diagrams and other categories ... Analysis is devoted to
developing the variables that capture social meanings rather than
necessarily 'telling it as it is'

(Brewer 2000: 107)

The work of Miles and Huberman (1994) typifies this approach in terms
of 'tight' rather than 'loose' organizing frameworks to enhance the validity
of the analysis. A clear-cut case for prestructured designs is made, while
conceding that emergent designs 'might' make 'good sense' 'when experienced researchers have plenty of time and are exploring exotic cultures,
understudied phenomena, and complex social phenomena' (p.17). But the
advocacy of a structured approach for *most* ethnographies is clear from
the promotion of diagrams and matrices for data display:

> to assemble organised information into an immediately accessible,
> compact form so that the analyst can see what is happening and either
> draw justified conclusions or move on to the next step of analysis
> the display suggests may be useful ... The dictum 'You are what
> you eat' might be transposed to 'You know what you display' ...
> We advocate more systematic, powerful displays and urge a more
> inventive, self-conscious, iterative stance towards their display and
> use.

(Miles and Huberman 1994: 11)

'Humanistic' ethnographers (Brewer 2000) also want to capture the
'inside' of educational experience, but overwhelmingly from the perspectives
and 'words' of 'insiders', a theme revisited by us in Chapter 6. The contrast
with the previous approach is quite marked. Here, the emphasis is upon
the extended text as a story told by insiders, with minimum 'interference'
from diagrams, matrices, or the imposition of the formal language of the
researcher. The validity of this approach rests upon staying close to the
stories of research participants who tell it as it is. For such ethnographers,
the key to their 'disappearance' from the research account is to 'write' the
insiders' words and actions as if unaffected by the researcher's presence. Is
this possible? The approach has been contested on epistemological and
technical grounds, Hammersley and Atkinson (1995) arguing, for example,
that such a 'reality' *cannot be*:

> Once we abandon the idea that the social character of research can be
> 'standardised out' or avoided by becoming a 'fly on the wall' or 'full
> participant', the role of the researcher as active participant in the
> research process becomes clear. He or she is the research instrument
> *par excellence*.

(p.19)

Miles and Huberman (1994) prefer to base their critique of 'poor' humanistic ethnography on technical grounds of bulky texts which may 'drastically overweight vivid information ... that jumps out [and] in which the criteria for weighting and selecting may never be questioned' (p.11). Such ethnographies, it is argued, present problems for readers; the long text 'can overload humans' information processing capabilities' and 'preys on their tendencies to find simplifying patterns' (Miles and Huberman 1994).

Ethnographies assigned the labels 'postmodernist' and 'post-postmodernist' (Brewer 2000) deny realities of either the positivist or humanist variety. Rather, there are:

> competing versions of reality and multiple perspectives that the analyst must address. Moreover, the data are seen as created in and through interactions that occur between the researcher and people in the field, and analysis must therefore illustrate the situated or context-bound nature of the multivocal meanings disclosed in the research.
>
> (Brewer 2000: 108)

However, in its post-postmodern forms, analysis is not splintered into the multiple relativist forms of postmodernism, but instead offers prospects for 'subtle realism' (Hammersley 1992b) or 'ethnographic imagination' that are systematically and rigorously grounded. Such concerns link us directly to the key importance of *reflexivity* in research. Following Brewer (2000: 108), ethnographers need to 'turn inwards' to:

- relationships developed in the field;
- the characteristics of the researcher, and how these relate to the people in the field;
- time and circumstances in which the research was carried out;
- the methodology and fieldwork practices used; and
- broader educational, socioeconomic, and political contexts in which the research took place.

All this suggests that there are *some* features that are common to all ethnographic analyses, and these are now considered.

Common features

Despite a range of perspectives, many ethnographies in educational settings have a particular 'feel' and are framed by a number of common features.

First, all ethnographers share an interest in bringing order to the data they collect by looking for patterns, categories, descriptive units and themes, even if:

on the face of it, there may be some irreconcilable couples – for example, the quest for lawful relationships (social anthropology) versus the search for 'essences' that may not transcend individuals, and lend themselves to multiple compelling interpretations (phenomenology).

(Miles and Huberman 1994: 9)

Second, the appeal of *grounded theory* (Glaser and Strauss 1967; Strauss 1987; Strauss and Corbin 1990) is widespread. However, despite frequent citation, it has been suggested that researchers have focused on the *desirability* of its appeal to make theory from data rather than upon detailed use as the basis for ethnographic analysis (Bryman 1988; Bryman and Burgess 1994; Richards and Richards 1994). Notwithstanding its role as a kind of ethnographic manifesto rather than analytical blueprint, grounded theory 'stands for' a range of approaches that are based upon the following premises. These feature more strongly in some versions of ethnography than others. (Denscombe (1998: 214–16) offers these as basic premises for *all* qualitative data analysis that draws upon grounded theory.)

1 Ethnography is 'pragmatic'. This does not imply an abrogation of meth-odological rules but rather an avoidance of standardized 'methods [that] . . . would only constrain and even stifle social researchers' best efforts' (Strauss 1987: 7).

2 Ethnography (usually) includes the generation of concepts and/or theories. This moves ethnographic analysis beyond descriptions of people, events and phenomena based on insiders' perspectives, to the ways in which researchers make sense of the information they collect and transform through analysis into data. Some ethnographers focus more intently on theory generation than others (discussed again in Chapter 5); some use sensitizing concepts to drive research design and process.

3 Emergent theories should be 'grounded' in empirical data. *But*, as Bryman and Burgess (1994) contend, such 'an iterative interplay of data collection and analysis rarely' reveals 'clear indications' of theory generation (p.221).

4 Ethnography is a journey of discovery. 'Preconceived theory that dictates, prior to the research, "relevancies" in concepts and hypotheses' (Glaser and Strauss 1967: 33) are/should be absent. Again, as the example from Roach and Morrison (1998) highlights, it is the word 'dictate' that is significant; ethnographers do not begin with an empty sheet.

5 Among the implications of likening ethnography to a journey of discovery or exploration is that it may be impossible, even undesirable for many ethnographers to identify, prior to fieldwork, precisely who or what might be included as phenomena for investigation. This can be unsettling for researchers and those who supervise them. Again, this does

not preclude the importance of recognizing the boundedness of discrete locations for our studies and the limiting and delimiting elements of the human and physical resources at our disposal.

6 In grounded theory, *theoretical saturation* occurs when additional analysis is unable to add anything 'new' to our understanding of those phenomena (Strauss 1987: 21).

If some of these premises are not found in all ethnographies, even in diluted forms, then how do we continue to reconcile the oft-quoted connection between grounded theory and many types of ethnography? (Postmodernists may have already severed the main artery of that connection.) An epistemological view would be that grounded theory approaches continue to resonate with the underpinning principle that guides much of educational ethnography, namely, remaining 'true to the data' (Brewer 2000: 109). A pragmatic view would be that the connection continues to provide a practical reminder of the need for ethnographers to be systematic and rigorous (Seale 1999: 85) in data analysis that is 'grounded' in the language of the subjects, and where the researcher is centrally implicated.

As Pole and Lampard (2002: 206–09) remind us, such approaches are not without challenge. Ethnography has been accused of relativism. How are the conceptual frameworks used by ethnographers to be judged? Is all knowledge gained equally 'true' or of equal merit? And, how do we know when we have reached the point of conceptual 'saturation'? Such questions are located in two features at the heart of ethnographic data collection and analysis. First, its propensity to yield masses (literally) of qualitative data, and second, the ongoing 'intimate relationship between researcher and data' (Pole and Lampard 2002). Our stance is not to advocate any 'slavish' adherence to the approaches of Glaser and Strauss (1967) but rather to point out that educational ethnography is notable for applying the 'essence' of such grounded approaches to analyses. While ethnography cannot apply the same procedures to determine reliability and validity as quantitative approaches (even if this was considered desirable), it remains essential that its analytical procedures and audit trails of evidence remain transparent, systematic, and open to public scrutiny (Glaser and Strauss 1967).

Where to begin

All analysis involves the efficient management of data. Denscombe (1998: 209–10) offers useful practical guidance:

- As far as possible, get all materials in similar format . . . This helps with storage and when sifting through the materials;
- Where possible, the raw data should be collated in such a way that allows researchers' notes and comments to be added alongside;

- Each piece of 'raw data' material should be identified with a unique serial number or code for reference purposes . . . The importance of this is two-fold. First, when analysing the data it is vital that the researcher is able to return to points in the data which are of particular interest . . . Second, on a very practical note, when you are sifting through mounds of papers or record cards, it is easy to muddle the order or lose the place where the piece of raw data was originally located;
- Make a back-up copy of all original materials.

As a preliminary to systematic filing procedures, data are read and re-read in order to organize them into manageable 'bits' or units to which codes, initially described as index codes, can be attached. In initial stages, codes are 'labels' attached to data; ethnographers make decisions about where and how to file them. One of the advantages of the computer (discussed later) is that it facilitates the process of filing materials, suitably coded or labelled, in different files. Ethnographers produce and obtain very large amounts of data; these need to be variously filed. Codes can also be sub-coded and cross-referenced; in effect, this signals an almost imperceptible movement from coding as labelling to coding as analysis.

One way in which early reading and writing can facilitate thorough exposure to the data is through the process of writing summaries or memos attached to data bits. Again, the computer can help to overcome an aversion among some ethnographers to reducing data 'too soon'; the computer allows full versions of data bits to be recovered under their respective codes as quickly as the summaries. Some aspects of this aversion to summaries may be ill-founded, if based on the assumption that summaries contaminate 'raw' or 'natural' data. As Atkinson (1992) explains, all aspects of ethnographic reading and writing about and in the field are textual productions. He comments:

> The field is not merely reported in the texts of fieldwork: it is constituted by our writing and reading. I do not mean that there are no social beings or acts independent of our observation. Clearly there are. Rather, my view is that the 'field' of observation is the outcome of a series of transactions engaged in by the ethnographer . . . First, it is constructed through the ethnographer's gaze. Second, it is re-constituted through his or her ability to construct a-text-of-the-field. Third, it is reconstructed and recontextualised through the reader's work of interpretation and contextualisation.
>
> (pp. 8–9)

This applies to fieldnotes (inscriptions) that are constructed, interpreted and re-interpreted by various acts of reading and writing, and also to data (transcriptions), like interviews and diaries, that are deemed to report 'factually' what people say or write, and yet are also subject to textual conventions and representations (Arkinson 1992). The processes of ethnographic reading are interactive. Dey (1993) refers to the importance of 'the interactive quintet' – Who? What? When? Where? Why? – as anchor points for (re)reading, and the 'stock-in-trade' of the analyst. Bogden and Biklen (1982) prefer a list of substantive concerns to guide analysis: settings, definitions, processes, events, strategies and relationships. Interactive reading can usefully involve ethnographers asking 'what if' questions (Dey 1993, on transposition). *What if* this school was urban rather than rural? *What if* this teacher was in her induction year rather than experienced? *What if* this headteacher was male instead of female? *What if* this event had occurred at an 'all white' rather than at a multiethnic school? One outcome of detailed content analysis is the development of *qualitative description*. This describes key events, people and institutions, and provides vignettes that may also have numerical features.

Categorizing data also means that the ethnographer needs to move *backwards and forwards* through the data. This dialectic between category and data occurs during as well as after data collection; it is the essence of the iterative process. As an analytical strategy, what does moving backwards and forwards through the data actually mean? And what kinds of qualitative descriptions might be produced? In the following sections we draw upon two examples from educational settings to illustrate the processes and the description.

Moving backwards and forwards

First time ethnographers in education often seek guidance on the initial stages of analysis, and, for the most part, have looked in vain for examples of what has sometimes been misconstrued as 'intuition' (even though analysis may, of course, have intuitive elements). In the following extract, we explore the ways in which Morrison shares with readers some approaches to analysis, in particular the early juxtapositions between messiness and orderliness, in order to illustrate that a non-linear approach to analysis does not necessarily mean it is non-systematic. Extracts from fieldnotes and analytic memos come from a project entitled *Libraries for Learning: Approaches to Book Resources in the Primary School* (Morrison and Scott 1994). The research methodology combined qualitative and quantitative approaches; the qualitative element was ethnographic case studies of two primary schools, in which each researcher spent three days a week in one school for two terms.

The following fieldnotes were taken mid-term in one primary school. Fieldnotes and analytic memos are illustrated; the latter were usually written during the evenings that followed fieldwork and are shown as italicized text. The extracts are drawn from data that was collected during week 4 of one term. But first, the scene is set as follows:

Context

Primary School A is a large urban multiethnic primary school with a designated space called the 'library' and designated areas in each classroom that are described variously by teachers as reading or library corners. Morrison had conducted five interviews in week 2: one with the head, one with the library coordinator and three with class teachers.

During week 2 Morrison had sought permission from the head to spend three days in the school library in week 4. The head said that library observation was 'fine' although she was unclear whether 'much would be going on'. The researcher persisted, noting that the opportunity to spend time studying the book stock and classification systems would complement her observations of children at work there.

At a later date, Morrison would be welcome in school to talk with parents about 'books and things' (headteacher) if that would help. This was agreed as part of ongoing negotiation of access as a process rather than as a one-off event.

Interview analysis: early themes

Morrison drew upon thematic issues from her interviews with staff to provide an early conceptual map for the planned observation. So she did not start with a blank sheet for observation since, first, interim analysis of survey data was ongoing; second, a draft literature review had taken place; and third, early interviews had been transcribed and recurrent themes extracted. This took the form of themes/ideas noted initially on each transcript, transcripts compared and similarities/ differences noted. What were the recurrent themes to have emerged from the five interviews? Four thematic headings were identified as: school, pupils, parents and teachers. These were further divided into sub-themes as shown below and would be used to inform her observations in the library.

Theme: School
Sub-theme: school policy
Features:

1   A written school policy on the role of the school library had been agreed jointly by all staff (identified by four interviewees, one 'not sure' about its existence).

2   Key role of library co-ordinator (LC) identified. 'Still a need to convert the unconverted' (LC), although this was not a view shared by the headteacher (HT) who commented that 'all staff are committed to our library' (HT).

3 Target for fundraising. Enhancement of library resources had been a recent target for governors.

Theme: Pupils
Sub-theme (a): a curriculum for pupils
Features:
According to the interviewees, the school library was a 'key' to:

1 language development;
2 literacy;
3 meeting the requirements of the national curriculum.

Sub-theme (b): pupils' learning
Features
According to the interviewees, primary school libraries encouraged 'joy' in:

1 discovering reading;
2 finding out;
3 celebrating all cultures.

Sub-theme (c): pupil empowerment and enhanced responsibilities
Features:
Interviewees considered that the library gave the children a sense of:

1 responsibility – as library monitors;
2 empowerment – children were responsible for wall plans and displays in the library.

Theme: Parents
Sub-theme: home–school relations
Features:

1 Funding target for money raising efforts among parents.
2 Library loans encouraged 'shared reading' at home.

Theme: Teachers
Sub-theme (a): constraints
Features:

1 Not enough time to use the library (the national curriculum 'fall-out').
2 Not enough resources in the library (other priorities linked to national curriculum).

Sub-theme (b): teachers' doubts
Expressed variously by all interviewees, except the head:

1 Limitations – 'Books are old-fashioned.' 'We need computer suites not libraries.'

2   Utility – 'The library is a nice room but there's nothing in there that I can't do with the children in the classroom'.

Observations

Such themes were used to inform a 3-day observation in the school library. Further objectives were to collect data about the layout and contents of the library and its use during a school day. In total, three people used the library during the period of observation the cleaner who 'tidied up' and two pupils who worked together for 20 minutes. In addition, one class (6b) passed through the library six times a day because for them the library was the only thoroughfare to and from their classroom. What sense did Morrison make of her observations? Fieldnotes were taken at intervals during the day and analytic memos were drafted in the evening. Hopefully, the extracts below provide readers not only with a sense of 'what happened' but also about the ethnographer's feelings about what happened (or did not happen!)

Extracts from fieldnotes – day 1:
. . . This is eerie, no-one's been in. I'm making loads of headway in auditing the stock and looking for classification patterns (sheet attached) but nobody's using this. I've sketched a map of the layout. How can I capture its brightness and interesting corners for the children? Will bring in camera tomorrow. Orange cushions, new carpet, wall displays look impressive, children's texts and artwork linked to books they've read and liked. Also a seasonal feature. Children from 6b walk through at regular intervals. Several give me a wave, otherwise I'm pretty well ignored by all including Mr Child [class 6b form teacher] who seems determined to avoid any glance in my direction . . . into staff room for lunch. Friendly enough. Mr. C. says he could do with my job. 'What qualifications do you need?' Seemed a good point to request an interview(?) A date agreed three weeks hence: 'too busy till then' . . .

That evening – towards analytic memos:
Some links with interview themes, and some useful data for sponsors concerning library layout and stock but where are the 'keys' and the 'joys'? What happens when I've no-one to observe?

Like being on a film set: the library 'world' would be delighted with the stock and the layout. Library guidelines are full of advocacy about this kind of stuff.

But no people. Can I make links between *visibility* of the library *space* and the *invisibility* of library *learning*, gaps between pol./practice, rhetoric and reality? Need to think a way through here. Several avenues to pursue:

- Check this 'reality' with teachers. Can raise this at end of classroom observ. periods. Can raise this with Mr. C.
- What do parents know about library use? (include in parent interview schedule)
- What do the children understand by library use? (use in group interviews)
- Check with school secretary about this week's timetables. Perhaps classes are out on visits this week? If so, week 4 may be untypical.

Theme: Library
Sub-theme: physical space
Features:

1 visibility;
2 layout;
3 book stock;
4 displays;
5 pupil thoroughfare.

Sub-theme: learning in library
Features:

1 invisibility;
2 evidence from displays.

Extracts from fieldnotes – day 2:
Lunch in staff room. Library co-ordinator says she's planning to do some work with her class in the library next week. Would I like to observe? Yes, please . . .

2.30 and no-one's been in [the library]. I'm feeling a bit panicky. Bet David's [other researcher] getting loads of data at [] school. Need to catch him on Thursday to discuss. Need to stay until after school, just to check my classroom observation with Mrs T. [a class teacher] . . .

What have I achieved today so far? Written up part of my audit, and sharpened up my illustration. Taken a photo. Bring in my lit. review tomorrow for reading/some gaps to fill . . .

3.30 Cleaner's come in. Talk . . .
    4 Cleaner exits. Notes. Mrs. S [the cleaner] says hello: asks me what I'm doing. Brief explanation. She says 'it's a nice little school'. Her daughter attends. Loves cleaning the library, it's such a 'special room'. There's been fund-raising events to make it

that way. The head likes her to keep the library 'nice' and it's a treat compared to the toilets. Children 'wee up the walls' – not the children's fault, it's the parents. A few 'rough 'uns have moved in'. Back to 'the library'. Parents are shown round the library when they come and look at the school with their children, so she likes to 'keep it nice'. Final plumping of cushions. Leaves, wishing me luck. Might see me again?

That evening – towards analytic memos:
What a day! School secretary confirmed that nothing unusual by way of outside trips going on. So the emptiness of the library *is* a finding that needs further exploration. The space is also being used to demonstrate not only what the school stands for, but also as a potential marketing tool for prospective parents – need to link to parental interviews, school brochure . . . Bring interview transcripts in tomorrow. Look again. Can I afford to spend more days like this? . . . Libraries for learning – libraries are both an 'approach' to learning as well as a physical 'space'. Space visible: approaches invisible. Maybe libraries as 'an approach' is being interpreted by teachers as learning that can be confined to the classroom, or needs to be confined to the classroom, because of other constraints, or is it that the library is not seen as a space for learning. What's the space for? – Explore with teachers, and in classroom observations.

At least, one activity planned with LC – illuminating (hopefully), but how regular, how integral to teaching and learning is/should library use be?

Theme: Library
Sub-theme: image
Feature:

1   cleaner's image

Sub-theme: physical space
Features:

1   'special', different;
2   marketing tool;
3   focal point for school–parent relations;
4   absence of pupils or teachers.

Extracts from fieldnotes – day 3:
11.30 Two children enter the library. Exchange greetings and names. Jenny and Darren have finished all their work so Mrs Y (year 5) has sent them to library to find out about butterflies, and they can draw one if they've got time. They've got paper with the

words butterfly, caterpillar or larva, and pupa on it. They work
quickly and efficiently through the Dewey system and locate 3
texts. They share the writing of definitions and a pencilled sketch
of a butterfly. 8 minutes before lunch, no need to get back to the
classroom too soon, so spend the last few minutes in quiet chatter
and giggling. Jenny tells me she's a library monitor 'on Fridays'.
Usually the monitors do it, sometimes it's the teachers. 'Depends'.
Classes borrow books 'in turns' . . .

That evening – towards analytic memos:
Only use of library today appears to be as a reward for children
completing classroom work tasks – Develop with teacher
concerned. I'm observing in her class. The two pupils seemed
adept at using the library for information seeking. Where had
they learned those skills? Develop further understandings about
the library as it relates to children developing *knowledge and
skills* (teacher and pupils interviews, also parents' role) . . . Have
decided can afford to do only two more days' 'open' observation
(confer with David), and need to ensure that a Friday is included.
At end of today, have two further 'closed' observations in the
pipeline linked to curriculum activities planned by teachers in the
library space, and to which I am invited. Are the concepts 'open'
and 'closed' useful in this context? How do teachers 'book' the
library for sessions? (Loop back to library co-ordinator and
school secretary.)

Theme: Library
Sub-theme: physical space (cont.)
Features:

1 open or closed access;
2 for pupils and/or teachers;
3 library access as reward for work completed.

Theme: Library
Sub-theme: learning
Features:

1 pupils gaining knowledge;
2 pupils' information skills;
3 pupils as library monitors (what does this mean in practice?);
4 library visit as a 'reward' for classroom 'learning'.

As is shown above, themes from the original interviews inform the subsequent observation, and understandings about some, but by no means
all, of the interview themes are extended by the observation. New themes

and questions emerge and are looped – *back* into earlier data, *across* to complementary data and *forward* into the next stages of fieldwork. Observation notes are also interwoven with the personal concerns expressed by the ethnographer. Is she 'seeing enough'? Is she 'wasting' time? Is this 'typical' or . . .? The themes are given codes. Some are further sub-divided; some will remain without sub-division or further fragmentation. For some codes, the frequency of referral would decline – this did not necessarily diminish their potential value as data since they might become the 'unusual' or 'exceptional' data 'bits' that required further explanation elsewhere.

Qualitative description

An ethnographer's key task is to describe and explain that which has been observed in the field. Some writers like Lofland (1971) have focused upon a series of headings as the focal point for descriptive attention: acts, activities, meanings, participation, relationships and settings. Others draw upon the codes that are developed out of the earliest stages of analysis (Miles and Huberman 1994) and use these as frameworks for the qualitative descrip-tion upon which coded talk and activities rest. Ethnographers use a range of rhetorical devices to convey its analytical themes through qualitative descriptions of examples, vignettes and cases. In the following example, we see how Burgess and Morrison (1995) used ethnographies of food and eating in schools as a major feature of an Economic and Social Research Council (ESRC) funded project called Teaching and Learning about Food and Nutrition in Schools. This was part of a larger research programme: *The Nation's Diet: The Social Science of Food Choice* (Murcott 1998). A key aspect of the project was the use of a sociological perspective to examine the interrelations between a range of understandings about food use in schools, explored through interviews, observations and diary use with teachers, pupils, dinner ladies and parents.

An emerging theme was the significance of food use used as a *punishment* or *reward*, and, as such, part of an ongoing *struggle for control*. In the following extract, qualitative descriptions about lunchtime arrangements in a school called Brook Street Primary are used to illustrate the issue of *control* (Morrison 1996b; Burgess and Morrison 1998). What is described by Burgess and Morrison is not a single event. We use their words here to highlight ethnographic analysis as synecdoche, as the account attempts to describe and exemplify patterns of eating in school. Extracted as micro-analysis, excerpts from the text provide 'thick' descriptions of lunchtime arrangements in one school. In the first excerpt, the 'scene' or context for the narrative analysis is set:

230 children out of 360 children on roll stayed for lunch. Of these 58 brought packed lunches and the remainder ate meals provided by the city's School Meals Service. Seventy three per cent of the children received free school meals. Adults, that is, dinner ladies, supervised by a lunchtime superintendent, were in charge . . . Children were not allowed to save spaces for friends. The superintendent would also oversee the quantity and quality of the packed lunches . . . The non-involvement of the teaching staff reinforced the segregation of lunchtime as a non-educational activity. Lunchtimes were staggered, allowing the youngest children to enter the dining hall before the majority. The sociability of eating resembled a conveyor belt system, with queuing, eating at speed, a minimum of talk, and throughput, its salient features. While most dinner ladies ate at the same tables as children, stewardship was exercised with minimal discourse and included patrolling to maintain order. 'Eating up' was of paramount importance. Queuing served as a control as well as a labelling function, and daily lists of children in receipt of free school meals reinforced a perceived need among adults to encourage children to eat up.

(Burgess and Morrison 1998: 222)

The narrative mode is being used here to portray what happens at Brook Street School and we note that Burgess and Morrison 'translate' fieldnotes into text using what Hammersley and Atkinson (1995) describe as 'a narrative construction of everyday life' (p.250) that, following Richardson (1990), is 'valued as a basic tool in the ethnographer's craft' (1995: 250). A picture is painted that juxtaposes individualized eating experiences with daily eating rituals of pupils. They continue:

The process of individualised eating in an institutionalised setting had specific features at Brook Street. Because dinner ladies viewed eating and conversation as incompatible, the latter was discouraged and persistent offenders were isolated at smaller tables. Deviant children were those who resisted rules about queuing, eating up, talking, or fighting. Control was maintained with different degrees of success by dinner ladies who befriended, joked, cajoled, ordered, shouted, and, in one case, ranted at children. An extreme case is recorded:

The dining room is noisy. Screaming Mrs. B [a dinner lady] adds to the noise level. She doesn't differentiate her screaming for different levels of reprimand. Consequently, at times her screaming is ignored by the children . . . I find it more and more difficult to ignore her (Morrison: fieldnote).

(Burgess and Morrison 1998: 222–3)

In educational ethnography, qualitative description frequently treads a careful path between vignettes of the 'familiar' and the 'strange', in order to evoke a range of understandings about 'what is going on here', and, as in the above example, the researcher's fieldnotes are included. This gives readers a sense of the researcher (Morrison) 'being there'. Moreover, contrasts are sometimes evoked as part of the narrative. In the next extract, 'conventional morality' (Hammersley and Atkinson 1995: 251) is contrasted with the 'situated moralities' (p.251) of a school dining room in which:

> the rationale for keeping control was dominated by practical and institutional concerns to feed large numbers in a relatively short time span. Dinner ladies also invoked other kinds of rationale. These included the view that children who had 'free school meals' should 'eat up' not only because it was 'their only meal' but also because 'other people's taxes' paid for them. Those children whose parents paid were also chivvied to 'eat up' to fulfil parental expectations, and in the belief that to waste food and money was wrong.
>
> (Burgess and Morrison 1998: 223)

An illustrative vignette is used to reinforce the point:

> One day, Thomas from the reception class was observed as follows:

> > Thomas eats all his meals (eventually) . . . but breaks the cardinal rules – he eats slowly and wants to talk. Sit next to Thomas. Reprimanded four times for talking . . . Reception class told to sit outside on the grass once they have finished. I asked Mrs C. [lunchtime superintendent] why. Slow eaters, humid weather, high noise levels in the hall. So young children wait outside for others to finish. This doesn't work for Thomas . . . he finally leaves the dining hall at 1pm (plate still not empty.) I shadow him across the playground. Thomas has a problem since detention in the dining hall has meant that . . . play groups have already been established and he finds it difficult to break in . . . finally he finds two boys who are playing hide and seek – he joins them before the bell (Morrison: fieldnotes).
> >
> > (Burgess and Morrison 1998: 224)

In this ethnographic account the concept of control is also used to frame descriptions about what happens in the school dining room *and* what was eaten as a school meal, and again actual fieldnotes are interspersed with the descriptive account, as is shown in the following extract which focuses upon control over what pupils eat, how this is variously thwarted or resisted, and by whom:

> The School Meals Service made central decisions about the choice of menu which included attention given to cultural food preferences. In the dining hall, such decisions were reinforced *and* thwarted by counter staff and dinner ladies, and by the children. Membership of

the 'meat' and 'non-meat' queue was rigidly enforced [during the first week in school the youngest pupils wore labels which read 'meat' and 'no meat']. Omnivores had to state a preference and remain consistent. Blanket 'no meat' assumptions about mainly 'Asian' diets could pose problems for children as the following fieldnote indicates:

> Ravi (year 2) joins me at the table. Tells me dinner ladies are – points finger to head and twists finger. I look quizzical enough for him to continue 'They keep telling me I'm "no meat" but I do eat meat'. Anyway, today he has secured some chicken pie. Do you eat meat at home I ask? We establish that meat at home comes from a special shop (Morrison: fieldnote).

Adults and children also thwarted central attempts to control the nutritional balance of meals. The overriding adult view was that eating something was preferable to not eating at all, and so children's food trays might contain a combination of supplementary dishes rather than any 'main' dish on the menu. This could mean . . . combinations of boiled, mashed, and chipped potatoes. Being labelled 'meat' could also restrict choices. In theory, children could choose a vegetarian dish. In practice, adults controlled choice by discouraging specific choices if it was felt that the vegetarian allocation might be used up.

(Burgess and Morrison 1998: 225)

Through an ethnographic exploration of lunchtimes, it was possible to learn about control strategies and resistance among children and adults in school. At Brook Street, Burgess and Morrison report that a conveyor-belt system was reflected in patterns of adult and child behaviour. This showed degrees of opposition to, and some accommodation with, the more widely recognized models of meals as social events. 'Next steps' in the research would be to look for similar or different patterns in segments of the data that pertained to the other school sites, looking for patterns, for example, across the primary/secondary, rural/urban, monoethnic/multiethnic and socioeconomic dimensions of the four schools.

In such ways, we see that qualitative description is not the end point for ethnographic analysts. Searching for patterns is what Dey (1993) describes as the 'building blocks' of analysis which are assembled and re-assembled to produce 'an intelligent, coherent and valid account' (p.51).

Patterns and classifications

In ethnographic analysis much interest has been given to producing *theoretical descriptions*. Writing in 1990, Hammersley was critical of the limited extent to which ethnography produced theoretical descriptions, and, if they *did*, what kinds of theories were produced. His suggestion was that the distinctiveness of theoretical approaches in ethnography should lie both 'in the explicitness and the coherence of the models employed, and *the rigour of the analysis*' (1991: 28, our emphasis).

For Miles and Huberman (1994) a key aspect of rigour is the attention given to the patterns and ordering of the data. Dey (1993) depicts this process as an iterative spiral which moves from collecting data to describing it, classifying it and making connections between the classifications in order to arrive at a qualitative account of the research. A number of steps are suggested (Dey 1993: 52, our emphasis):

- In *classifying*, we establish logical connections between categories.
- Once *categorised*, we can look for *patterns* in the data.
- Statistics can help identify *singularities, regularities*, and *variations*.
- Regularities can be suggestive but not conclusive evidence of *connections*.
- To establish connections requires a qualitative analysis of *capabilities* and *liabilities*.
- *Graphic representation* is useful in analysing concepts and their connections.
- *Theories* can contribute direction and order to the analysis.

In education, ethnography often tries to get to 'the parts' of educational experience that other research approaches cannot reach. Even so, there is a series of steps in which the formation of patterns and classifications are readily discernible. This is seen clearly in a published account by Jeffrey and Woods (1996) where they report on their exploration of classroom 'climate' or 'ethos' as aspects of long-term research into creative teaching in schools. In previous work with secondary schools, Woods (1990b) had characterized ethos as 'a moving set of relationships within which different groups and individuals are constantly engaged in negotiation. It is expressed largely in symbolic form, notably in language, appearance, and behaviour' (p.77). Subsequently, Jeffrey and Woods sought to understand the 'quality of ethos or climate' in primary school contexts. Adopting a qualitative approach, they record that classroom-focused research took place in depth with five teachers for one day a week for up to three terms, and with 12 teachers overall, and where the researchers were expected to engage in limited participation in the classroom. Methods used included observations and conversations with teachers and pupils recorded by photographs, tape recordings and fieldnotes. Interviews with pupils took place individually and as groups. Teachers were invited to act as respondent validators to the extent that that they were given all papers from the project for comment.

The study illustrates the various ways in which research draws upon qualitative data to illustrate, in tangible textual form, analysis of school 'realities' that might otherwise be viewed as intangible or abstract (even unresearchable). In this example, the 'intangible' is 'the subtle art of teaching' researched against the backdrop of the wider policy contexts of the 1990s. Jeffrey and Woods' (1996) value positions are clear; they focus readers' attention upon the 'meanings' of teaching as viewed by teachers, and the 'desire' to teach (p.166). Our summary of their work illustrates a number of patterns and classifications in which the study of classroom climates is sub-divided into two thematic aspects – 'atmosphere' and 'tone'.

Atmosphere

Here, illustrative examples are used to explore the ways in which teachers 'create' and 'sustain' atmospheres that are conducive to learning. A range of themes and patterns for classifying classroom climates are developed. Following the examples drawn earlier in this chapter, one interpretation (ours) would be as follows:

1　*Anticipation and expectation*
　　Sub-themes:　construction of classroom situations;
　　　　　　　　sense of timing;
　　　　　　　　visual aids;
　　　　　　　　sense of theatre;
　　　　　　　　taking learning into the community;
　　　　　　　　bringing the community into the classroom.

2　*Relevance*
　　Sub-themes:　　pupils contribute to classroom learning activities;
　　　　　　　　　pupils involved in classroom learning activities;
　　　　　　　　　teachers take account of cultural, race and gender distinctions;
　　　　　　　　　teachers relate learning to pupils' feelings;
　　　　　　　　　teachers evoke a sense of purpose for the learning.

3　*Achievement and success*
　　Sub-themes:　　mood of achievement and success.
　　Sub-sub-themes:　use of praise and commentary;
　　　　　　　　　dialogic engagement between teacher and pupil;
　　　　　　　　　clear distinction between praise and encouragement.

4　*Satisfaction*
　　Sub-themes:　　teachers' sense of a job well done.

Tone

Jeffrey and Woods (1996) apply a musical analogy by referring to tone as 'the sound quality and levels, rhythm, pace and tempo of classroom life. In these respects an artistic lesson has affinities with a piece of music with its variations designed for effect, its range of instruments to produce them, and with the teacher as orchestrator and conductor' (p.161). For purposes of analysis the researchers group the data under three headings 'andante', 'legato' and 'spiritoso', analytical distinctions drawn upon by using metaphors to illustrate differences in teachers' use of physical and subjective space to encourage learning. It is also illustrative of the propensity to use metaphor to construct and reconstruct qualitative accounts of people, experiences and situations.

1 *Andante* (to be performed in moderately slow time):
   The mood generated by the teacher is to establish seriousness and create tension, and is described as 'creeping quietness' (1996: 162) A specific illustrative vignette is used by the researchers to illustrate a teacher's sense of timing, of drama, and of capturing an 'emotional as well as cognitive engagement of the [pupil] audience, so that all are captured in the spirit of *communitas*' (p.164).

2 *Legato* (smoothly and connectedly, no gaps or breaks):
   This tone is adopted as the general working atmosphere of the classroom in which there is a 'quiet buzz' and 'working noise' as children engage in individual and group activities with the teacher as orchestrator 'keeping the rhythm and smooth pace going' and 'sets the tone for dialogue and inquiry' (p.165).

3 *Spiritoso* (with spirit):
   'A *spiritoso* mood involving animation, vigour and liveliness generates excitement, joy, interest and enthusiasm. There is much humour, and many smiling faces. It is commonly used to "arouse appetite" (Hargreaves 1982)' (p.165).

Connections

Patterns shown in previous sections are identified when the ethnographer looks for connections. Again, Dey (1993: 176) takes readers helpfully through a number of *stages*. Each are facilitated by the use of a computer:

- Concurrence – do data bits concur?
- Overlaps – do data bits overlap?
- Sequence – are the data bits consecutive?
- Proximity – are the data bits within a given distance?
- Precedence – does one data bit precede another?

Evolving classifications commonly involves the development of typologies and taxonomies that are, in turn, part of the processes of interpretation. As both Dey (1993) and Brewer (2000) remind us, classifications and typologies are always developed with research purposes and objectives in mind, and are, therefore, never 'neutral' (Brewer 2000: 116). Miles and Huberman (1994) are enthusiastic supporters of classification systems; humanistic ethnographers are moderate exponents as long as schema keep as close as possible to the 'words' and meanings of the research subjects.

For positivist ethnographers, the question of *why* things happen is uppermost. The notion that ethnography is 'only' useful for exploration and developing hypotheses is strongly countered:

> We consider qualitative analysis to be a very powerful method for assessing causality ... Qualitative analysis with its close-up look, can identify mechanisms, going beyond sheer association. It is un-relentingly local, and deals with the complex network of events and processes in a situation. It can sort out the temporal dimension, showing clearly what preceded what, either through direct observation or through retrospection. It is well equipped to cycle backwards and forth between variables and processes showing that stories are not capricious but include underlying variables, and that variables are not disembodied but have connections over time
>
> (Miles and Huberman 1994: 147)

Miles and Huberman draw upon examples of displays: *explanatory effects matrices* (that look at outcomes and processes), *case dynamics matrices* (for considering what leads to what) and *causal networks* (which pull together independent and dependent variables into a coherent pattern). Final steps include looking for negatives cases. There needs to be systematic scrutiny of *all* the evidence, including the negative examples (see Jeffrey and Woods 1996, above).

Towards outcomes

For positivist ethnographers (Miles and Huberman 1994), analysis can be extended to making *predictions*. So in relation to a school improvement research programme, a prediction exercise was built into the study and the mechanics that involved research informants are fully outlined. There is little here of the tentative statements sometimes evident in other ethnographic studies, or of a language that 'suggests' or 'indicates' or describes 'tendencies towards'. (Not that such language is necessarily problematic; there are always dangers in claiming 'too much' from analysis – see below.) Arguing that prediction acts as 'a powerful validating device' (p.170), Miles and Huberman (1994) do note, however, a number of drawbacks in their attempts to build prediction into their research model for school improvement: reliance on the 'site informants' for feedback, for example, and 'wrong' predictions that were unconnected with the internal validity of the analysis. To this, we might add the difficulties in working towards predictive analysis within some of the limited time frames facing ethnographers in current funding climates.

For researchers of the postmodern turn, all classification schemes, patterns and typologies are personal to the researcher and the research team. Negative 'cases' are, therefore, not the reverse of positive 'cases' since it is the diversity in understanding about ethnographic realities that is of prime interest. An example from Stronach and Maclure (1997) exemplifies the contrast between the tightly structured 'objective' approaches highlighted above, and a diversity of conclusions and outcomes from postmodern analysis. In a chapter entitled, 'Jack in two boxes: a postmodern perspective on the transformation of persons into portraits', Stronach and Maclure report on a portrayal of Jack, a primary school headteacher approaching retirement, and analyse three lengthy life history interviews that were conducted by Maclure but written up separately by Stronach and Maclure as part of a research project on teachers' lives and careers. A humanistic approach to ethnography would be one in which the ethnographer facilitates the self-expression of Jack, leaving as much control in the hands of Jack as possible. In contrast, what emerges from a 'postmodern embrace' is two rather different accounts produced separately by each of the authors, based on the same data, that are further mediated by Jack in follow-up discussions. For the authors, this raises the question of whether 'methodological questions' could ever be 'reducible to textual ones' (Stronach and Maclure 1997: 56) in which there is a single or final representation of reality. They comment:

> We do not seek to dismiss methodology but rather bring its textual properties to light; to ask what sorts of stories are implicated in a particular methodology, and what sorts of stories are suppressed or made 'untellable' . . . Narratives that promote coherence, singularity, and closure, and which aim to set up a cosy camaraderie with the reader, are ultimately conservative and uncritical of prevailing ideological and representational arrangements. If we refuse to interrogate these forms we run the risk of promoting an uncritical research practice which, in seeming to describe teachers as they 'really are', simply perpetuates whatever iconographies of teacher-hood happen to be circulating in the various professional cultures (research, practitioner, academic) at any given time.
>
> (Stronach and Maclure 1997: 57)

If all this suggests that educational ethnography continues to be challenged and stimulated by competing epistemological traditions, we might also consider the extent to which this has been exacerbated or reduced by recent developments in computers. What has prompted the development and acceleration of computer aided analysis? In the next section some underlying principles are introduced. We sketch out some intellectual tendencies towards analytical convergence and consider practical implications.

Computer-aided analysis

Proponents and exponents of the computer-aided analysis of ethnographic data (Tesch 1990; Miles and Huberman 1994; Richards and Richards 1994, 1998; Stroh 2000a,b; Fielding and Lee 1995; Kelle 1995; Lee 1995) are growing in number. Advocacy rests upon three main advantages:

1 its ability to manage data;
2 its capacity to assist the actual process of analysis, and
3 its approximation to (or emulation of?) quantitative or positivist approaches to research.

Managing data

For ethnographers, a major challenge lies in the management of vast amounts of textual data. Computer use greatly assists in (Miles and Huberman 1994: 44; Brown and Dowling 1998: 99):

- making notes in the field;
- writing up or transcribing fieldnotes;
- editing: correcting, extending or revising fieldnotes;
- coding: attaching key words or tags to segments of text and making them available for inspection;
- storage: keeping text in an organized database;
- search and retrieval: locating relevant segments of the text and making them available for inspection;
- content analysis: counting frequencies, sequences or the location of words and phrases.

Assisting analysis

Some exponents (Richards and Richards 1998) claim much more than this by arguing that computers can assist *directly* in the process of analysis. Computer packages facilitate the exploration of links which, when combined with the creativity of the researcher, can help to generate theories. The 'value-added' is that computers have vast organizing potential that mechanical processes cannot match. This suggests that the larger the ethnographic project, for example, in multisite school studies and/or among large research teams, the greater the 'value-added'. Key aspects include (Miles and Huberman 1994: 44; Brown and Dowling 1998: 99):

- data linking: connecting relevant data segments and forming categories, clusters or networks of information;
- memoing: writing reflective commentaries on some aspects of the data for deeper analysis;
- data display: placing selected or reduced data in a condensed, organized format, such as a matrix or network for inspection;
- conclusion drawing and verification: aiding the analyst to interpret displayed data and to test or confirm findings;
- theory-building: developing systematic, conceptually coherent explanations of findings;
- testing hypotheses;
- graphic mapping: creating diagrams that depict findings or theories.

Credibility

The *coup de grâce* is that computer-aided analysis allows ethnographic findings to become *replicable*. As ethnography becomes more 'scientific', it is argued, the potential for ethnography to be parodied as 'anecdotal' or 'singular' diminishes. Ethnography gains respectability and finds increased favour with funders, including research councils (Fielding and Lee 1998: 58–9). Prospects are magnified when the potential for combining qualitative and quantitative approaches to research is also enhanced (Dey 1993: 4). In 1998, Fetterman (1998: 82) produced a helpful list of programs and their best uses. This includes Kwalitan, QUALPRO and The Ethnograph (for finding, displaying, and retrieving coded data), HyperRESEARCH and NUDIST (for theory generation) and Atlas-ti (for theory testing). Subsequently, NVivo has been developed and marketed (Bazeley and Richards 2000).[1]

Caution

The issue of whether the logic of the computer is the most appropriate basis for the analysis of ethnographic data has been controversial and we will return to this. (However, as qualitative computing enters the mainstream, sponsors appear to find efficiency and proficiency in use, rather than controversy, the main issue.) Meanwhile, readers who may be first time ethnographers, engaged in small-scale research in educational settings are invited to exercise some caution on a number of practical grounds, as indicated below. (This is *not* to take a Luddite position.) We invite you to ask:

- How many of the tasks discussed above could be accomplished on a word processor?
- How much time and resources are available to learn multi-access packages like NUD*IST, for example? (But see Stroh 2000 a and b) for

very useful introductions to this computing software that includes hands-on exercises.)

- Most importantly, consider carefully the uses to which the selected packages can be put. As Brown and Dowling (1998) note: 'much time and/or expense can be wasted putting data in the required form and working through it using a program only to discover that the form of analysis towards which you are being led is not appropriate' (p.100).

Other criticisms are more than exhortations not 'to bite off more than you can chew', and it is to these we now return.

Contested representations and computing

We have already noted connections between ethnography and grounded theory. Coffey and Atkinson (2000: 35) contend that the latter has been 'received in two ways', first as a 'general strategy of social inquiry' (as in earlier sections of this chapter) and second, as a 'method which can be reduced to prescriptive recipe-knowledge'. In this sense, it is argued, 'computerized' ethnographic analysis has the potential to lose some of its connections to humanistic ethnography and commitments to 'deep' and 'thick' understandings of the subjective world of educational actors, and also to aspects inherent in the postmodern insistence upon the importance of multiple voices and perspectives.

This critique rests not on a view that qualitative computing necessarily prescribes particular epistemological approaches. Rather, issue is taken with the assumptions on which analysis is assumed to rest, in particular the emphasis upon *coding*. Now many sponsors of applied educational research are seeking confirmation from research proposal writers that qualitative computer software will underpin analysis. What are the challenging elements of 'this emergent orthodoxy'? For Coffey and Atkinson (2000: 36–7) five propositions are discernible:

1 grounded theory depends on an inductive approach to analysis;
2 analysis depends on the retrieval of coded segments;
3 coding consists of data reduction into categories;
4 analysis depends on the retrieval of coded segments;
5 a search and retrieve strategy is therefore the implementation of grounded theory inquiry.

In response, they argue that:

None of these propositions is uncontested and we do not agree with all or indeed any of them in any simple sense. They do not entail one another ... Grounded theorizing is more than coding ... The point is not about the full potential of CAQDAS [Computer

Assisted Qualitative Data Analysis Software], nor about the true nature of grounded theorizing. Rather, the danger lies in the glib association between the two, linked by an emphasis on data coding procedures.

(Coffey and Atkinson 2000: 36–7)

Accordingly, it is argued that a 'sub-culture' of computerized analysis has evolved that lends itself to a specific and converging way of thinking about and representing qualitative data, and this is supported and reinforced by burgeoning expertise and published manuals. In contrast, computer use that departs from coding and search and retrieve procedures, and allows experimentation with the use of text, *is* advocated (see also Chapter 5).

Meanwhile, as a counterpoint to the celebratory and evangelistic tone contained in much of the computer literature is Sprokkereef *et al.*'s (1995) critical evaluation of the use of Ethnograph for funded research purposes. Meanwhile, Fetterman (1998: 72) continues to advocate computer use for 'traditional' ethnographic purposes, such as literature searches and reviews, and through the increased use of the Internet.

Making ethnographic sense

Interpretation is part and parcel of the ethnographer's work in educational settings. How do we assess the 'goodness' (Miles and Huberman 1994: chap. 10) or 'truthfulness' of our analysis? Even if we accept the postmodern argument that there is no single 'truth', but rather a range of polyvocal stories told in and about educational settings, all ethnographers are engaged in one of more readings of 'truths' that are derived from analysis. Ethnographers are, above all, 'meaning finders' (Miles and Huberman 1994). The question is: do ethnographers find the 'right' meanings? Ethnographers with positivist intent have suggested a number of approaches for confirming the 'quality' of derived meanings. Increasingly, computer assisted 'quality assurance' demands that ethnographers address a range of questions as they engage in analysis and move towards reporting outcomes. Miles and Huberman (1994: Chapter 10) identify a range of issues:

1 What goes with what? Using data patterning, thematizing and clustering.
2 What's there? Using counting, literary devices (like metaphors) as aspects of partial theorizing.
3 What does this mean? Making contrasts and comparisons, sub-dividing variables, finding relations between variables and finding intervening variables.
4 How can we move towards coherent conclusions? Building a logical chain of evidence and developing conceptual/theoretical coherence.

Whether or not we wish to consider ethnographic data as 'right' or 'wrong', many ethnographers would wish to confirm that some ethnographic truths are more 'right' than 'wrong', or vice versa. Hammersley (1992b), for example, discusses what he considers to be the two most important criteria for assessing the outcomes of ethnographic analysis, namely its 'validity' and 'relevance', as a counterpoint to 'naive realism'. By which criteria might we judge validity? Given existing educational knowledge, the claims made by ethnography, he argues, need to be judged first in terms of their *plausibility* and *credibility*:

> If they [the claims] are themselves beyond reasonable doubt, we can simply accept them. If they are not, we must ask if the claims are credible, by which I mean whether it is of a kind that we could reasonably expect to be correct given what we know about the circumstances in which the research was carried out.
>
> (Hammersley 1992b: 70)

The second criterion concerns the *centrality* of the claims that ethnographers make. So, 'where a claim is central, more convincing evidence will be required than where it is marginal. This is analogous to the common-sense tendency to require more evidence where a costly decision is involved' (p.71).

The third criterion concerns the *types* of claim(s) made. Given that ethnographies in educational settings frequently involve 'definition, descriptions, explanations and theories', ethnographers will, for example, need to distinguish between 'descriptive' and 'theoretical' claims. It is argued that the second type is more complex than the first, since

> in trying to support a theoretical claim then [ethnographers] will need to produce descriptive evidence about some case (or more likely, cases) relevant to the theory, which documents the correlation of instances of the type of phenomena produced with the type claimed to produce them. In addition, though, we will have to try to show that, *in this case and others*, the occurrence of the first type of phenomenon is not a product of factors other than the ones claimed.
>
> (Hammersley 1992b: 71–2)

To what extent is it possible for ethnographers to meet these criteria? A number of research methods texts provide a range of checklist approaches to allow ethnographers and others to address such concerns (Miles and Huberman 1994: 263; Denscombe 1998: 223; Brewer 2000: 124).

An amalgam of approaches would include:

1 *Checking* with informants, but also adopting a critical attitude towards what informants say. (*Action*: check for representativeness; weight the evidence by checking across data and methods deployed; check with alternative studies.)

2 *Seeking* alternative explanations. (*Action*: look for phenomena that do not appear to fit; follow up unusual or typical 'cases'; check for 'spurious' or 'rival' explanations.)

3 *Checking* ethnographer effects. (*Action*: be reflexive – but see below.)

4 *Representing* the range of voices in the field. (*Action*: how this is done will vary among researchers. 'Feeding back' data for matters of factual accuracy, for example, is a rather different order of representation to feeding back models, typologies and/or taxonomies, for example, to informants in order to achieve a negotiated account.)

In combination, such approaches provide counterpoints to tendencies towards:

- holism: seeing educational phenomena as more patterned than they are;
- elitism: overweighting evidence from articulate or high-status informants rather than from the less articulate or lower-status;
- 'going native': 'losing the plot' because of 'capture' by (particular) informants.

Reflexivity

For the purposes of this chapter reflexivity provides the link between ethnographic analysis and the final account as ethnographic text. This is not to argue that reflexivity is confined to analytical and/or the end processes of ethnography. Reflexivity or being reflexive is rather easier to define than it is to enact or to be. At one level, reflexivity denies the possibility of ethnographers ever achieving an entirely objective position in relation to research (see also Morrison 2002), because researchers are part of the social and educational worlds they are studying. From the perspective of reflexivity, such awareness is not just implicated in the kinds of ethnography in which we are engaged, but also in the way such orientations affect all aspects of research design – from the selection of research topics through to writing up and dissemination. Such awareness is self-evidently challenging since it brings to the fore features of educational research that may hitherto have remained hidden, assumed or denied. Reflexivity is neither easy nor straightforward. We might return to Hammersley's (1992b) earlier arguments about the descriptive and theoretical claims upon which ethnography might be assessed, in order to look for 'descriptive' as well as 'analytical' or 'theoretical' reflexivity in the accounts produced.

For Griffiths (1998), for example, both kinds of reflexivity present the ethnographer with the continuing prospect of 'getting things wrong and having to put them right again' (p.142); she also berates researchers who pay limited attention to reflexivity by engaging in processes described as 'intellectual tourism'. On the one hand, this includes 'the seduction of [researcher] autobiography and self-gaze', and on the other, 'an apparent performance of reflexivity by a series of cosmetic moves' (1998: 143). An example of the latter might be describing an ethnography as 'feminist' or 'anti-racist' without engaging in any of the major debates in those areas as part of the research design or process (1998: 143). An example of the former is when ethnographers write in the 'confessional mode', a not uncommon practice that occurs several years (or more) after the original account has been published.

In brief, the task of the ethnographer in educational settings is to engage in reflexivity as a means of substantiating 'interpretations and findings with a reflexive account of themselves and the processes of their research' (Altheide and Johnson 1998: 292). This moves ethnographers beyond what Griffiths (1998) regards as the 'self-deceiving rather than hypocritical' mode of bringing back tales from the field, towards a greater sensitivity to ethnography's twin challenges of representation and legitimation. Brewer (2000: 132–3) provides a useful summary of issues in which all ethnographic presentations make explicit the:

- wider relevance of the setting and the topic researched;
- features of the topic and the setting that remain unresearched and why;
- theoretical framework used and developed;
- ethnographer's value framework.

And will also include critical assessments of the:

- ethnographer's integrity as a researcher and author;
- iterative processes of data collection and analysis;
- data's complexity.

Centrally implicated here are all the processes in which the ethnographer is engaged that require reading and re-reading, as well as writing, rewriting and writing up. It is to writing, as an aspect of analysis, that our attention now turns.

Writing as analysis

General issues of representation and writing will be discussed in Chapter 6. We introduce it here because, for ethnographers, writing and representing are also part of analysis. Assumptions that the 'writing up' of ethnographic observations can ever be final arbiters of all theoretical and methodological aspects of ethnography has long been challenged. As Atkinson (1992: 38) points out, 'however factual or realistic a text appears to be, it is inescapably dependent upon the conventions of reading and writing that its producers and consumers bring to bear'.

Little has been written so far in this chapter about what Woods (1985: 86) describes as the 'pain threshold' which occurs when 'creative' ideas about data collected are transformed through textual analysis into written text. (Advocates of computer assisted analysis see an important aspect of that assistance in terms of pain reduction!) However, if we retain the notion of the ethnographer as central to the creative processes of analysis, it 'may be helpful to conceive of the [writing] problem not so much in terms of what you do to the data but what you do to yourself' (Woods 1985: 87). Are there specific aspects of ethnographic research that make moving beyond the 'pain threshold' especially challenging?

There appears to be two levels at which the pain barrier needs to be crossed. The *first* is at the level of debate about which kinds of ethnography are the most appropriate for educational research – and we have positivist, humanist, postmodern and post-postmodern versions of this debate to choose from. This will be reflected in and affected by the styles of and formats for writing (see below). At the micro-level, the challenge for individually researched small scale ethnographies has also been those identified by Woods (1985: 104–5):

- emphasis on the investigator as the chief research instrument, which tends to make problems more personal than they really are;
- nature of the research as a process: an open-ended dialogue between data collection and theory, where the search for ongoing dialogues mitigates against early foreclosure; and the
- necessity, in view of this, to regard the 'writing up' process as important an inducement to the production of ideas as to their communication.

Perhaps 'writing up' is most usefully considered in relation to three concerns:

1 What to include and why include 'this' data bit rather than 'that' data bit.
2 How to write, and why 'this' format rather than 'that'.
3 What status is claimed for the ethnography by the analyst/writer, whether *technically* or *procedurally* in relation to other methods deployed within a research project (potentially critical in research programmes where ethnographies are part of a combination of approaches to address a research problem), or *theoretically*, in terms of the status of the ethnographic text?

A number of publications give clear guidance and advice on writing in particular approaches that engage the reader and intended audience(s) (Becker 1986; Wolcott 1990; Dey 1993; Woods 1999; Burton 2000). Good writing begins with good planning and does not preclude writing creatively (see Wolcott 1990: 16). Educational ethnographies of the past were especially noted for 'thick description' (Hargreaves 1967; Lacey 1970; Ball

1981; Burgess 1983). The lesson for ethnographers who may be engaged in smaller-scale ethnographies and/or studies of shorter duration may be not to 'over-do' description to the extent that it substitutes for analysis.

Views on the use of the first or third person in ethnographic writing are also mixed. Advice to write in the third person and past tense for 'academic' reasons, we think, needs to be carefully balanced against the use of the first person, to position 'I' as integral to the research design, process and account. More recently, Woods (1999) provides further advice for writing 'on' and writing 'up'. His list of don'ts is especially helpful (pp. 64–7):

- *Don't* use words to persuade without evidential support.
- *Don't* construct 'straw persons'. This works on a principle of contrasts, where in order to highlight one's own argument, an opposite version is constructed that does not really exist.
- *Don't* overclaim and overstate the case (even though the pressure in applied educational research, with its emphasis on problem solving, is considerable). 'Overclaiming' can be linked to 'sloppy' writing.
- *Don't* underclaim, whether through modesty or failure to perceive possibilities. 'Underclaiming' can also be linked to 'sloppy' writing.
- *Don't* put forward Utopian possibilities instead of practical possibilities.
- *Don't* be over-zealous. An example might be where over-zealous attention to methodological rigour reduces opportunities for the researcher to develop creative ideas.
- *Don't* overdo the use of metaphors, but use them when they add to the reader's understanding of the text, for example, consider Jeffrey and Woods' use of '*andante*' '*legato*' and '*spiritoso*' earlier as a way of classifying forms of creative teaching.
- *Don't* iron out all the messiness of ethnographic research.
- *Don't* be content with under-theorized description.

Educational ethnographers are divided about the status of their texts. The most obvious dichotomy is between the realists and anti-realists. The former hold the perspective that it is possible to employ an authoritative style, whether on the basis of telling it as it is or through strict adherence to methodological procedures that 'accurately' represents the truth. Anti-realists deny that any one story can be privileged over another. And between these poles are the post-post modernists and critical realists in which thick description is mixed with analyst constructed taxonomies. Thus, Miles and Huberman (1994) write about a balance in the 'mix' between 'stories' and 'variables', and between thinking derived from the 'paradigmatic' and the 'narrative' 'texts' and 'displays'. Following Hammersley's (1990, 1992b) concerns about the plausibility and credibility of evidence, then ethnography is/might also be written in ways that allow readers to assess ethnography on those grounds.

Are there new, imaginative and/or divergent trends for ethnographic analysis? Some innovative forms of ethnography have begun to re-address the 'what?' and 'how?' questions about writing and reading ethnography. One way might be to write an account that is not primarily concerned with the truth, whether in single or multiple forms, but presents 'fiction' as a way of describing/explaining educational phenomena. Atkinson (1992: 49–51) comments:

> A small number of [postmodern] authors have taken the use of 'literary pastiche' and invention to the point where they cease to represent or reconstruct recognisable and plausible social worlds in any conventional sense ... Tyler (1987) suggests that the distinction is not between 'fact' (ethnography) and 'fiction' (literature) but between fiction and 'fantasy' ethnography.

From this perspective ethnography ceases to become a representation of 'reality' but instead analysis 'evokes' images that free ethnographers from striving to adhere to outmoded scientific principles. There may be something of a 'straw person' syndrome here (see Woods 1999). In rejecting cruder forms of representation, ethnographers could lose important reference points to the educational world or, in Atkinson's words, become 'increasingly self-referential' (1992: 50). Is this taking insight and innovation to extremes ... or ...?

Meanwhile, some ethnographers are now writing up analysis as ethno-drama or as poetry. In addition, some ethnography is being written in dialogic forms either as fiction, with the researcher talking to 'self' or another, or where there is a juggling of 'real' text, in which it is argued, outcomes become closer to rather than distanced from the complexities of individual experience (see, for example, Coffey *et al.* (1996) on the use of Hypertext as a way of representing data in non-linear or non-sequential forms, a theme re-visited in Chapter 5 on using ethnography). For an interesting example of the dialogic form, in particular the use of irony, consider the following extract from Cooper and Woolgar (1996) – a dialogue between a director of research and a research fellow in a research centre, in which the wisdom to be derived from published texts on research methods is juxtaposed with 'what goes on here':

Research fellow:	It is extraordinary that almost all ... methods texts assume that researchers work on their own, make their own decisions and otherwise proceed in isolation of the demands of their colleagues, their institution and discipline.
Director:	Doesn't sound like what goes on in this centre.
Research fellow:	It's such a misleading picture of the research process especially when you think that this is what is being taught to newcomers to research!

Director:	Researchers have to learn that textbook versions of research don't tell anything like the whole story.
Research fellow:	And it's curious isn't it, that so few of those terribly sophisticated discussions in and of postmodernism engage with the nitty gritty of what it's like actually to do research . . .
Director:	Yes, all those terribly interesting questions: Can we escape totalising discourses? Is the world experienced as a mere simulation of itself? What are the consequences of eroding the social? And so on. But hardly anyone bothers to bring these concerns to bear on the day-to-day realities of research practice.
Research fellow:	It's as if all those discussions of postmodernism take place in a . . . vacuum.

(Cooper and Woolgar 1996: 148)

Summary

It will be clear from previous sections that there are a number of choices facing the ethnographer as she or he writes up the analysis of her or his account, and many of these are linked to the type of ethnography the researcher is engaged in. Perhaps 'choice' is too strong a word. Increasingly, ethnographers who work in applied policy fields will need to present their analyses in prescribed formats, if not prescribed lengths. This is less a lament than a realistic assessment of the compromises required of ethnographic research in educational settings since the mid-1980s. Ethnography *is* 'alive and well' in education, but in relation to funded research it continues to 'fight off . . . relegation to a technician role' (Finch 1985: 125) and/or being used to provide supplementary if 'interesting' data for illustrative purposes.

Does/must the account of ethnographic analysis draw upon a distinctive reporting style? There is something of a mismatch between generic styles of research reporting (most research methods textbooks provide guidance on suggested outlines) and ethnographic reporting, although this *may* be less of a challenge for a doctoral candidate (as long as examiners recognize the academic genre they are examining) than it is for researchers presenting findings to external sponsors who want the main points summarized 'in a maximum of eight sides of A4, thank you'. So, key issues will include awareness about the kind of audience the ethnography is addressing when they present the crucially important audit trail for scrutiny, and the effects that ethnographers hope their analyses will have upon readers. Indeed, a possible outcome of such awareness may be that different kinds of accounts will be necessary for different audiences.

Miles and Huberman (1994) distinguish between a range of general reporting 'stances' – *aesthetic, scientific, moral* and *activist* (1996: 300) – and van Maanen (1988) has identified a number of ethnographic 'voices' – *realist, confessional* and *impressionist* – each of which might be embedded in broader genres of 'tales from the field'. Reproduced by Miles and Huberman (1994), they include:

- *Critical genres*: where the focus is upon the meaning of local events embedded in larger social, educational, economic and political structures;
- *Formal genres*: that apply systematic use of inductive and inferential logic to develop theory;
- *Literary genres*: where theatrical and emotion arousing accounts are shaped by authors, with little reference to theory;
- *Jointly told genres*: that are texts produced jointly by the ethnographer and the research informant(s).

While not mutually exclusive, some genres are more likely than others to engender prospects for ethno-dramatic, fictional or poetic accounts than others. As a note of caution, readers might also like to consider the possible effects of 'innovative' formats upon those within and outside the educational community who, from a range of starting points, are already critical of its recent outputs (Hargreaves 1996b; Tooley with Darby 1998).

Meanwhile, are there any minimum guidelines for ethnographic reporting beyond providing a clear audit trail of data collection and analysis? We think so. Notwithstanding the propensity for a wide range of formats, the final accounts of systematically produced ethnography will still contain most or all of the following features:

1 Tell readers what the 'story' is about. (Does it clearly explain themes and relationships?)
2 Give readers a clear sense of context – social, political, economic and educational (Does it avoid over-generalization and over-simplification?)
3 Enable the reader to trace and track the history and the progress of the research (Will the reader know when key decisions were made and why, and what effect they had on the collection and analysis of data?)
4 Illustrate how and why key insights and concepts emerged. (This will be more than a 'list' of methods as the reader asks: what account was taken of other studies or alternative explanations?)
5 Provide data clearly. (What use was made of textual accounts, vignettes, data displays, photographs . . .?)
6 Provide conclusions which show clear connective links to the educational

worlds in which the research operated. (What does this mean for policy-makers? ... headteachers? ... classroom practice? ... parents? ... pupils? ... and so on as appropriate).

Answers to these questions remain critical if ethnography's value for education is to represent educational phenomena as accurately *and* engagingly as possible, and be conducted by ethnographers who are committed to evoking authoritative rather than authoritarian voices.

Note

1 Readers should note the propensity for such lists to become rapidly out of date, although they provide useful indications of the range of software packages available.

5 | Using ethnography

Introduction

In previous chapters we have looked at the range of definitional and operational criteria by which ethnographic data can be collected and analysed and at the ways in which such criteria also underpin judgements about ethnography as research. We have also pointed out that such criteria are often disputed, not least by ethnographers themselves. Yet, in a variety of ways, ethnography retains its key focal points while remaining open to change. In important respects, then, as Scott (2000) points out, ethnography is not unlike all 'knowledge-producing activity' in which research 'initiates' are provided with a set of methodological criteria, which, if followed, will distinguish the ethnographer 'practitioner from a non-practitioner' (2000: 74).

While ethnography has travelled far to become accepted and sustained in the academy, 'especially in the UK and the US,' it still struggles for sustained recognition in policy-making circles. While the extent to which ethnographers have been excluded from policy-making and educational macro-politics may have been exaggerated (see Scott 2000), the uses and usefulness of ethnography by and for stakeholders in and beyond education have been under-reported. In part, the struggle for recognition lies in the Janus-faced fitness for specific purpose that is at the heart of ethnography. In this chapter, we re-examine various aspects of this fitness for the tasks that education demands of it. We begin by revisiting ethnography's core claims.

The utility of ethnography has long rested upon *depth* of insight and understanding – its success in plumbing the meanings and activities that educational actors, including researchers, bring and apply to educational situations and experiences. All research, in its concern to make a contribution to theoretical knowledge and/or practical action, focuses on its originality and innovative features. Ethnography is no exception. Its contribution has tended to pivot upon its 'naturalistic profile' (Miles and

Huberman 1994) in order to study specifically situated aspects of educational lives and experiences. Depth, it is argued, *can* be accompanied by breadth, when research leads to theoretical inference or empirical generalization, although the emphasis has tended to remain with the former.

Denzin and Lincoln's (1998: 3–4) description of ethnographers as 'bricoleurs' conjures images of educational researchers as house builders who draw on a range of building approaches and materials that best fit clients' needs for a house to meet the specific purposes required of it. Yet this potent mix of methodological fitness for purpose combined with a hesitation, even denial, that such individual designs might be appropriate or useful for all kinds of house dwellers, or indeed equally for all inhabitants of the same house, has posed a number of challenges for educational ethnography. Part of that challenge lies in the *boundedness* of ethnographic accounts; another is concern about prioritization among multiple '*voices*' including the researcher's; and, still further, the well-aired 'problem' of *generalizability*. As Connolly observes (1998: 122), ethnographers tend to be caught in a 'no win situation': condemned if they fail to develop generalizations that can be used and developed for all relevant and related practice, and condemned if they attempt to offer recommendations beyond the specific social, political, locational and historical contexts in which the educational ethnography takes place.

Usefulness

If ethnographers choose to ignore aspects of empirical generalizability, does this lay bare the usefulness of educational ethnography beyond specific circumstances? As ethnographers have faced and countered attacks among various protagonists of positivism, realism, humanism and postmodernism, the usefulness of ethnographic research has been variously acknowledged: first, as critical insight into educational processes and practices; second, as a sensitizing device or source that can be used in subsequent studies; and third, in the development of theory that is grounded in empirical investigation. Most of the arguments are well rehearsed elsewhere (Hammersley 1992b) and include those which relate to grounded theory, its application in ethnography and its misapplication as a kind of theoretical whitewash (Glaser 1992). Such arguments will be summarized here in so far as they provide a prelude to other interests and concerns that you may have as a small-scale or first-time user of ethnography.

Meanwhile, although educational ethnography no longer struggles for legitimacy, except among the academies of those countries where ethnography is still seen as insufficiently rigorous as a 'scientific' endeavour, new challenges proliferate. In terms of rapidly changing local, national and global milieux, and, as importantly, the interconnections between them, there are emerging concerns about whether 'conventional' educational ethnography has begun to look a little outdated, 'small' even, in relation to the 'big' global world 'out there', and 'in' our homes and places of work and study. So, our discussion about the use and usefulness of ethnography extends beyond methodological and theoretical argument and counter-argument previously encompassed in debates about the particularity and generalizability of ethnographic evidence, and towards more novel questions posed by writers such as Eisenhart (2001: 16, 19) when she asks: 'How should we adjust our conceptual orientations and methodological priorities to take into account apparently changing human experiences and priorities?' And: 'How can we conscientiously encourage more ethnography, even use it as a standard bearer of good qualitative research, if its methods no longer fit the life and experiences of those we are trying to understand?'

In this chapter we explore the challenges facing ethnography that have followed an intense period of postmodern deconstruction, post-postmodern navel gazing within the academy and accelerating globalization beyond it. Our arguments rest upon an insistence that it is still possible to use ethnography to make pertinent representations about education that are grounded in the aims and objectives of this book and elsewhere. However, in doing so, we introduce representations that have been less commonly foregrounded in terms of their utility for education other than in specialist texts. Such forms may challenge readers to think about new ways of using ethnography to make links between local and wider educational milieux.

But to begin with we address ethnography's twin purposes to creating knowledge: whether 'just' or entirely for that purpose and/or for practical purposes. Brewer (2000: 147) describes 'use' in terms of:

> Knowledge for knowledge sake because the knowledge is interesting in its own right, sometimes knowledge for practical purposes. This purpose can be to build theory or engage in empirical generalisation, and these empirical or theoretical inferences can have practical effects, one of which is to affect public policy.

Two terms act as useful entry points to discussion, those of generalizability and authenticity.

Generalizability

In education as elsewhere, ethnography has been used to investigate the local and the small scale. The core interest may be to address questions like 'what is going on here?' and 'how are such "goings-on" understood and by whom?' inside a classroom, a physics department of a secondary school, the head's office, an education department in a university and so on . . . in order to address a specific research problem(s). Purposes may or may not lack any *primary* intention to draw theoretical inference or empirical generalization as outcome indicators of usefulness.

Some educational ethnographies are akin to Gubrium's (1988) typologies of ethnography as 'structural' (what is going on?) and 'articulative' (how is it understood?). When ethnography moves beyond either or both to address the question 'what do we need to do to make the situation or activities of people better?', ethnography might be described better as 'practical' (Gubrium 1988) or as 'advocacy' (Burgess 1984).

Where the appeal is to uniqueness, ethnographies have engendered support and critique in equal measure, especially where the 'one-off' is accompanied by 'indifferent conceptual structure or theory' (Shipman 1981: 1) or sloppiness in methodological application. Simultaneously advocated for its appeal to the 'common sense' understandings of practitioner researchers working in the 'illuminative' mode of ethnographic educational practice and evaluation (Parlett and Hamilton 1972; Walker 1981) and condemned as reductionism to 'common sense' idiosyncrasy or as a 'methodological cop-out' (Atkinson and Delamont 1985: 208), part of its utilitarian appeal for the last 30 years has been for evaluative purposes.

Some ethnographic accounts have focused upon theoretical inference or empirical generalization or both. The extent to which it is possible to make empirical generalizations from in-depth studies of one or a small number of cases has been hotly debated (Gomm *et al.* 2000). Some proponents have argued that the kinds of inferences or generalizations that can be drawn from small scale scrutiny are different in type (rather than absent) from those that might be drawn quantitatively, or from the large-scale scrutiny (Yin 1994). For writers such as Stake (1978), what really matters is the use other researchers make of published ethnographies, whether towards 'naturalistic generalisation' and/or as working hypotheses that might link certain ethnographies to other studies and/or applications to policy-making, under the umbrellas of 'fitness for purpose' or 'transferability' (Guba and Lincoln 1989).

In his book, *Case Study Research in Educational Settings*, Bassey (1999) contends that educational research, including ethnographic case studies, should not pretend to produce generalizations of 'scientific' or 'statistical' kinds; instead he focuses upon a concept of 'fuzzy generalisation' that 'carries an element of uncertainty. It reports that something has happened in one place and it may happen elsewhere. There is a possibility but no surety.' There is an invitation to 'try it and see if the same happens for you' (p.52).

Subsequently, Hammersley (2001) argues that all generalizations are a matter of degree, especially in educational and social research where there are 'a multiplicity of interacting variables operating in most situations' (2001: 223). Accordingly, he argues, the usefulness of 'fuzzy generalisations' far from being specific to qualitative research is to alert us to the prospect that 'even scientific laws can be no more than the resources available for use, along with those from other quarters, to make sensible judgements about what is *likely* to happen, about what is the best course of action for us to take' (Hammersley 2001: 224, our emphasis).

Contested activity?

Such concerns can be both contentious and contested when considered in relation to applied studies. The issue of linkage between the small-scale and its application for wider purposes is a feature of applied educational studies that give primacy to qualitative approaches. In a project (Osler and Morrison 2000) funded by the Commission for Racial Equality (CRE), the researchers took a mainly qualitative approach to examine the extent to which Ofsted school inspection reports consistently applied those sections of the reporting framework that related to race equality, and the quality of those applications. An examination that was primarily qualitative and secondarily quantitative was subsequently denounced by Ofsted as 'qualitative' (Klein 2000). Criticized in part for focusing upon a 'small' number of reports and interviews, concerns resonated with earlier published debates about applied forms of qualitative research by commentators like Tooley (1997), for example, who, according to Ozga (2000) would prefer that qualitative research provided only the supplementary 'addition of human colour'. And critics chose not to scrutinize and report on the careful construction and enactment of the methodological approach taken and its audit trail. Subsequently its usefulness has been reported, if not necessarily acknowledged, by all stakeholders (Morrison and Osler 2002). In this sense part of 'the wider relevance of the findings may be conceptualised [or contested] in terms of the provision of vicarious experience, as a basis for "naturalistic generalisation" or "transferability" ' (Gomm *et al.* 2000: 4).

Authenticity and voice

In previous chapters we have noted the importance attached to ethnographic studies in terms of the privileging of accounts by research participants. Indeed, the appeal of ethnography for readers of this book may be primarily to capture the unique voices of those you are intending to research or those with whom you work and study. This position has been debated as ethnographers have faced criticism for our capacity to tell it as it is by critical theorists, *and* to tell it as if it were a one storied interpretation of reality(ies) by postmodernists and by policy makers who may prefer to judge outcomes on the basis of whose voice is worth listening to here, or is this your voice or the participants'? Nonetheless, the telling of key moments in a research 'story' especially when core statements or actions encapsulate the symbolic 'heart' of qualitative inquiry is frequently seen as part of its authenticity. Thus, it is the use and usefulness of ethnography for practical purposes, especially where application is linked to policy making, and the research and evaluation of practice arising from policy, that has been increasingly under the spotlight, and we now examine this further.

Applied ethnography

Brewer (2000: 156–7) is among writers to have noted a movement towards applied ethnography first advocated by Finch (1986) many years earlier. This growing 'penchant for applied ethnography' is described both in terms of the 'ethos of accountability' demanded by sponsors who fund educational ethnography, but also as part of a recourse to (or retreat from?) relevance once postmodernists have attempted to deconstruct all other ways of judging data produced by ethnography (Brewer 2000: 156). Whether to collect data to inform policy making, to provide solutions to predefined problems or to retain an independent approach to policy making (the empiricist, engineering and enlightenment approaches outlined by Bulmer (1982) and noted by Brewer (2000)), the seminal ethnographies of Hargreaves (1967), Lacey (1970), Ball (1981) and Burgess (1983) now appear to represent moments in the history of educational ethnography. As importantly, among established writers of ethnographic case studies are those who question whether there has been an over-proliferation of the individualistic, unconnected and small scale (Bassey 1999).

In the UK, there is renewed emphasis upon training researchers in both quantitative and qualitative skills, a growing demand for research that illustrates 'combinations' of methodological approaches, a pendulum swing towards measurable outcomes from educational research and a 'cementing of alliances' between policy-makers and researchers who focus upon such outcomes (Scott 2000: 75). Similarly, in the US it is argued that:

> Young scholars have compelling critiques of conventional [ethno-graphic] methods but little in the way of fresh insights on methods to offer. At the same time, some funding agencies confused by the proliferation of qualitative methods and debates surrounding them, are poised to deny ethnographic research proposals – along with other forms of qualitative research – on the grounds that the methods are not 'reliable and rigorous'. And legislation to require that all federally funded educational research projects include randomised field trials has recently been under consideration in Congress.
>
> (Eisenhart 2001: 16)

The globalization factor

Moreover, in the light of increased globalization of knowledge and experience, questions arise not just about whether local ethnographies remain pertinent as exemplars of cultures that are 'clearly bounded and determined, internally coherent, and uniformly meaningful' (Eisenhart 2001: 17) but also about whether we may need to broaden the scope of 'traditional' ethnography to provide more settings and/or broader perspectives. Such questions have distinct as well as overlapping elements.

Our contention is that educational ethnography needs to persist in its concern to map the local and the specific even when many (but by no means all) educational experiences are becoming increasingly mediated by the global (if not necessarily in the same way). For instance, no one would doubt the potential for the massive changes wrought by information and communications technology (ICT) to impact upon the processes and outcomes of schooling. However, this does not deny the critical importance of studying ICT implementation at the level of the individual, the institution and the locale, not just to investigate its prospects for (or threats to) the enhancement of teaching and learning, but also to investigate a diversity of meanings and understandings, that might include integration, resistance and/or impediments to use in and beyond school. School ethnographies can make an important contribution in understanding 'what is going on here' as teachers and learners negotiate and renegotiate the relationship between global, local and institutional learning spaces and times via the World Wide Web and the Internet.

A not dissimilar argument would apply to citizenship education. Its incorporation into mainstream curricula is emerging, if variously subsumed under sub-headings such as personal, social, and health education (PSHE), personal and social development, and human rights and global citizenship education. But as we note from research instigated by Morrison and Watling (2002) in an evaluation for citizenship project in Northern Ireland, for example, the meanings applied to citizenship education needs to be understood at the interface between specific, local and institutional identities, and more widespread general declarations and assertions about human rights and citizenship.

Moreover, challenges in defining the bounded, localized nature of ethnographic cases are not unique to ethnography. Addressing practitioner researchers in education, Brown and Dowling (1998), for example, criticize Stake's (1978) view of case studies as bounded independent systems in terms of:

> a mythologising of research and a romanticizing of the world in general. The natural world is presented as thinkable in terms of a collection of mutually independent (bounded) systems which are

nevertheless transparently knowable to us . . . and is also mythologizing in terms of its reference to the singularity of the case study. The expression 'single actor' may seem clear enough. But what is to be the context in which the actor is involved. Will educational research consider the behaviour of the subject in their domestic and leisure activities as well as the classroom? Will it address the entire life cycle and, indeed, family history of the subject? . . . The fact of the matter is that even a single actor participates in a multiplicity of research sites upon which research acts selectively, which is to say, it samples.

(Brown and Dowling 1998: 166)

This still begs the question about whether the 'traditional' methods of ethnography, including studies of 'single actors' or schools, encapsulated by ethnographic approaches are sufficient for understanding complexities at the interface between the institutional, local, national and global. At one level, of course, constraints faced by single-handed, small-scale researchers are necessarily restricted by the time, resources and expertise at their disposal. But, new ways of *doing* ethnography may encourage us to begin to reconceptualize new ways of *using* ethnography. Eisenhart (2001) helps set the scene before we introduce some changing forms of ethnography.

'Tangled-up'[1] ethnography?

According to Eisenhart (2001) ethnographic accounts that are guided by changing views about the relationship between the institutional, local and global are becoming more commonplace. She writes:

If we are going to trace relationships that stretch across time and space; and if we are going to analyze activities and cultural forms that are taken up locally but formed or controlled elsewhere, we would seem to need some new ways of doing ethnography, or at least some different methodological priorities . . . Ethnographies will have to include ways of exploring connections among sites that together make up arenas of social practice.

(Eisenhart 2001: 22)

Drawing upon Nespor's study (1997), she explores the ways in which the author traces what happened in a specific school 'upwards' and 'outwards' as part of networks of larger social systems and 'downwards' and 'inwards' to see how cultural forms become part of individual pupil and teacher subjectivities and imaginations. Nespor (1997: xiii) explains:

School ethnography is a familiar genre, but what I do with it in this book is a little unusual. Instead of treating the school as a container filled with teacher cultures, student subgroups, classroom instruction,

and administrative micropolitics . . . I look at one school as an inter-
section in social space, a knot in a web of practices that stretch into
complex systems beginning and ending outside the school . . . I want
to give the school its due, but not on its own terms – to treat it not
as the focus of the study but as the point of entry . . . to the study
of economic, cultural, and political relations shaping curriculum,
teaching, and kids' experiences.

Hence, as Eisenhart (2001: 23) points out, the 'tangled-upness' of Nespor's
study refers to a school ethnography that 'is not seen as a microcosm
adapted to a particular society' nor as 'a coherent entity to be compared
with home and community' but rather ' "tangled up" with them in
numerous overlapping ways'; but *still* ethnography.

If ethnography is to continue and develop its contribution to basic and
applied forms of educational research, we may need to ask whether there are
new dimensions of usefulness to influence either or both. In the remaining
sections of this chapter we introduce two forms that are described as visual
and virtual ethnography.

Visual ethnography

At one level there is nothing new about the visual in ethnography. From the
anthropological tradition, photographs, sketches and paintings have been
used for many years, and are reviewed in Chapter 3. Margaret Mead (1963)
used both film and photography but, like Becker (1974), she noted the
tendency in the social sciences to give more attention to words in describing
observations and, therefore in constructing knowledge, than to the visual.
More recently, Harrison (1996) notes a continuing tendency to use the
visual as a supplementary aid to the written text rather than the reverse.
Notwithstanding practical, technical and ethical issues (challenges that
may take a particular form in the visual, but are no more or less than for
other ethnographic methods?), she points out that researchers can use
existing visual materials as resources for representation as well as stimuli to
encourage subjective interpretations. Following Foucault (1977), she argues
that if we accept that:

> the visual has and can be used in strategies for power and control . . .
> [then researchers] should cease to be paralysed by a heritage of claims
> about 'realism' in visual data and accept the challenge they offer . . . [in
> enabling] investigation into the ways our social world is constituted,
> reproduced, and experienced, in which seeing is as important as saying
> and doing.
>
> (Harrison 1996: 91)

It is, then, expansion in the various forms of the visual that should interest us as ethnographers, in particular the increased potential for the use of photography, video and film, and hypermedia. Most recently, Pink's (2001) book, *Doing Visual Ethnography*, illustrates the various ways in which ethnography and visual studies contribute to one another. Not primarily designed as a text for educational researchers, it is, nevertheless, key reading for ethnographers wishing to use the visual as a core element of their studies. As importantly, it provides fascinating insights into the ways in which the visual is interwoven with debates about the role that educational ethnography can and might play in basic and applied studies, and in the relationship between theory, method, and the visual.

What is an ethnographic image? In agreement with Pink's assertion that ethnography is more than a method and more of a methodology that involves 'a process of creating and representing knowledge . . . based on the ethnographers' own experiences' (2001: 18), then we might also ask what this entails for ethnographers in education. Perhaps the first point to make is that there is no one image of your school, your teacher, your pupils, your university and so on that is essentially 'ethnographic'. A key issue is that it will be defined in negotiation with others through interpretation and context. Such interpretations are influenced by the understandings we, as ethnographers, bring to the visual. This may be our theoretical understanding about what constitutes valid research and how we see our roles as women, men, children and adults, as well as our technical understanding about the potential and actual use of the visual in our daily lives, including work and study. This suggests that there may be at least three ways in which educational researchers might use the visual as ethnographic.

The first is making use of found visual artefacts in order to provide one point of access to individuals or groups or situations even though we have not met them, seen them or have any direct evidence of their existence other than the images left behind.

The second occurs when we record our own images of other people and other situations. In educational ethnography, as elsewhere, lightweight, relatively cheap ways of recording data, like handheld VHS cameras for example, have made this easier. The act of creating visible images, of course, also makes us visible in ways that the traditional ethnographer (with his or her post-observation reflective notebook) was, in part, invisible. So Pink's advice (2001: 35–6), to consider not only the technical aspects of the visual apparatus we use and the expertise required, but also the impact of our own identities and those of others 'in the field', is apposite.

The third approach involves us in collaborating with others to produce visual images, whether still or moving. Again, the approach alerts us to theoretical and ideological as well as technical aspects of the visual in ethnography. Watling (2002a) expresses this well:

Some people would argue that 'taking' someone's photograph is an act of appropriation. You do not have to believe that it literally 'takes' something from them, as if they were spiritually diminished by your act. But it is very easy to slip into a discourse that talks about 'my project', 'my data', 'my photographs' or, even more problematic, 'my subjects'. Of course you would ask people to sign consent forms if you were to do this kind of work . . . But some researchers are still wary, and seek to address these issues of ethics and ownership from the beginning. Rather than asking how images can help them understand other people, they are inclined to ask how the production of images can help people understand themselves, in a process which *includes* them and the researcher.

Such work has an affinity with action research, with community and professional development, with collaborative investigation, and more generally with research which tries to empower and enable people to study their own communities.

(Watling 2002a: 9)

An example of this kind of approach is found in Watling (2001), where the focus is upon the visual interpretation of aspects of a primary school curriculum by teachers and pupils. Another is in the work of Schratz and Steiner-Loffler (1997) in Austria in which they report on research where children use photographs as part of a school self-evaluation.

So far, our discussion of the visual has concerned itself with the usefulness of still and moving images and for a variety of purposes. Most recently, electronic hypermedia offers new potential for ethnographers. But it also challenges us to rethink the ways in which ethnographic representation takes place and/or might be possible. For the purposes of this chapter, we introduce some of the possibilities and challenges for use. Readers wishing to develop a deeper understanding should refer to specialist texts like Hine (2000), Pink (2001) and Prosser (1998).

Hypermedia

What is electronic hypermedia text? Following Pink (2001: 156), publications are usually sets of interlinked files with written words, moving and still images, sound or a combination of these, and include features like:

- Inter-linkages between files or places within files to support the inter-activity of the media.
- Hyperlinks represented as words or symbols to enable users to move through files.
- Different forms of interaction with different texts depending on the software used.

The usefulness of hypermedia for and as ethnography is as for other visual forms, but 'conventional' ethnographic text, even within hypermedia, still predominates over visual imagery. This may change. For the purposes of this chapter, however, a key issue is the way that hypermedia texts challenge the more conventional use of *linear* writing styles in ethnography. Again, as Pink (2001: 164) reports: 'Hypermedia's capacity for multilinearity and layering information allows reflexivity to develop differently and can represent the historical development of ethnographic research and interpretation in ways that written text and film cannot.'

One way in which digital technology may advance the use of ethnography, therefore, is not just in enabling the reader and viewer to see and hear how ethnographic analysis proceeds but also for readers and viewers to take their own 'journeys' through the data. This is not to argue that educational ethnographies become (irritatingly?) unfinished texts, but to allow an up-dated open-endedness and connectivity to other and wider representations, 'stories' and uses. This may provide an interesting counterpoint to Bassey's (1999: 7–13) earlier concerns about a lack of coherence and connectivity in educational research, especially that which focuses upon the singular or small scale.

Meanwhile, all of the above needs to be seen in relation to changing ethical relationships between producers and consumers of hypermedia texts and changing technologies, from CD-ROMs to DVD, and faster Internet use. We may also need to be reminded that technologies that are commonplace in some educational cultures may still be almost unknown in others. This means that both conventional and novel forms of ethnographic representation need to develop in tandem rather than in opposition. Nonetheless, such developments offer the potential to visit and revisit the local – global nexus (Sklair 1999) in ways that are new and exciting for ethnography.

In its conventional forms, ethnography has maximized its usefulness in terms of the *face to face* interactions between and among individual and groups in specific situations and locales. The Internet provides ways of transmitting information about others and ourselves in the absence of any close physical contact. Moreover, it opens the possibilities for children, young people and adults in all educational sectors to 'converse' globally with others in ways that even five years ago would have been rare or unknown. Where does this leave educational ethnography, or, put another way, how and to what extent might the usefulness of ethnography be adapted to the virtual? These are the contexts in which we consider using ethnography in the final sections of this chapter which draw heavily upon Hine's (2000) key text entitled *Virtual Ethnography*.

Virtual environments for ethnographic research

Virtual environments in education comprise all those forums for teaching, learning and its organization that occur across a computer network. This can occur in many forms. Computer-mediated communication (CMC) is a catch-all term to refer to the kinds of communication that occur when teachers, learners and educationalists communicate with one another across computer networks. Such communication can be synchronous (both parties are present simultaneously) or asynchronous (parties need not be); inter-action can be one to one, one to many or many to many; the form of communication can be text-based or video or audio transmitted.[2] The kind of debates discussed about doing and using ethnography in education in this book and elsewhere open up the possibilities of moving educational ethnography into virtual settings.

How might this take place? Ethnography could, for example, have a specific appeal, in studies about how individuals and groups engage with computer networks in educational settings. An appropriate research question in relation to recent changes in lecturers' engagement with students in higher education, for example, might be the extent to which CMC between colleagues and among and with UK and international students affects the nature, understanding and experience of professional work in university settings. Such a study might, in process and outcomes, follow, in part, the conventions of traditional ethnography, where the ethnographer, in an 'off-line' face to face relationship with research participants (lecturers), studies what participants do and understand when they engage with others (colleagues and students) on- and off-line. We could envisage, for example, a research design in which ethnographers observed, tracked or shadowed, interviewed and photographed lecturers as they engaged in daily educational activities, and/or invited them to keep journals for reflective discussion of such activities that included email correspondence and on-line communica-tions with students. But what would happen if *our* research was pursued entirely on-line, that is, all of our engagement with research participants occurred on-line, in the same way as the engagement between lecturers and distance learning students was on-line? It would seem that a number of issues might emerge, some of which might be common to all ethnography and some distinctive to virtual ethnography (see Hine 2000, especially chapters 1 and 2).

Commonalities?

Some features of virtual ethnography – how much to record, how many lecturers to sample, the scope of the 'snapshot' – might be considered design issues that are common for all ethnographic research. Issues for virtual and traditional ethnography might also include physical limits to researcher's stamina, concentration and access to people and resources. Whereas in 'traditional' ethnography the issue might be how long one should remain with participants and at which levels of engagement, the issue in a virtual environment might be how long to stay logged on, especially where the potential is for 24 hour contact. Like traditional ethnographers, virtual ethnographers would still prioritize access to and engagement with participants but the focus of that engagement might shift (see below).

Ethical issues remain important for all ethnographers although in virtual ethnographies they would need to be framed rather differently. As in traditional ethnography, the need to protect the anonymity and confidentiality of participants is critical; in virtual environments such issues might also relate to passwords and access to conferencing and chat rooms.

Distinctiveness?

Ethnographers working in virtual environments would no longer have to share the same time frame as their key informants, although they might choose to do so. (Different time frames may also apply in some traditional ethnographies, such as when researchers draw upon archival and documented evidence, as outlined in Chapter 3.) However, what might be identified as a professional 'problem' by lecturers in terms of the potential for 24-hour contact from students, could present itself as a 'flexible' opportunity for the researcher to contact informants, in this example lecturers, over flexible time frames.

With the possibility of working in asynchronous and synchronous time frames, the approach to data collection might shift. Virtual ethnographers might be less likely to be engaged in selectivity of data during the event (as when researchers make notes in an interview, for example). On-line selection from texts could take place *after* the creation of the text(s) by the research informants.

Without the face to face presence of the ethnographer in the setting, opportunities to mislead or misinform the ethnographer might appear to multiply, and there will be subtle shifts in the nature of the engagement with participants (as occurs, for example, among those lecturers who spend much longer 'composing' and engaging in email correspondence with students than if they were engaged in more 'spontaneous' face to face conversation).

Moving beyond our specific example, some general issues are noted. Negotiation of access, and the positioning of the ethnographer in the ethnography, have been viewed as fundamentally important aspects of ethnographic engagement and representation, and this takes a rather different turn in virtual settings. The potential to be a hidden participant (or 'lurker') in a virtual environment, whether as researcher or participant, would appear to be greater (although an analogy with covert ethnography is illustrative of common elements). Moreover, ethnographic engagement in virtual environments might presuppose that all participants receive and participate in CMC in homogeneous ways. Again, Hine (2000) reminds us that this is not always the case – whether technically or culturally (see also below).

So far, we have considered a potential 'virtual' study in comparison to a more 'traditional' ethnography. We may also need to consider whether and to what extent prevalent ethnographic relationships between research subjects, and with ethnographers and readers, might need to be reconfigured in virtual environments. Hine identifies three aspects (2000: 43–63): first, the role of face to face interaction; second, the relationship between text, technology and reflexivity; and third, 'the making of ethnographic objects'.

Face to face interaction

Traditionally, ethnographers have relied heavily on face to face interaction, whether this involves travelling to Japan to study the impact of educational reform upon schools as did the authors of this book in 1993, or whether they remain 'close' to schools with which they are familiar and need, therefore, 'to make strange'. Part of that 'making' occurs when ethnographers explain to readers what it feels like to negotiate access into familiar and strange settings. The anchoring of 'self' in the text occurs, for example, in an ethnographic study of food and eating in school, when we note how Morrison (1996b) explains what it is like to eat daily in primary and secondary school dining rooms in England, and at a later date describes what it is like to experience eating in Japanese schools (Morrison and Benn 2000). In contrast, Hine (2000) comments that: 'Far from getting the seats of their pants dirty, Internet ethnographers keep their seats firmly on the University's upholstery' (p.45). But, for ethnographers, 'travelling' and 'arriving' do not tell the whole story; ethnographers select, analyse and interpret parts of a 'holistic experience'. And this is where writers like Hine make the strongest claims about the commonalities between actual and virtual contacts between researchers and participants, arguing that virtual ethnographers, like others, also need to negotiate a relationship with participants in cyberspace and select, share and negotiate aspects of experience in specific ways.

Texts, technology and reflexivity

Oral interactions are predominant in ethnography, though not to the exclusion of written interactions in the form of documents, diaries and life histories, for example. In virtual ethnography far more attention is given to written (and/or visual) texts and, in operation, these involve specific kinds of technical and technological skills. As in other ethnographies, careful attention is also given to interpretation and interaction. Two challenges are foreseen (Hine 2000: 50–7). One is about the ethnographer 'going native' with participants in cyberspace, since in order to interpret the texts, ethnographers are required to engage fully with both the technology and the production and reproduction of the texts. The other may be the danger in losing a sense of reflexivity. To counter this, three strategies are advocated by Hine. The first is to place participants' texts alongside the researcher's texts rather than privileging the former. The second strategy includes the need for the researcher to articulate clearly how the ethnographer has come to write his or her account (readers might wish to consider the point at which this could become self-indulgence or something else). A final counterpoint is Hine's insistence that *all* ethnographers, including those who operate in virtual environments, continue to think and engage in new ways of 'writing' and 'writing up' ethnography and in the 'making of ethnographic objects' (Hine 2000: 58–63). This takes us to the third point.

Virtual environments as objects of study

Individuals, groups, schools and education systems are frequently understood in specific spatial and temporal terms. Classroom ethnographies, for example, are much more commonplace in educational ethnography than ethnographies of teaching and learning that might be experienced, for example, as new flexible forms of open-ended and on-line learning as exemplified by approaches like *Learn Direct* in the UK. Virtual environments provide a promising arena for ethnography and for extending the range and types of methodological tools. Equally importantly, they may also suggest additional roles for ethnographers. Previously, the ethnographer has acted as an intermediary between his or her world (mostly but not always of the academy) and the world of subjects (teacher or pupil participants in an English or Japanese secondary school, for example, in which the ethnographer is physically present in each setting for prolonged periods). A changing local – global nexus may require us to rethink our approaches. In such ways, using the Internet as an ethnographic tool *as well as* studying Internet connectivity and connections ethnographically may, as Eisenhart (2001) suggests, have a specific appeal.

Summary

This chapter began by reaffirming the key use of ethnography in bringing a *depth* of understanding and meanings to educational research that is accompanied by *breadth* of understanding through theoretical inference and/or specific approaches to the 'problem' of generalization. We have examined the use and usefulness of ethnography as a *process* and as an *outcome* and have explored potential as well as actual intellectual and practical challenges. Drawing upon specific examples, we have examined the ways in which ethnography retains its utilitarian appeal not only in terms of 'knowledge for knowledge sake' (Brewer 2000) but also its contribution to educational policy and practical action and new ways of thinking about the usefulness and relevance of educational research. Few methodologies have been the subject of such intense critique but ethnography's survival, in part, continues to depend on a core of methodological principles that are adaptive to changing circumstances. Our contention remains that educational ethnography needs to persist in its insistence to map the local and the specific even when either or both are increasingly mediated by broader issues whether regional, national or global. To this extent, we acknowledge and welcome the questions raised by Eisenhart (2001) about the past, present and future of educational ethnography.

At the start of 2003, localized settings still provide the entry points as well as the containers for studying and capturing vicarious educational experience. Conventional as well as novel forms of visual ethnography provide one access point; virtual ethnography suggests new and complementary approaches to more widely recognized forms of ethnographic representation. In combination, *using ethnography*, as a process and outcome in all its adaptive forms, allows us to research education in ways that continue to provide deep and critical understandings about what it means to teach and learn and experience education in myriad forms.

Notes

1 Nespor, J. (1997) *Tangled-Up in School: Politics, Space, Bodies, and Signs in the Educational Process*. Mahwah, NJ: Lawrence Erlbaum.
2 Hine (2000) provides a full glossary of relevant terms.

6 | Writing and representing ethnography

Introduction

At the outset of this book we identified an ambiguity in the term ethnography in that it is used to refer to both a process and a product: we simultaneously talk about doing ethnography and about producing and consuming (reading) ethnography. The former implies that there is an approach, or at least a set of methods, which constitute a distinctive kind of research which we call ethnography, the latter that there is a product of the research which again is distinctive and also called ethnography. So far, the various chapters of this text have engaged largely with the process of ethnography in educational research by looking at the different research methods which the ethnographer might use and the ways in which she or he might analyse data collected by those methods.

In this chapter our concern is with ethnography as a product. It is here that we shall seek to establish what is meant by ethnography as an outcome of research. This takes us into the realms of epistemology, thinking about what is distinctive about the kind(s) of knowledge which ethnographic research yields, and into important questions of the way(s) in which ethnographers choose to represent the data and to fashion an ethnography.

Ethnography and representation

Central to our understanding of ethnography as a product is an appreciation of the relationship between the researcher (ethnographer), the data and the way in which the ethnographer chooses to represent the data in the product. The key concept here is that of choice. We have already established that ethnographic research in education, as in any other area of social life, is a human process about which choices are made. The path a particular research programme takes is largely down to the decisions the researcher makes about it. Ethnographic research is not a slave to rigid formulaic method. It does not follow a predetermined path established at the outset of the programme. Rather it requires flexibility and the capacity of the researcher to engage with the data as they are gathered, as they are generated or as they emerge, and to make decisions about the progress of the research project. This is not to imply that ethnography is ad hoc, casual or without structure. It is, however, to imply that the process of ethnography reflects its essential human quality, in that researchers make decisions about the best ways of observing, documenting and reporting human behaviour as it happens. If it is to do this successfully, the research methods must follow the behaviour which they seek to witness and to document. This requires decisions to be made by the researcher, often at short notice, not only about what research tools to use and when to use them, but also about research focus and what it is he or she hopes to be able to say about social life as a result of the research.

The process that the researcher goes through in coming to such decisions we refer to as one of reflexivity (Hammersley and Atkinson 1995). In this we recognize that the research process not only reflects the decisions made by the researcher, but also the research product, as the two are clearly interdependent. Consequently, we also argue that what results from ethnographic research cannot be divorced from its relationship with the researcher. That is, ethnography as product is a reflection of the ethnographer in terms of his or her biography, the intellectual tradition(s) that have influenced his or her approach to research and to the decisions he or she makes about the research process as it progresses. In making such a statement, we may leave ourselves open to charges of relativism and to concerns about the capacity of ethnography to yield data that are not only rich and detailed but also that reflect the reality of the situation that it seeks to understand, not merely the opinion of the ethnographer. These are important charges which need to be taken seriously, for if we regard research as a search for some kind of truth, or at least truths, then presumably our objective is to present our research product, our ethnography, with some degree of confidence that what it says is in some way correct.

For many social scientists working outside of a positivist framework, this notion of truth and reality in research product is difficult. While we recognize this and emphasize that we also generally regard the complexity of social life as beyond reduction to one single truth or absolute certainty, and by no means subscribe to a positivist perspective, we do, nevertheless, like Hammersley (1995), see research as the search for information which will take us further towards a truth. Why else would we advocate the careful collection, recording and painstaking analysis of data? In saying this, we are not subscribing to a notion of blind empiricism, but simply pointing to what we see as a logical outcome of the ethnographic research process. Another way of saying this would be to assert that ethnography goes beyond conjecture, opinion and dogma to produce accounts of social life that are substantiated in the lived experience of that social life, by the actors who construct it. In reading an ethnography we want to feel confident that those responsible for producing it are working from firm foundations of data, analysis and interpretation. Unlike the quantitative researcher, we cannot subject our material to tests of significance to establish how confident we can be that our findings are correct. Nevertheless, the issue of reliability remains as important for the ethnographer as it does for the quantitative researcher. The need for reliability and confidence are what distinguish the ethnographer from some types of journalist, the novelist or other writers of fiction.

Implicit in our discussion so far is the idea of the ethnographer not merely as a conduit for data collection and the emergence of convincing accounts of social life, but as an active participant in the construction of those accounts. We have asserted that the ethnographer makes decisions throughout the research process about what she or he should focus upon, what research methods to use and how to approach the analysis of the data. It is these decisions that shape the research product. As a result, we would argue that ethnography, as a product, is equally dependent upon choice as is ethnography as a process.

Ethnography and relativism

By introducing notions of choice, construction, researcher biography and decision making as key contributors to both the ethnographic research process and, therefore, inevitably to ethnography as a product, charges of relativism in respect of the knowledge yielded or produced are easily levelled against ethnographic research. In making such charges, critics assert that ethnography is incapable of providing knowledge or truth which is independent of the process that produced it. Central to that process, we have argued, is the ethnographer himself or herself. Consequently, ethnography is incapable of providing knowledge undistorted by the researcher, or of independent verification and validation. The logical extension of such charges is that the knowledge to come from ethnography lacks any authority which is external to the researcher responsible for its production. As a result, that knowledge is no more reliable than that produced by anyone else, for example, a journalist or a novelist. Such charges intend to invalidate ethnography as a product by asserting that it is little more than conjecture anecdote or a story.

Our response to such charges against ethnography is not to rebut them by arguing that the knowledge it yields is, or can be, independent of the researcher, as to do so would be to fail to understand the significance of the researcher as an actor both in ethnography as process and as product.

Rather, our view would be that in many respects the relationship between ethnographer and his or her research process and product is little different from that between researchers working within other research traditions and their process and product. All research relies on the researcher to decide what to focus upon, what questions to ask, who should ask them, when and how they should be asked. It relies on many decisions relating to the direction of the research, the research problem, the politics (Hammersley 1995) and the feasibility (Delamont 1992) of the study, that can only be taken by those responsible for its conduct. In these respects, we argue that ethnography is similar to other approaches to social research. Where it is different, however, is in its recognition of the centrality of the researcher to the research process and product. However, its acknowledgement that research is in itself a social process, which inevitably requires decisions and choices to be made, does, we believe, set it apart from those approaches which see the unearthing of knowledge about social life untainted by the researcher as achievable, or as something to be striven for. Equally, we see those kinds of research which fail to recognize and, through a process of reflexivity, account for the impact of the researcher, as unrealistic searches for a version of truth which is neither available nor appropriate to the social sciences. If ethnography is guilty of a form of relativism then this is due to its capacity to represent the complexity of knowledge about the social world in ways which recognize that this knowledge is rarely, if ever, uncontested and certain.

Representation and persuasion

Concerns about the relativism of ethnography as a product are important to the reflexivity which underpins ethnography as a process. Such concerns are in themselves an important way of ensuring that ethnography is not reduced to dogma or the unsubstantiated musings of the researcher. Nevertheless, in our defence of ethnography as a legitimate and important way of knowing about social life, it is not our intention to suggest a role for the researcher merely as a conduit for information. To do so would be to ignore the role that he or she has as the person responsible for presenting and representing his or her research.

As we have shown in earlier chapters of this volume, ethnography relies on the careful collection of detailed data of different kinds. Alongside data collection there is equally careful and detailed analysis which looks not simply for confirmation of hypotheses, concepts and theories within the data, but also for evidence which challenges them. In doing this, the ethnographer seeks to make a case for his or her research findings and conclusions. In making a case, the ethnographer does not act as an advocate or some sort of social scientific evangelist, rather he or she seeks to put forward a convincing case for the conclusions drawn from his or her research. Back (1998), who draws on Atkinson's (1990) influential text in this area, refers to this aspect of the research process as one of persuasion which is based on the careful deployment of rhetoric. However, in referring to the product of research in such a way, Back stresses that he is using the term 'rhetoric' in its historical and philosophical sense, rather than as an allusion to 'insincere oratory or sloganeering'. In his or her use of rhetoric, the ethnographer seeks authority for his or her research knowledge, for ethnography as a product.

It is the use of rhetoric in this historical and philosophical form that distinguishes the ethnographer from those who may tend towards the more commonly understood sloganeering form of rhetoric. It is also the use of rhetoric as persuasion which helps the ethnographer to guard against charges of relativism and vested interest. In seeking to persuade his or her readers, the ethnographer does not engage in a process of displaying or giving undue emphasis to those data which confirm a particular view or finding, as this would clearly reduce ethnography to an act of meaningless insincerity. The use of the term persuasion in the context of ethnography may be seen as akin to a doctor examining a patient. He or she knows there is something wrong with the patient but does not know exactly what it is. The examination of the patient, consideration of various symptoms and results of tests lead the doctor towards a diagnosis. Like the doctor, the ethnographer engages in a process of self-persuasion. The doctor gains nothing by reaching the wrong diagnosis and neither does his or her client (the patient). Similarly, the ethnographer gains nothing from advancing an argument about which he or she is not convinced, and neither does his or her client (the readers).

In using a medical analogy it is not our intention to reduce the way in which social scientists choose to represent their research to a crude functionalist model, in which we present social knowledge as merely the sum of its parts or to equate it to a crude positivist approach to medical science. By using the analogy we simply seek to illustrate that there are issues around evidence and proof which are in some ways common to both the medic and the ethnographer. For the medic, the search is for the underlying cause of an ailment and at the early stages of diagnosis there may be competing accounts of what this may be. Seeking a second opinion from a different doctor is common practice among patients and disagreement among doctors is common, sometimes leading to different treatments. The process of diagnosis is a human process, based on analysis and interpretation. For the social scientist the process is similar. The use of evidence in analysis, in which different degrees of emphasis will be given to some forms of evidence over others, is similar to the means by which the medic reaches a diagnosis. Similarly, different social scientists may reach different conclusions about the particular topic of research. However, while we may argue that there are such similarities between medical and social science there are also significant differences. In medicine, there is usually a belief that a cause or root of an illness, disease or complaint can ultimately be identified. It may not be possible to treat it effectively, but at least there is knowledge of its cause and the process of different interpretations and second opinions are seen as part of that discovery of the cause. If doctors are not able to find the cause and so offer appropriate treatment then this is commonly seen as unacceptable. Medical science is seen to have failed. From the patient's perspective there is no place for ambiguity and uncertainty. It is the role of medicine and its practitioners to deal in certainties.

While ethnographers do not deal in certainties in quite the same way as doctors, and we might argue that for individuals upon whom their research focuses, the personal stakes are not so high, there is nevertheless an expectation that they will also 'get it right'. As we have seen throughout this text, the process of analysis and interpretation upon which ethnography rests cannot be separated from the person(s) who conducts it. However, this is not to imply that ethnography is a means of legitimating personal opinion or biases on the part of the researcher. The process of persuasion which we discussed above is rigorous and demanding. Ultimately, in seeking to persuade the readers, the ethnographer is making a statement about his or her confidence in his or her own work. The confidence refers to the conduct of the research, to the analysis and interpretation of the collected data and to the integrity of the ethnographer. In this respect, ethnography is little different from other forms of social research. However, the nature of ethnographic data, and the relationship of the researcher to it are different. For example, none of the tests for significance, reliability or confidence which can so readily be deployed by the quantitative researcher lends itself to ethnography. Neither is there the possibility of generalization and comparison across populations and research sites to which other more quantitative research lends itself.

Ethnography, narrative and truth

In spite of all of the discussion above, the question remains, how can ethnographers persuade their readers that they should have confidence in their work? Or put more directly, how can we be sure that the findings of ethnographic research are true and, therefore, worthy of being taken seriously?

From our discussions earlier in this text, especially in Chapter 5, it should be clear by now that we believe that there are no simple answers to these questions. Alternatively, the discussion so far may have lead us to the conclusion that ultimately, there is no way of knowing whether ethnographic research findings are true or not and consequently it is not possible to have confidence in them. However, to take this view would in our opinion lead to a rejection of ethnography as being of no value, having no role to play in attempts to understand the social world. Clearly, this is not a view that we hold.

To begin to understand ethnography's capacity to provide useful accounts of aspects of the social world, it may be useful to consider the ways in which ethnographers have chosen to represent their work. While it is important to draw attention to the fact that ethnographers do have a choice in how to represent and present the results of their research in as far as they are not required to work to any prescribed scheme or format of representation, it is also relevant to our discussion to note that the dominant method of representation is via the written medium. While this may seem an obvious statement to make and for some researchers the written medium is clearly the only way of representing their research, our discussion earlier in this book of the use of a range of different kinds of data and data collection methods open to the ethnographer makes clear that written accounts are by no means the only method of representing ethnographic research. Developments in the area of visual research, which include the use of still and video photography, have led some ethnographers to represent their work through a visual medium. The work of Pink (2001) on the meaning of home and Grimshaw (2001) on children's experiences of the city are notable examples of recent work which does not rely on the written medium as its principal means of representation. Similarly, earlier work on schools and school culture by Prosser (1998) also makes considerable use of still photography. For these researchers, the written medium has been deemed to be less effective that the visual. While in each of these examples the visual is supported by some written text, it is the visual representation which takes precedence. As developments in video and digital photography have continued apace over the past few years, the possibility of using a visual means of representation is probably within the scope of most ethnographers. The simplification of the technology means that there is no longer a need for an expert photographer or film maker to produce filmic ethnographic accounts of aspects of social life. At the same time, falling prices of cameras and other equipment make this an option for increasing numbers of ethnographers. Evidence of this can also be taken from a number of recent studies which have combined visual and written means of representation. For example, Mizen *et al.* (1999), Bolton *et al.* (2001) and Pole *et al.* (1999) used photography as a means of self-reporting by children engaged in paid employment, and Allatt and Dixon (2002) used similar methods to document children's workloads in school and part-time employment. In these cases, photographic images were a central aspect of the ethnographic accounts of children's lives which, the researchers argued, conveyed data and an understanding which went beyond that conveyed by conventional written accounts. Similarly, as we have seen in Chapter 5, Hine (2000) examines the implications of technological development for ethnography at length in her interesting book on virtual ethnography. Among other things, Hine considers the role of the Internet in providing a 'voice' for ethnography, not just as an additional location for conventional written ethnography, but also as a cultural artefact which incorporates an element of performance.

Despite these different and developing media through which it is clearly possible to represent ethnography, the dominant form of representation remains the written account. While what may be seen as a conservative approach may be due, in part, to researchers' lack of familiarity with new and alternative media and the fact that they are comfortable with that with which they are familiar, this cannot solely account for the pre-eminence of the written account. This may in fact be due to what both ethnographers themselves and the readers of their work expect from an ethnography, not only in terms of its substance but also its form. For example, we have already seen that an ethnography has, to some extent, become defined by its capacity to provide highly detailed accounts of social action. Much of this is descriptive, but it also entails painstaking analysis in order to provide explanation and understanding which goes beyond the description, to construct conceptual and theoretical accounts of aspects of the social. In order to do this ethnographies have often become lengthy documents, in which a case is argued on the basis of the presentation of data and evidence of the data analysis. In this sense, ethnography as a product is not only about the findings and the conclusions of research but it is also a necessary showcase for the process which has led to those findings and conclusions. We say 'necessary' in recognition that ethnography's 'legitimacy' as a research process and product comes, in part, as we have argued above, from its capacity to persuade its readers that it can provide truthful accounts of social reality. To do this it is seen to require careful, detailed and often lengthy argument. In this sense, ethnography's form and substance has become part of the discourse of science, which in its need to be accepted as serious and respectable is itself a conservative discourse. Consequently, in order to fulfil this need to be accepted as a legitimate and serious mode of research, ethnography has, in most cases, embraced a tried and trusted mode of representation and has avoided experimentation with others which may lead to challenges of both its substance and form.

Having identified textual representation as dominant for ethnography we feel it is useful, in our attempt to understand what ethnography seeks to achieve in terms of process and product, to take the discussion further at this point. In particular, we wish to refer to the dominant textual or written form within which ethnography is represented, that of narrative. By this, we refer to a specific format to which the writing tends to adhere. In identifying narrative as the dominant written form in ethnography, however, we stress again that we do not wish to suggest that all ethnographers write to a formula or template. Indeed, there are growing numbers of ethnographers (for example Ellis and Bochner 1992, 1996, 2000; Ellis 1993; Richardson

1995, 1997, 2000; Richardson and Lockridge 1998) who are concerned to experiment with different written forms. They advocate not only the use of a number of writing genres including poetry, plays, stories and extended metaphor as a means of representing ethnography but, specifically in the case of Richardson (2000), promote writing as a method of inquiry in and of itself. Richardson sees writing in different formats, which might include the use of different fonts and constructive use of layout and colour as a 'way of knowing a method of discovery and analysis'. She states:

> Writing as a method of enquiry, then, provides a research practice through which we can investigate how we construct the world, ourselves and others, and how standard objectifying practices of social science unnecessarily limit us and social science. Writing as a method does not take writing for granted, but offers multiple ways to learn to do it, and so nurture the writer.
>
> (Richardson 2000: 924)

However, having noted these alternative means of writing and representation, our argument is that within the written mode of representation it is the narrative approach that forms the dominant discourse. In perhaps over simple terms we refer to narrative as story telling in which ethnography follows a linear path, adhering to particular conventions which have become acceptable to the ethnographer as a means of representing his or her work to meet the requirements of reliability in the ways that we discussed above, and to allow a persuasive account of the research and its findings to be produced. In addition, the narrative is a form of representation familiar to readers of ethnography which, consequently, puts them in a position in which they are able to evaluate its reliability as a contribution to knowledge about the social world. Moreover, the idea of ethnography as narrative is a useful one in that it conveys something of the research process because it rests not on one instance of story telling but on several. In this sense, narrative forms of ethnography become multilinear, rather than unilinear, through successive story tellings.

In the first instance, those who provide the data tell the story to the ethnographer. This may occur quite literally as a story in the form of an interview or conversation, or metaphorically where the ethnographer is given access to situations in which he or she is able to watch and experience the story unfold at first hand. The story is then retold by the ethnographer in the textual accounts he or she constructs based on those data. In fact, the ethnographer will usually retell the story several times in a textual form. For example, starting with brief fieldnotes taken in situ, moving on to much more detailed and analytical field accounts upon which the final or published written account draws.[1] Furthermore, Bruner (1986) extends the story telling analogy to the reader, by claiming that each time the ethnography is read constitutes a retelling of the story, and that each telling draws on those that have gone before. He states: 'Each telling depends on the context, the audience and the conventions of the medium. A retelling is never an exact duplicate of the already told story, for it takes into account previous tellings the conditions of which are never identical' (1986: 143). We might also add at this point that implicit in the act of reading or retelling is a process of interpretation and understanding. These too vary from one reader or teller to the next. Despite this idea of continual telling and retelling and of multiple interpretations, we would argue that many aspects of the story remain constant, and that these aspects are, and should be, the ones told by those upon whom the research focuses. These stories told at first hand represent the primary data upon which the ethnography relies. For ethnography and the ethnographer, the data are paramount and it is this aspect of the story that must remain constant with each telling. Each telling represents an interpretation of the reality of the situation being studied. Inevitably, there may be different and competing accounts of the same situations and events provided by research participants. Consequently, these may be seen as competing versions of reality. However, part of the process of analysis will be the selection and interpretation of the data for the purposes of narrative construction. Consequently, readers can, usually, only read what has been selected for them by the researcher in producing the narrative. If this is the case then concerns about researcher bias in the selection, interpretation and telling process should also be addressed in coming to tentative conclusions about what each story is able to tell us.

Bruner (1986) engages with these issues by contrasting the work of Chatman (1978), which asserts that the same story told in different versions inevitably draws on a core narrative which is independent of the teller and the conditions under which the story is retold, and that of Herrnstein-Smith (1980) whose position privileges the social context of the story telling at the expense of the story itself. Bruner steers a middle course in this debate, which in our view is the most useful in that it holds on to the notion of the core to a narrative, but at the same time acknowledges that there are many ways in which the telling, interpretation and understanding of the core may be affected by a range of factors. Nevertheless, there remains a recognizable telling to the story on each occasion. Bruner states: 'My position is that the story is prior to, but not independent of, the discourse. We abstract the story from discourse, but once abstracted the story serves as a model for future discourse' (Bruner 1986: 143).

In Bruner's analysis, narrative is maintained as a useful characterization not only of the way in which much ethnography is represented, but also of the ways in which it is read, consumed or used. Moreover, it brings into question the authorship of ethnographies. If a process of reconstruction occurs each time they are read or told, does this in fact constitute a re-authorship of the narrative? Or are all tellings merely a reworking of the narrative core which is provided by those on whom the research focuses?

If this is the case then does this inevitably mean that the authors of any ethnography can only be those who provide the original data upon which it is based?

Whatever our answers to these questions, the ethnographer remains central to the construction and reconstruction of the narrative. The ethnographer is simultaneously an author of the ethnography and a voice for other authors of different versions of the same ethnography. Establishing any definitive author of the narrative is, therefore, impossible as it is the interaction of the different authors in the narrative process that is responsible for the narrative product rather than a single act of writing or telling. Again, Bruner (1986) is instructive here:

> The ethnographer appears not as an individual creative scholar, a knowing subject who discovers, but more as a material body through whom a narrative structure unfolds. If myths have no authors (a la Levi-Strauss), then in the same sense neither do ethnographic texts.
>
> (1986: 146)

In one sense, questioning the authorship of the narrative and suggesting that it cannot be attributed to one single individual, but results from the interactions of several, serves to democratize the process of ethnographic construction in that it is no longer possible to see it as a whim of the researcher. Rather, the process becomes more complex where, with each telling or rewriting of the narrative, a different interpretation may arise. If this is the case, however, it does not necessarily remove ethnography from charges of relativism. On the one hand it could be argued that the relativism of the narrative is shared among the various contributors to its construction who consequently act as a means of restraint on any individual source of bias. On the other hand, it could be argued that recognizing the role of the different contributors to the narrative increases the opportunity for relativism. If we adopt the latter view then we risk characterizing ethnography as at worst a meaningless pot-pourri of opinion, whereas the former view may help us get closer to a reliable account of the given situation. Whichever of these positions we adopt, we return to questions about the reliability of ethnography and the authority of the narrative on which it rests. If ethnography is to be accepted as having the capacity to provide reliable and hence persuasive accounts of social reality then it must find a means of distancing itself from these charges of relativism.

The authority of the author

Having suggested that ethnography is in fact represented by the interaction of several authors rather than one acting in isolation, it may seem erroneous to continue our discussion under a sub-heading which includes reference to a singular author. However, we do this in an attempt to regain some of the ground that may have been ceded to those who accuse ethnography of meaningless relativism, in our discussion under the previous sub-heading in this chapter.

In using the term 'author' in this context, we refer only to the person responsible for producing the published ethnography. Although we recognize that others may be involved in retelling the ethnography, we place a primacy on the role of the ethnographer or researcher as author, as it is he or she who provides the analysed and constructed text, which may stand alone as the authoritative account, or will be the basis of subsequent accounts or retellings. We do this not because we reject the legitimacy of retellings of the narrative, or the credentials of those who retell them, but because of the central role we believe the researcher has in the construction of the ethnography, as should be evident from our discussions throughout this text. In all of our discussion so far, we have attributed to the ethnographer a role which is central to all aspects of ethnography, both process and product. Consequently, we would argue that this centrality yields authority.

In the first place, the ethnographer has detailed first-hand experience of the subject of the research. The direct participation and/or observation of events and activities means that close contact with those actors upon whom the research focuses not only yields detailed data, but also provides the ethnographer with a perspective on the social action which is unavailable to other researchers.[2] While this may be broadly identified as the ethnographer's attempt to achieve an insider's view, we would wish to take this further by suggesting that this may also be characterized as a heuristic perspective. Such a perspective affords an understanding of social action within the specific context in which it is performed or takes place. It is a perspective which is engaged with the actors and the social action within the field under study. At the same time it is a perspective which remains sufficiently detached from the actors and the social action to facilitate comprehensive and systematic data collection, which provide a basis for thorough analysis. It is, therefore, a perspective which is shaped by the physical and metaphorical use of place by the ethnographer.

Geertz (1988) also recognizes this authority of place in his conception of 'being there' when he states:

> The ability of anthropologists to get us to take what they say seriously has less to do with either a factual look or an air of conceptual elegance than it has with their capacity to convince us that what they say is a result of their having actually penetrated (or, if you prefer, been penetrated by) another form of life, of having one way or another, truly 'been there'.
>
> (1988: 299)

While stressing the importance of 'being there' to the authority of ethno-graphic accounts it could also be argued that this is not solely the preserve of the ethnographer. Inevitably, it is an a priori condition of ethnography that those at the centre of the social action, the researched, must be there in order for the ethnographer also to be there and for an ethnography to be produced.[3] However, important differences between these two types of actor and their experiences of 'being there' are two-fold. First, the reasons for being there are different. For the researched their presence is part of the social action that is being studied and hence might be seen as a natural state of 'being there'. However, for the ethnographer this is not the case. For the ethnographer 'being there' facilitates the collection of data which will be central to his or her concern to understand the social action that is being witnessed. In this sense, although by his or her presence the social action is inevitably changed, 'being there' is not part of the 'natural' social action, and is consequently an artificial or contrived state of being. The only reason for the ethnographer's presence is to seek to understand the social action, not to take part in it for its own sake.

Second, a further difference between these two types of actor within the given situation, and hence the difference in their types of 'being', is that the ethnographer is a trained researcher. This may seem an obvious point to make but it is, in our view, pivotal to the debate about the author and the authority of his or her text. Different ways of being in any given situation will inevitably make for different ways of seeing that situation. However, the researcher will attempt to see the situation in ways which pose searching questions about the action that is witnessed. He or she will not take for granted what is seen and experienced, will adopt ways of systematically recording what is seen and experienced and, subsequently, will subject this collected data to rigorous analysis. In addition, he or she may also seek to place the action in a wider social context by looking at the structures within which the action takes place. In essence, the ethnographers' training as a social researcher should, simultaneously, enable him or her to achieve both a degree of intimacy with the focus of the research and the researched, and a capacity for analysis which is not tainted by vested interest or personal subjectivities. Moreover, the importance of reflexivity to the process of ethnography, which we discussed earlier in this chapter, should ensure that if such influences do come to bear on the research, they, like the inevitable impact made by the very presence of the ethnographer, are accounted for in the process of analysis.

As a result of these differences between the researcher and other social actors in the research setting, we would argue that the researcher occupies a privileged position. By virtue of his or her training and structural relationship to the social action, which is the focus of the research, the ethnographer as author of the narrative, has both a technical and epistemo-logical authority which is not shared by the researched. This authority provides ethnography with its legitimacy and a means of challenging charges of relativism which may be levelled against it. Moreover, it is upon this authority that the heuristic capacity of ethnography rests. That the researcher has exacted a systematic, careful and diligent process of research imbues ethnography, as a product, with a capacity for explanation and understanding of social action. Furthermore, in making a case for the authority of ethnography in this way, we have maintained the centrality of the role of the researcher to the entire ethnographic research process. This we feel is important as it also continues to emphasize the significance of interpretation to ethnography and allow the narrative as the dominant mode of its representation to be maintained.

Summary

Our discussions have lead us, therefore, to a position which strengthens the relationship between the ethnographer and the ethnography as a product. In earlier chapters we established the close relationship between the ethnographer and ethnography as process. Part of the objective of this chapter has been to explore whether that relationship becomes any more distant as the account of the process is produced for public scrutiny. While assumptions may have been drawn as to whether as the ethnographer engages in analysis and representation he or she seeks to stand back from the ethnography in the name of science, our argument does not uphold such an assumption. Rather than bringing into question the scientific and reliability credentials of the ethnography, we see the proximity of the ethnographer to the ethnography as product as central to its reliability and authority as an account of social life.

We have established a role for the ethnographer based upon Geertz's (1988) notion of 'being there' where the first-hand experience of social action, combined with the researcher's training and experience, what we might term his or her ethnographic eye, and with assiduous analysis, provide an authority and validity for the account of that social life that is produced by the ethnographic research process. The role that we have identified for the ethnographer does not lend itself to a neat and tidy formulation. We cannot construct a list of instructions to be followed which will result in the production of a perfect ethnography. Moreover, we have also sought to stress that the ethnography is produced only as a result of the interaction of the ethnographer/researcher with the researched, as such, ethnography is the result of collaboration of actors rather than the actions of a lone scholar. It is this idea of collaboration that emphasizes the role of construction in ethnography as a product and which links it to a narrative structure. Unlike the archaeologist or the lab-based scientist, the ethnographer does not merely 'uncover' research findings. As we have seen, they are produced or constructed (Berger and Luckman 1967) by means of a social process. Moreover, if we accept that the role of ethnography, as with all social research, is to provide information which will enlighten and help us to understand aspects of social life, then the narrative approach to this endeavour would seem appropriate.

As the dominant medium of communication, narrative is familiar to us all as intelligent social actors. Its capacity to explain, reveal, build an argument and persuade its readers is implicitly well known, if not always acknowledged, as we read without thinking about the nature of the medium through which the message is conveyed. We would argue that because narrative is able to do all of these things it is, therefore, a familiar, convenient and extremely effective means of representing ethnography. However, recent years have seen challenges to narrative representation, in particular from postmodern writers (Scheurich 1997; Stronarch and Maclure 1997) and from those, some of whom would also be identified as postmodernists but who, at the same time, are more creatively experimental in their approach to representation (Lather 1991; Burrows 2001). For these writers narrative accounts of social life, located in their pursuit of enlightenment, can never do justice to its complexity and uncertainty. Nevertheless, despite or perhaps because of such challenges, it is the narrative which has remained the dominant form of representation for ethnography. We believe this is quite simply due to its accessibility as a medium and its capacity to convey rich and detailed accounts of social action, which are at the heart of ethnography. Moreover, Bruner (1986) suggests that, inevitably, the existence of narrative as the dominant mode of representation means that ethnographers approach their task with a narrative in their heads which structures their approach in the field. As such, the narrative is inescapable. In addition, we have also stressed the important role of the reader to the construction of the ethnography in terms of the telling and the retelling of the ethnography. For the ethnographer to communicate with an audience, therefore, the narrative may be simply the most accessible and straightforward approach. It has the power of persuasion and rhetoric through which the ethnographer seeks to convince his or her readers that his or her story is authentic and reliable.

Notes

1 Delamont's (1992) account of Bernard's cough during a cookery lesson provides an excellent example of the 'career' of a fieldnote as she demonstrates the progress from rough note taken in the classroom to the place the incident takes in published work.

2 In the case of auto-ethnography (Ellis 1997, 1998; Ellis and Bochner 2000) where the life and emotional experiences of the ethnographer are a topic of investigation in their own right, the issue is not one of getting close to social action, but of

finding a way to analyse it while being its principal protagonist. Some of the 'experimental' approaches to writing and representing ethnography which we discussed earlier in this chapter offer interesting and challenging possibilities here. Unfortunately, we do not have the space to pursue these at present.

3 Again, auto-ethnograph presents a different situation where researcher and researched are one and the same.

7 | Ethical considerations

Introduction

Throughout this volume we have sought to go beyond a conventional text-book approach to ethnography by focusing not simply on the ways of doing ethnographic research in educational settings, but also on encouraging critical thought about the nature of ethnography. In particular we have been keen to focus on the strengths of ethnographic research in terms of what it might contribute to knowledge about education and other aspects of social life. At the same time, however, we have also been concerned to identify its limitations. For example, we have endeavoured to ensure that the claims we made for ethnography, about the nature of the knowledge it is capable of generating, are realistic. We have stressed its relationship to the specific circumstances of where and when the data upon which the knowledge is based are collected. In addition, we have been at pains to emphasize that the whole process of ethnography relies on the capacity of the ethnographer to interact successfully with those who are at the centre of the research and to manage the total experience of 'being there' (Geertz 1988) within the specific research location.

Ethnography is, therefore, a human process which relies on first-hand experience of other people's lives. Of all approaches to educational research, ethnography is perhaps the most notable in sharing the lives and feelings of educational 'others', whether they are teachers, pupils, students or parents. This can and does frequently engender feelings of vulnerability and insecurity for all parties. Such concerns about the exposure and exploitation of ourselves and others can be apparent regardless of whether ethnography in education is conducted as *basic* research – a knowledge-creating activity that concentrates upon the social scientific characterization of educational phenomena – or as *applied* research, in order to seek practical and profes-sional solutions to educational 'problems', however defined. Ethical frame-works to guide the conduct of ethnographic research are a feature of much ethnographic writing, although often framed as confessional post-research reflections.

Such concerns surface frequently among small-scale first-time ethnographers. While writing the early draft of this chapter, for example, one of the authors was interrupted by a student who wished to discuss what we call the many *what if, how much* and *how many* questions that emerge when first time ethnographers prepare to enter the field. In combination such questions are as much ethical as they are practical. In this case the student was returning to her home country in the Far East to conduct in-depth primary school studies. Research methods training had allowed her to access all the basic issues of ethnographic research in theory and in discussion. Now research was to be 'for real'. Permission to research had been obtained from the relevant Ministry of Education. But: *what if* individual principals 'limited' her work in specific ways? *How many* levels of access should she negotiate in school – with the head of curriculum and the head of student affairs, with all the classroom teachers . . .? *How much* should she inform each participant about her research – to the point at which teachers might become alarmed, bored, defensive or 'too aware' about the project's concerns so that they amended their views and actions or . . .? *How much*, if anything, should she tell pupils, and *how* should she frame this telling? *What if* the teachers granted her interviews and then withdrew permission to use the data? *What if* she returned the data to them to confirm the accuracy of her transcriptions and they made substantive alterations to initial responses? *What if* rapport declined to the point at which she needed to seek out new participants? *How many* 'new' respondents should she approach? What should she tell them, and *how many* would be 'enough'? And all this in a country which, until recently, considered the main route to research truth to derive from a model of the natural sciences rather than through the in-depth study of discrete locations through first hand experience.

While ethical issues are aspects of all research (and indeed *all* aspects of research that starts with our need to distinguish between what is do-able and what is desirable to do), the outpourings from a nervous if enthusiastic first time ethnographer suggest that notions of ethics and morals take a particular 'turn' in ethnography. Advocacy for individual researchers to develop, use and highlight their own personal codes of conduct has become increasingly common in all forms of research. More recently, associations of researchers like the British Educational Research Association (BERA) and the British Sociological Association (BSA), for example, have listed and advocated codes of conduct for research which have specific resonance for ethnographers and also implications for the various disciplines to which some ethnographers might specifically adhere, whether this is to 'education' or 'sociology' or 'psychology' and so on. Indeed, for some forms of funded research, refusal to acknowledge or abide by such guidelines would, in effect, scupper the chances of such proposals being funded.

Quite rightly so, readers might argue. A fundamental respect for human dignity and the need for mutually agreed ethical and moral underpinnings to guide all research, including ethnography, should be viewed as sacrosanct. Not that all writers would support the notion that ethics and morals are indistinguishable. For example, Pring (2000: 141) regards ethics as 'the philosophical enquiry into the basis of morals and moral judgements' and morals as 'what is the right and wrong thing to do'. Moreover, Busher (2002) warns us against overly technicist formulations of principles that are designed to protect *us* (researchers) rather than, or from, *them* (research participants and/or research sponsors). Commenting on the need for researchers to make and remake practical moral decisions in specific situations and locations he writes about the need to:

> go beyond the search for 'rules of conduct' that Simons (1995: 436) pursued in order to allow researchers to defend their work in par-ticular social and political contexts. Such technicist solutions imply an autocratic style of managing research that privileges the views of some people, researchers. This view of managing has 'at its core a set of values: a disrespectful and distrusting view of people as the cogs or components in the machinery of organisations' (Shipley and Moir 2001: iv).
>
> (Busher 2002: 73)

Does this mean that 'anything goes' as long as it all 'works out' in the end with minimal damage and maximum benefit for all concerned? We think not. Instead, we prefer to embed general principles for guiding ethnography in the 'contemporary and historical social, political, and cultural frame-works' (Busher 2002: 74) in which they are located, what Pring (2000: 141) describes as 'the dispositions and character of the researcher', together with 'personhood, i.e. the individuality and autonomy . . . of the researched . . . for which researchers are said to have a duty of care . . . to avoid harm to them' (Busher 2002: 74).

Let us, then, consider some of the specific ethical implications for educational ethnography. The following list of issues is not exhaustive. Moreover, it needs to be counterbalanced against, rather than exacerbate, what some might see as excesses in ethical 'navel-gazing' by ethnographers (Sammons 1989; Brewer 2000) to the extent that the relation between ethics and other approaches to research, like quantitative approaches, have been underemphasized. (Indeed, as Sammons has suggested, it may be precisely because sponsors and readers of quantitative research are sometimes inclined to bestow upon it more external validity, and/or because readers may lack the skills of statistical analysis to interpret its outcomes, that we may need to be *more* ethically conscious about such approaches.)

Informed consent

Respect for 'personhood' in educational ethnography is often associated with the importance of 'informed consent'. Mason (1996: 166–7) notes that such consent has two core features, one of which has been the subject of more comment than the other. The first relates to the in-depth engagement between researchers and the researched that can evoke a sensitive (and sensitizing) intimacy of engagement between them. Ethical issues of getting in, getting on and getting out of ethnography, together with considerations about 'what's in it' for researchers and the researched, loom large. We note, for example, how Morrison and Galloway (1996) retrospectively express concerns about the use to which supply teacher diaries were put in their study of supply teachers in English schools (Galloway and Morrison 1993) especially when they comment:

> At a general level, there was agreement among researchers and diarists about the purposes of the accounts. Diarists knew these were important bases for recording and analysing lives within and beyond school, and that their work would be presented using pseudonyms. For several, the act of writing raised consciousness about complexities at the public/private interface, yet mechanisms to support that consciousness remained beyond the research agenda . . . The contribution of writing was not fully formulated. Indeed at this stage of the work the research team could not reliably predict the nature of the data or how it might be appropriate to use this information.
> (Morrison and Galloway 1996: 53)

This last sentence amplifies the second of Mason's (1996) points, which relates to the ways in which research interests can change in direction and emphasis as research progresses.

To what extent is the framing of such issues comforting or disconcerting for the first time researcher we introduced in the opening passages to this chapter? We think (as does Silverman 2001: 55) that Mason's opening guidelines are helpful when, in addition, she offers three pronged advice for ethnographers in the early stages of their ethnographies:

1 Decide what is the purpose of your research (Is it to bring about changes in teachers' professional practice? Is it to empower a group of women . . .?)
2 Examine which individuals or groups might be interested or affected by your research topic. (Consider our first time ethnographer's need

to negotiate and renegotiate access at levels which start at the national and end with individuals . . . and may involve negotiated feedback in a number of formats.)

3 Consider what are the implications for these parties of framing your research topic in the way you have done.

(Mason 1996: 29–30)

To these we would add the need to consult the ethical guidelines of the professional association to which the first time ethnographer and/or readers of this book may belong.

Hammersley and Atkinson (1995: 264) write about the need for research participants to give their 'unconstrained' consent. This has been debated in a number of ways. Let us begin with the BERA (1992) guidelines. Here, under items 7–11, researchers' responsibilities to participants are characterized as follows:

- Participants in a research study have the right to be informed about the aims and purposes and likely publications of findings involved in the research and of potential consequences for participants and to give their informed consent before participating in the event.
- Care should be taken when interviewing children and students up to school leaving age; permission should be obtained from the school and if they so suggest the parents.
- Honesty and openness should characterise the relationship between research participants and institutional representatives.
- Participants have the right to withdraw from the study at any time.
- Researchers have a responsibility to be mindful of cultural, religious, gendered and other significant differences in the planning, conducting, and reporting of their research.

Such guidelines (still voluntary) contain the seeds of both clarity and ambiguity. The depth of information needed for an informant to be or become informed is not fully specified, and likely outcomes, publications and consequences are assumed to be known from the outset, or at least in the early stages. Such assumptions are questionable. The 'care' taken when interviewing children appears to suggest that the right to 'informed consent' rests with teachers and parents rather than with children. This is contested and contestable, for example, by those who conduct ethnographies *with* rather than *on* children, for example Davis *et al.* (2000) who apply ethnographic methods to explore 'the learning lives of disabled children' from the starting point of children as social actors and frameworks for childhood in which 'children become constituted as children and also actively constitute themselves' (Christensen and James 2000: 3–4). The notion of honesty and openness is also open to interpretation when 'complete' honesty or 'lack of constraint' (in Hammersley and Atkinson's (1995) terms) might lead the ethnographer into physical danger, for example. And at which point in the research participant's right to withdraw from a research programme do we confront a tension or contradiction with a subsequent BERA (1992) guideline (item 15) that concerns the public's 'right to know' and where 'educational researchers should remain free to interpret and publish their findings without censorship or approval from individuals or organisations, including sponsors, funding agencies, *participants*, colleagues, supervisors, or administrators' (our emphasis)?

For ethnographers such issues have loomed largest in concerns about covert and overt research and it is to this we now turn.

Overt, covert and researcher identity

Some writers have argued that covert research is 'wrong' – full stop. Covert research is unequivocally wrong because it infringes participants' rights to informed consent, and it is 'bad science' (Erikson 1967, 1968, 1982; Homan 1980, 1982, 1991). At the macro-level, covert ethnography is also deemed to contribute towards a society of 'cynics, liars, and manipulators' (Warwick 1982: 58, in Hammersley and Atkinson 1995: 264).

Other writers take more of an 'it all depends' stance, that is also mediated by concerns about the extent of deception in relation to ends that are variously viewed as achievable or desirable. The relation between 'white lies' and 'whopping lies' may be one of degree and interpretation. However, Burgess (1984), in educational settings, has noted that the former may be advisable where telling the truth exposes colleagues, clients and sources to whom confidentiality has been promised.

Often covert research has been deployed in terms of what Silverman (2001) has described as ethnographies about 'underdog' sub-cultures (2001: 56) in which subterfuge, it is argued, may become an ethnographic necessity. Even here, covert research is not without its critics. Recorded in Silverman (2001), is Dingwall's (1980) suspicions that covert ethnography adds an element of 'radical chic ... to liven up the humdrum lives of academic inquiry' (Silverman 2001: 874) and there is a flavour of this in Brewer's (2000) writing when, in discussing his own covert research about fascists he comments:

> On the whole postgraduate researchers ... bold and foolish enough
> ... are more likely to engage in this sort of research, although
> less likely than they once were. Warren (1988: 66) notes that ageing
> ethnographers tend to retreat to interview research [!]
> (Brewer 2000: 97, our exclamation)

Realistically, most educational ethnographies are about degrees of overtness rather than about location at either end of an overt–covert continuum.

There are several reasons for this. We have already alluded to the challenge in identifying both for ourselves as well as for the researched the 'definitive' directions and outcomes for research outcomes in educational settings. But as we have already suggested in earlier chapters, research participants also bring to educational experiences their own sets of understandings and meanings about the research, as well as about the role that we, as ethnographers, play. In another sense, of course, this multiplicity of meanings, exhibited by a range of actors in educational settings, is part of ethnography's strength. It is also what makes research ethically complex. Moreover, whether educational actors are willing to tell you their story will be as much about the kind of person they perceive you, the reader and ethnographer, to be as it is about you telling them the 'whole' problem or rationale that underpins your research project. Part of the ethical problem, then, is not 'just' about degrees of overtness but involves reflexivity on the part of the ethnographer. Part of that reflexivity is recognition and interpretation of the ways in which your identity as male or female, outsider or insider, youthful or mature, affects and is reflected in the collection and analysis of ethnographic data.

Avoiding harm

The BERA (1992) guidelines suggest the importance of our being 'mindful' (item 11) of the need to 'protect' (item 13) participants from harm. Items 11 and 13 are aspects of research process, outcome and/or derive from research publications, the ramifications of which might extend, in extreme cases, beyond the discrete locations and people that are hallmarks of educational ethnography, towards the uses to which other people and organizations put the findings. Not that all educational researchers are averse to such disclosures and uses. Arguably, in a research world that is progressively narrowed and confined in scope by those who are powerful enough to define what counts as worthwhile knowledge, critical ethnography can and does provide an effective counterpoint for interpreting and reinterpreting education. Nonetheless, ethnographers' micro-concerns have more usually focused upon ethical dilemmas at the interface between the public and the private, and the need not 'to rock the research boat' to the extent that subsequent researchers may find it difficult to come 'on board'. Meanwhile, while what counts as *public* or *private* in educational settings is open to a variety of interpretations, for example, children's private spaces have been more likely to be seen as legitimate targets for public scrutiny than those of adults, and those of less powerful adults more than those of establishment figures of power and influence. Can we apply any comforting balm to first time ethnographers faced with such dilemmas? We can take some comfort from a perspective that:

in research relationships [ethnographic or not] there is no natural bargain that would be recognised as fair by all. Respondents are not fearful victims who open up their lives and souls because they are asked or told to. People have boundaries and strategies to protect themselves in research situations.

(Measor and Sikes 1991: 230)

And we may still need to recognize that not all research will be seen as fair or, indeed in similar ways, by every audience or by all participants in ethnography.

Looking ahead

As ethnographers we recognize that ethical issues will permeate every stage in the research process. There is no complete or single solution that is applicable to any one ethical dilemma or research situation. Hammersley and Atkinson (1995: 276–85) posit four positions which, they argue, are as much about assumptions concerning the nature of society and education that ethnographers bring to their research, as they are about researcher's particular values about how they should conduct research. It may be for you the reader to decide whether some approaches to ethnography, like covert observation and/or deception, must always be proscribed, or whether this is a matter for the researcher's judgement in context, or whether nothing should be done in opposition to the moral principles of the researched, or whether you think an insistence on informed consent would prevent the exposure of the ways in which educational organizations manipulate and control the policies and practices of education and its research. In the end, argues Busher (2002), there is no 'one' solution:

> Researchers have to take decisions about how to carry out research that makes the research as ethical as possible within the framework of the project, including the budgets and times they have available to them. These decisions include considering whether it is worthwhile . . . by weighing up the harm and benefit to participants and to society that may arise if the research is or is not carried out.
>
> (Busher 2002: 86–7)

For ethnographers, such decisions are affected by and reflected in the depth of understanding which they bring to the range of tools at their disposal and their respective abilities to apply and report them appropriately, a task that has been seen as core to the aims and purposes of this book.

Summary

At the beginning of this chapter we identified themes that can be traced throughout this volume: the centrality of the ethnographer's relation with research participants, ethnography's reliance on 'being there' (Geertz 1988), and the ethnographer's skills in managing relationships, situations and experiences in and beyond the field. Advocacy of, and indeed insistence upon, individually and institutionally approved ethical procedures are now common features of educational research conducted as part of under-graduate and postgraduate degrees in higher education, and are essential features of all applications for funded research. Ethics committees, formerly most common in medical research, are now more widespread throughout social science and education faculties of higher education. Recognized ethical guidelines provided by professional associations can be reassuring and helpful, but, as we have pointed out, also contain the seeds of ambiguity. Research processes can and often do engender feelings of insecurity and vulnerability for all parties, and we have illustrated how ethical issues loom large in ethnography and the ways in which they might be considered.

8 | Taking stock: ethnography as distinctive research

Introduction

Although the objectives of ethnographic research may, in the broadest sense, be similar to the approaches or outcomes of other kinds of research, in so far as all research seeks to discover or advance new knowledge about a given situation, we have argued that ethnography is different from other kinds of research. In essence, we see ethnography as distinctive on a number of counts which relate to its scope, the position of the researcher vis-à-vis the researched, the nature of the data yielded and the processes of analysis to which it is subjected. As a means of concluding our discussions, it may be useful to consider in a little more detail these characteristics which, in our view, make ethnography distinctive and mark it as the principal approach for educational research.

Scope of the research

By 'scope' we refer to the epistemological foundations upon which ethnography rests. For example, throughout this text we have seen how ethnography is concerned with detail, first hand experience and with what might broadly be termed 'an insider perspective'. From this we have sought to characterize ethnography as capable of yielding knowledge about the particular rather than the general, about processes rather than trends and about interactions rather than generalizations. At one level, therefore, the scope of ethnography may be seen as narrow, being temporally and spatially limited. On the other hand, the depth of knowledge about a given subject which it yields surpasses that from other approaches. Implicit in our characterization of the nature of the knowledge to come from ethnographic research is an assumption that the knowledge is reliable. By this we mean that ethnography as a product is capable of conveying a version of the truth about a given situation. However, it should be clear from our discussion in Chapter 6 that we do not hold on to the notion of what Hammersley (1990) has termed naive realism, where the ethnographer simply 'tells it like it is', representing social reality in a seemingly unproblematic fashion. Throughout our discussions we have sought to eschew this simplistic, positivistic conception of ethnography. In its place we have drawn attention to the centrality of the role of the researcher in producing or perhaps more appropriately constructing, a version of reality or truth. In doing this we have also drawn attention to research as a social process which is as much about selection and interpretation as it is about describing and representing social reality. However, at the same time we have attempted to avoid exposing ethnography to charges of total relativism. In this we have suggested that while recognizing the complexity of the concept of truth or certainty in knowledge about the social world, it remains nevertheless, the objective of any form of research to get as close to a version of it as possible. The careful collection and analysis of detailed data which are at the heart of ethnography is testimony to this.

Brewer (2000) terms these problems for ethnography and for the ethnographer, 'crises of representation and legitimation'. Our solution to them, which may be seen as somewhat predictable (Silverman 1997) but we believe still effective, is to refer again to the centrality of reflexivity for the process of ethnography. In this we adopt Hammersley and Atkinson's (1983) line in stressing the importance of the social context of the research in recognizing the role of the ethnographer not simply in constructing the research, but also in taking account of the ways in which he or she undertook the construction. More recently, Brewer (2000) has offered a wider definition of reflexivity to include a critical approach to many aspects of the research process. He says:

> Reflexivity involves reflection by ethnographers on the social process that impinge upon and influence data. It requires a critical attitude towards data, and recognition of the influence on the research of such factors as the location, of the setting, the sensitivity of the topic, power relations in the field and the nature of the social interaction between the researcher and the researched, all of which influence how the data are interpreted and conveyed in writing up the results. Reflexivity thus affects both writing up the data (called representation) and the data's status, standing and authority (called legitimation).
>
> (Brewer 2000: 127)

One conclusion to draw from the importance we attach to reflexivity could be that the knowledge which comes from ethnographic research is inevitably contingent upon the features identified in Brewer's definition of reflexivity. If this were the case then ethnographic knowledge could have no meaning beyond the particular circumstances in which it was constructed. However, an alternative and we think a more appropriate conclusion to draw, would be that it is the identification and taking account of the features that Brewer identifies that provide a greater legitimacy for ethnographic knowledge. The cultural and contextual features operate as a code against which the ethnographic narrative is both written and read. As such, reflexivity adds another layer of information to the account which is not otherwise provided. This does not mean that we can say that ethnography provides 'the truth', but it may mean that we are in a better position to judge whether it provides a convincing version of a truth. Is any form of research able to more than this?

Position of the researcher

Bearing in mind the caveats we expressed about naive realism and the dangers of assuming that ethnography has the capacity to 'tell it like it is', we still, nevertheless, regard the ethnographer's position within the social action as distinctive in social science research. It is this position which makes the ethnographer an inevitable participant in whatever is the focus of the study and, therefore, a contributor to the construction of the reality of the situation.

To a large extent, the position of the researcher vis-à-vis the researched has been addressed in our discussion of reflexivity and the scope of the research. Here we emphasized that the researcher is the principal instrument for the collection, interpretation and analysis of data and also for its representation in ethnography as a product. This is perhaps best characterized by Agar (1980) in his idea of the professional stranger. In essence, Agar refers to a relationship between researcher and researched which relies on the capacity of the ethnographer to play a dual role. In the fashion typified by anthropologists (Malinowski 1922), he or she participates, observes and witnesses social action from the inside. Seeking not merely to be in a position to record what is seen, heard and experienced but also to interpret and to analyse it. However, while the data are collected from within the social action, analysis and interpretation take place from a position which is slightly removed from it. The ethnographer's role is always one of social scientist and it is this that adds the degree of analytical distance between him or her and those who are the focus of the research. In order to engage in the process of ethnography the researcher must be a friend, but to produce the ethnography as a product he or she must not only be a stranger, but a *professional* stranger. In the second edition of *The Professional Stranger*, Agar (1996) offers a slightly different view of the ethnographer as stranger which reflects not only changes in ethnography but also in the social world more generally that have occurred in the 16 years since the publication of the first edition of the book. For example, he attaches considerable importance to ethnography as a profession and we believe it is here that he locates the critical distance between ethnographer and those upon whom his or her study focuses. It is the professional role which makes the ethnographer more than a participant. It gives the ethnographer a degree of authority which, in turn, is transferred to the ethnography as a product. Agar (1996) admits that critics may identify this view of authority more easily with the era of ethnography reflected in the first edition of his text (Agar 1980), rather than what he sees as modern or new era ethnography. However, he is quick to reject this and to assert that modern ethnography requires more rather than less authority than older ethnography. Here he is referring directly to the position of the researcher vis-à-vis the researched. As modern ethnography has sought to recognize the role of the ethnographer as an insider and to take account of his or her part in the construction of the social action which is studied, Agar (1996) argues that there is more of a need for the ethnographer to persuade readers that his or her perspective is legitimate and of value. In essence, the ethnographer needs to be able to draw on a form of professionalism which emphasizes that he or she is more than just a participant in the action upon which the ethnography is focused. As such, the ethnographer's professionalism offers a form of authority to the ethnography as product. Agar states:

> We can't let go of the responsibility to build an argument so that people can evaluate what we say. Besides, if one is committed to application of knowledge as well as its creation, one needs credible arguments to persuade sceptical people who are being asked to put themselves on the line ... Some who debate the newer model of authority would curl their lip at this point. One is supposed to diminish authority, not claim it. I don't think so. I think the new issues around doing ethnography call for more authority, more responsibility, not less. Ethnography is a profession after all. One trains for it for several years before one can do it competently.
>
> (Agar 1996: 17)

According to Agar (1996) authority in the text is what marks ethnographic accounts out from others which may also seek to give an account of social action, including those offered by research participants themselves, and professionalism is an important aspect of such authority. However, he also points out that authority and professionalism in modern ethnography are not predicated on positions of difference between researcher and researched, as may have been the case in traditional late nineteenth- or early twentieth-century anthropology. The distinction between 'emic' (from the native's point of view) and 'etic' studies (from an outsider's point of view), according to Agar, has become blurred.

The distinction doesn't make any sense anymore. People don't clump into mutually exclusive worlds. Ethnographers and others swim in the same interconnected global soup. They know things about each other even before they meet and start to talk.

(Agar 1996: 21)

In the context of educational research it is easy to see the point that Agar makes. Thinking back to some of the early school-based studies like *Social Relations in a Secondary School* (Hargreaves 1967) and *Hightown Grammar* (Lacey 1970), these classic studies provided a view of two different worlds which were unknown to many. Drawing on qualitative and quantitative fieldwork conducted in the mid- to late 1960s they provided the first detailed insight into postwar secondary schooling in Britain. A decade or so later *Beachside Comprehensive* (Ball 1981) and *Experiencing Comprehensive Education. A Study of Bishop McGregor School* (Burgess 1983) did the same in relation to comprehensive schools, when they were still relatively new and unknown to those who did not have direct experience of them, and even some of those who did, particularly parents, who were often kept at arms length by headteachers at this time. Twenty years on, however, comprehensive schools have become generally more accessible, positively encouraging participation from parents, business personnel and many other members of the local community. Moreover, schools have become sites for mainstream popular entertainment through television and film drama, popular fiction and, not least, through the lens of the documentary maker. The depictions of school life in *Grange Hill* or *Weatherfield Comp* may be fictional, designed primarily to entertain, but they do nevertheless contribute to what we think we know about present-day schooling. The school gates are now well and truly open, and teachers are no longer the 'other'. For the ethnographer of the twenty-first century, therefore, schools are not the foreign lands that perhaps they were for the ethnographers of the 1960s, 1970s and 1980s. Perhaps for these reasons, Agar's blurring of the emic and the etic rings true.

It is the combination of insider and outsider perspectives which we feel contributes to the distinctive nature of ethnography, giving the ethnographer a unique position vis-à-vis those at the focus of the research. In turn, this position makes a defining contribution to both the conduct of the research and to the knowledge constructed from it.

The nature of the data

As with the position of the researcher in relation to the research participants, consideration of the nature of the data within ethnography has been both explicit and implicit throughout this text. By now we hope that readers will be familiar with the possibilities that ethnography presents for data collection. Under the title 'Doing ethnography', Chapters 2 and 3 attempted to provide a comprehensive guide to what might constitute data in ethnographic research. While we remain confident that we have covered what are and will continue to be the enduring sources for ethnographic data, we should not rule out other sources which are at present unknown to us. For example, the impact of the Internet over the past decade or so has provided a rich source of data (Hine 2000) which 20 years ago, when many of the now celebrated texts on ethnography were first being published, was not foreseen. Taking this as a clear example of what was unknown becoming commonplace, it seems pointless speculating about future sources of data in any specific sense. It may, however, be feasible to speculate about the nature of the data, even if we cannot be sure of their source.

As long as the central concern of ethnography remains the fashioning of rich and detailed understandings of social action from within, we feel the essential qualities of the data upon which those understandings are based will also remain the same. If the objectives of ethnography change, then we would argue that it would be erroneous to continue to discuss ethnography in the ways in which we have done in this text. Undoubtedly there will be new forms of research which emerge and develop in years to come. They may not, however, be ethnographic in either their process or products. In making such a statement, we would not wish to be seen to be advocating a form of research Luddism, but simply to again emphasize the distinctive nature of ethnography by suggesting that although we have argued for a form of inclusive ethnography which perhaps extends to methods some ethnographers would not consider appropriate, we do nevertheless believe that there are boundaries to what can and cannot be considered ethnographic research. Those boundaries, we believe, do not necessarily relate to the nature of the data, at least not in isolation from the processes of analysis to which they are subjected.

It has been our concern throughout this text to emphasize that ethnography as a process is not simply about the collected data, but also about the analysis to which the data are subjected and the manner in which the data are used in constructing ethnography as a product. Consequently, the same data could conceivably be used very differently in different kinds of studies, for example, in a quantitatively based study compared to an ethnography, with different emphases leading to different kinds of findings. We would argue, therefore, that to speak of ethnographic data as though it were possible to separate it from other kinds on non-ethnographic data is to fail to understand the relationship between the nature of the data and the kind analysis to which they are subjected. Many, perhaps all, kinds of data have the capacity to contribute to ethnographic research. Whether such potential is realized or not will depend on the way in which they are analysed (ethnography as process) and used (ethnography as product).

Processes of analysis

In Chapter 4 we outlined our view of data analysis for ethnography. Underlying the examples used and the literature upon which we called in order to advance and justify our view is a concern that the processes of analysis should always privilege the detail in the data. By this we mean that analysis should be led by the content of the data and not by an external concern to apply a set of formulae or a computer program or even a particular theoretical framework. While all of these may be useful at some point during the process of analysis, our belief is that the essence of ethnography and hence of approaches to data analysis which pertain to it, are the data themselves and the capacity for the readers/users to engage with them. By this we mean, quite simply, that it is necessary for the readers/users of ethnography to be able to identify a clear link between findings and the data. This is not to suggest that findings should be merely descriptive of the situations and activities witnessed during the fieldwork, rather that they should be based on the concepts discovered from the data (Glaser and Strauss 1967). In this way, we return to notions of realism which we discussed in Chapter 6, where the ethnographer is the key instrument responsible for the research findings.

In locating ethnographic research findings firmly within the data, questions arise about the extent to which ethnographic analysis is able to produce knowledge which is able to generalize beyond the particular situation from which data were collected. While we would reject those views which suggest that widescale generalizations from ethnography are possible on the grounds that not only is such a view epistemologically flawed, but also that it fails to understand the rationale and scope of ethnography, this does not mean that we subscribe to a de facto position of parochiality. The emphasis which ethnography places on the identification of concepts grounded in the data succeeds in imbuing its findings with a significance which is capable of resonance beyond the specific case.

The emphasis on locating findings conceptually within the lived experience of social life allows readers/users to engage with those findings at a number of different levels. For example, they may wish to accept them at face value and see them only as relating to the particular situation from which the data upon which they are based was collected. Alternatively, they may look beyond those particular situations to engage the findings with other concepts and theories from other research in similar areas. A third option may be to reject the findings as irrelevant or simply wrong and by so doing seek to advance knowledge through an alternative perspective. Clearly, we would hope that the occasions when the third option was preferred would be much less frequent than the previous two alternatives which we identified.

Finally

It has been our intention throughout this text to encourage a careful and diligent approach to ethnography as a process, which would result in ethnography as a product, capable of enhancing understanding of particular aspects of social action specifically within educational settings, but also in other situations. Our position falls some way short of claiming that ethnographic research is able to yield generalizable findings, but as we have already stated, this is not an option for ethnography and as such we do not seek to make apologies for what researchers from a more positivistic tradition may see as a failing. The strength of ethnography as we see, it is in its capacity to offer conceptual and theoretical accounts of discrete social action. In doing this, we believe that ethnography is capable of engaging with issues which go beyond the particular and the discrete, not to general or macro-theoretical explanations but in such a way that there is connection and resonance with wider social behaviour, social processes and broader structural issues. Ethnography enables us to view education not in isolation but as part of the wider social and economic context of which it is a part, while at the same time holding onto the detail of the specific location, event or setting. While not ignoring the shortcomings of this approach, and every approach has shortcomings, for these reasons we have attempted to make a case for the use of ethnography for education.

References

Adler, P.A. and Adler, P. (1998) Observational techniques, in N. Denzin and Y. Lincoln (eds) *Collecting and Interpreting Qualitative Materials*. London: Sage.

Agar, M. (1980) *The Professional Stranger*, 1st edn. California: Academic Press.

Agar, M. (1986) *Speaking of Ethnography*. London: Sage.

Agar, M. (1996) *The Professional Stranger*, 2nd edn. California: Academic Press.

Allatt, P. and Dixon, C. (2002) Dissolving boundaries between employment, education and the family: the case of 17 year old A-level students engaged in full time schooling. Paper presented at British Sociological Association Annual Conference, University of Leicester, 25–27 March.

Altheide, D. and Johnson, M. (1998) Criteria for assessing interpretive validity in qualitative research, in N. Denzin and Y. Lincoln (eds) *Collecting and Interpreting Qualitative Material*. London: Sage.

Anderson, N. (1923) *The Hobo*. Chicago: University of Chicago Press.

Atkinson, P. (1990) *The Ethnographic Imagination. Textual Constructions of Reality*. London: Routledge.

Atkinson, P. (1992) *Understanding Ethnographic Texts*, Qualitative Research Methods Paper 25. London: Sage.

Atkinson, P. and Delamont, S. (1985) Bread and dreams or bread and circuses? A critique of 'case study' research in education, in M. Shipman (ed.) *Educational Research*. Lewes: Falmer Press.

Back, L. (1998) Reading and writing research, in C. Seale (ed.) *Researching Society and Culture*. London: Sage.

Baker C.D. (1982) Adolescent–adult talk as a practical interpretive problem, in G. Payne and E. Cuff (eds) *Doing Teaching: The Practical Management of Classrooms*. London: Batsford.

Ball, S.J. (1981) *Beachside Comprehensive: A Case Study of Schooling*. Cambridge: Cambridge University Press.

Bassey, M. (1999) *Case Study Research in Educational Settings*. Buckingham: Open University Press.

Bazeley, P. and Richards, L. (2000) *The NVivo Qualitative Project Book*. London: Sage.

Becker, H. (1966) Introduction, in C.R. Shaw (ed.) *The Jack Roller. A Juvenile Delinquent Boy's Own Story*. Chicago: University of Chicago Press.

Becker, H. (1974) Photography and Sociology, *Studies of the Anthropology of Visual Communication*, 1: 3–26.

Becker, H. (1986) *Writing for Social Scientists*. Chicago: University of Chicago Press.

Benn, T. (1998) Asma: The Struggle of an Asian Muslim Woman in Her Early Teaching Career. Paper presented to the Centre for Educational Development Appraisal and Research Case Study Conference, University of Warwick, Coventry.

BERA (British Educational Research Association) (1992) *Ethical Guidelines*. Edinburgh: SCRE for BERA.

Berger, P. and Luckman, T. (1967) *The Social Construction of Reality*. London: Allen Lane.

Bogden, R. and Biklen, S. (1982) *Qualitative Research for Education*. Boston: Allyn and Bacon.

Bolton, A., Pole, C. and Mizen, P. (2001) Picture This: Researching Child Workers, *Sociology*, 35(2): 501–18.

Brewer, J. (2000) *Ethnography*. Buckingham: Open University Press.

Brown, A. and Dowling, P. (1998) *Doing Research/Reading Research. A Mode of Interrogation for Education*. London: Falmer Press.

Bruner, J. (1986) Ethnography as narrative, in V. Turner and E. Bruner (eds) *The Anthropology Experience*. Illinois: University of Illinois Press.

Bryman, A. (1988) *Quantity and Quality in Social Research*. London: Routledge.

Bryman, A. (2001) *Social Research Methods*. Oxford: Oxford University Press.

Bryman, A. and Burgess, R.G. (eds) (1994) *Analysing Qualitative Data*. London: Routledge.

Bulmer, M. (1980) Why don't sociologists make more use of official statistics? in *Sociology*, 14: 505–25.

Bulmer, M. (1982) *The Uses of Social Research*. London: Allen and Unwin.

Bulmer, M. (1984) *The Chicago School of Sociology. Institutionalization, Diversity and the Rise of Sociological Research*. Chicago: University of Chicago Press.

Burgess, R.G. (1982) *Field Research: A Sourcebook and Field Manual*. London: Allen and Unwin.

Burgess, R.G. (1983) *Experiencing Comprehensive Education. A Study of Bishop McGregor School*. London: Methuen.

Burgess, R.G. (1984) *In the Field*. London: Routledge.

Burgess, R.G. (2000) Some issues and problems in cross-cultural case study research, in C. Pole and R. Burgess (eds) *Cross-Cultural Case Study*. Oxford: Elsevier Science for JAI Press.

Burgess, E. and Bogue, D. (eds) (1964) *Contributions to Urban Sociology*. Chicago: University of Chicago Press.

Burgess, R.G. and Morrison, M. (1995) *Teaching and Learning about Food and Nutrition in Schools*. Report to the ESRC on Grant no. L209252006. Swindon: ESRC.

Burgess, R.G. and Morrison, M. (1998) Ethnographies of eating in an urban primary school, in A. Murcott (ed.) *The Nation's Diet. The Social Science of Food Choice*. London: Longman.

Burrows, P. (2001) A trinity of dreamers – researched, researcher and 'reader,' in C. Boucher and R. Holian (eds) *Emerging Forms of Representing Qualitative Data*. Melbourne: RMIT Publishing.

Burton, D. (ed.) (2000) *Research Training for Social Scientists*. London: Sage.

Busher, H. (2002) The ethics of educational research, in M. Coleman and A. Briggs (eds) *Research Methods in Educational Leadership and Management*. London: Paul Chapman Publishing.

Carter, K. (1990) Teachers' knowledge and learning to teach, in W.R. Houston (ed.) *Handbook of Research on Teacher Education*. New York: Macmillan.

Carter, K. (1993) The place of story in the study of teacher and teacher education, in *Educational Researcher*, 22: 5–18.

Catterall, M. and Maclaran, P. (1997) Focus group data and qualitative analysis programmes, *Sociological Research On-line*, 2(1): http://www.socresonline.org.uk

Chatman, S. (1978) *Story and Discourse*. Ithaca, NY: Cornell University Press.

Christensen, P. and James, A. (2000) Introduction, in P. Christensen and A. James (eds) *Research with Children. Perspectives and Practices*. London: Falmer Press.

Coffey, A. (1999) *The Ethnographic Self: Fieldwork and the Representation of Identity*. London: Sage.

Coffey, A. and Atkinson, P. (2000) Hecate's domain: ethnography at the cultural cross-roads, in C. Pole and R.G. Burgess (eds) *Cross-cultural Case Study*. New York: Elsevier Science for JAI Press.

Coffey, A., Holbrook, B. and Atkinson, P. (1996) Qualitative data analysis: technologies and representations. *Sociological Research On-line*, 1(1): http://www.socresonline.org.uk/socresline/1/1/4.html

Coleman, C. and Moynihan, J. (1996) *Undergrounding Crime Data: Haunted by the Dark Figure*. Buckingham: Open University Press.

Connolly, P. (1998) 'Dancing to the wrong tune': ethnography, generalization and research on racism in schools, in P. Connolly and B. Troyna (eds) *Researching Racism in Education: Politics, Theory and Practice*. Buckingham: Open University Press.

Cooper, G. and Woolgar, S. (1996) The research process: context, autonomy, and audience, in E.S. Lyons and J. Busfield (eds) *Methodological Imaginations*. Wiltshire: Macmillan Press for the British Sociological Association.

Cressey, R.G. (1932) *The Taxi-Dance Hall: A Sociological Study in Commercial Recreation and City Life*. Chicago: University of Chicago Press.

Davis, J., Watson, N. and Cunningham-Burley, S. (2000) Learning the lives of disabled children: developing a reflexive approach, in P. Christensen and A. James (eds) *Research with Children. Perspectives and Practices*. London: Falmer Press.

Delamont, S. (1992) *Fieldwork in Educational Settings. Methods, Pitfalls, and Perspectives*. London: Falmer Press.

Denscombe, M. (1998) *The Good Research Guide for Small-scale Research Projects*. Buckingham: Open University Press.

Denzin, N. (1970) *The Research Act*. Chicago: Aldine.

Denzin, N. (2000) The practices and policies of interpretation, in N. Denzin and Y. Lincoln (eds) *Handbook of Qualitative Research*, 2nd edn. Thousand Oaks, CA: Sage.

Denzin, N. and Lincoln, Y. (1998) Entering the field of qualitative research, in N. Denzin and Y. Lincoln (eds) *Strategies of Qualitative Inquiry*. London: Sage.

Denzin, N. and Lincoln, Y. (2000) Introduction: entering the field of qualitative research, in N. Denzin and Y. Lincoln (eds) *Handbook of Qualitative Research*, 2nd edn. Thousand Oaks, CA: Sage.

Dey, I. (1993) *Qualitative Data Analysis. A User-friendly Guide for Social Scientists*. London: Routledge.

Dibb, S., Simkin, L., Pride, W. and Ferrell, O. (1997) *Marketing: Concepts and Strategies*, 3rd European edn. New York: Houghton Mifflin.

Dingwall, R. (1980) Ethics and Ethnography, in *Social Science and Medicine*.

Dwyer, K. (1982) *Moroccan Dialogue: Anthropology in Question*. Baltimore, MD: Johns Hopkins University Press.

Eisenhart, M. (2001) Educational ethnography past, present, and future: ideas to think with, *Educational Researcher*, 30(8): 16–27.

Elliott, J. (1990) Educational research in crisis: performance indicators and the decline of excellence, *British Educational Research Journal*, 16(1): 3–18.

Elliott, J. (1991) *Action Research for Educational Change*. Buckingham: Open University Press.

Ellis, C. (1993) Telling the story of sudden death, *Sociological Quarterly*, 34.

Ellis, C. (1997) Evocative autoethnography: writing emotionally about our lives, In W.G. Tierney and Y. Lincoln (eds) *Representation and the Text: Re-framing the Narrative Voice*. Albany: State University of New York Press.

Ellis, C. (1998) Exploring loss through autoethnographic enquiry. Autoethnographic stories, constructed narratives and interactive interviews, in J. Harvey (ed.) *Perspectives on Loss: A Sourcebook*. Philadelphia: Taylor and Francis.

Ellis, C. and Bochner, A. (1992) Telling and performing personal stories. The constraints of choice in abortion, in C. Ellis and M. Flaherty (eds) *Investigating Subjectivity: Research on Lived Experience*. Newbury Park, CA: Sage.

Ellis, C. and Bochner, A. (eds) (1996) *Composing Ethnography: Alternative Forms of Qualitative Writing*. Walnut Creek, CA: Alta-Mira Press.

Ellis, C. and Bochner, A. (2000) Autoethnography, personal narrative, reflexivity, in N. Denzin and Y. Lincoln (eds) *Handbook of Qualitative Research*, 2nd edn. Thousand Oaks, CA: Sage.

Erickson, F. (1986) Qualitative methods in research on teaching, in M.C. Wittrock (ed.) *Handbook of Research on Teaching*, 3rd edn. New York: Macmillan.

Erikson, K. (1967) A comment on disguised observation in sociology, *Social Problems*, 14: 366–73.

Erikson, K. (1968) On the ethics of disguised observation: a reply to Denzin, *Social Problems*, 15: 505–6.

Erikson, K. (1982) On the ethics of disguised observation: an exchange, in M. Bulmer (ed.) *Social Research Ethics*. London: Macmillan.

Evans, M. (1998) Using 'fictional' story in teacher research, *Educational Action Research*, 6(3): 193–502.

Faris, R. (1970) *Chicago Sociology 1920–1932*. London: Sage.

Fazzaro, C.J. (1998) Introduction. Paper presented as part of a larger presentation entitled Unmasking the White Knight: A Gramscian Image of Principal Haines at the Collaborative Action Research Network Conference, Anglia Polytechnic University, Chelmsford, October.

Fetterman, D. (1998) *Ethnography*. London: Sage.

Fielding, N. (1981) *The National Front*. London: Routledge and Kegan Paul.

Fielding, N. (1993) Ethnography, in N. Gilbert (ed.) *Researching Social Life*. London: Sage.

Fielding, N. and Lee, R.M. (1995) Confronting CAQDAS. Choice and contingency, in R.G. Burgess (ed.) *Studies in Qualitative Methodology Vol. 5: Computing and Qualitative Research*. London: JAI Press.

Fielding, N. and Lee, R.M. (1998) *Computer Analysis and Qualitative Research*. London: Sage.

Finch, J. (1985) Social policy and education. Problems and possibilities of using qualitative research, in R.G. Burgess (ed.) *Issues in Educational Research. Qualitative Methods*. Lewes: Falmer Press.

Finch, J. (1986) *Policy and Research*. Lewes: Falmer Press.

Firth, R. (ed.) (1957) *Man and Culture*. London: Routledge and Kegan Paul.

Foucault, M. (1977) *Discipline and Punish*. London: Allen Lane.

Galloway, S. and Morrison, M. (1993) *Supply Teaching: An Investigation of Policy, Processes and People in English Schools*. Report No. F215W. London: Leverhulme Trust.

Galton, M. and Delamont, S. (1985) Speaking with forked tongues? Two styles of observation in the ORACLE project, in R.G.. Burgess (ed.) *Field Methods in the Study of Education*. London: Falmer Press.

Geertz, C. (1973) *The Interpretation of Cultures*. New York: Basic Books.

Geertz, C. (1988) *Works and Lives: The Anthropologist as Author*. Stanford: Stanford University Press.

Glaser, B. (1992) *Emergence Versus Forcing*. Mill Valley, Ca: Sociology Press.

Glaser, B. and Strauss, A.L. (1967) *The Discovery of Grounded Theory*. Chicago: Aldine.

Gold, R. (1958) Roles in sociological field observation, in *Social Forces*, 36(3): 217–23.

Gomm, R., Hammersley, M. and Foster, P. (eds) (2000) *Case Study Method: Key Issues, Key Texts*. London: Sage.

Goodson, I. (1983) The use of life history in the study of schooling, *Interchange*, 11(4): 62–76.

Goodson, I. (ed.) (1990) *Studying Teachers' Lives*. London: Routledge.

Goodson, I. and Sikes, P. (2001) *Life History Research in Educational Settings*. Buckingham: Open University Press.

Griffiths, M. (1998) *Educational Research for Social Justice. Getting Off the Fence*. Buckingham: Open University Press.

Grimshaw, A. (2001) *The Ethnographer's Eye. Ways of Seeing in Anthropology*. Cambridge: Cambridge University Press.

Grint, K. and Woolgar, S. (1997) *The Machine at Work: Technology, Work and Organization*. Cambridge: Polity Press.

Guba, E. and Lincoln, Y. (1989) *Fourth Generation Evaluation*. Newbury Park, Ca: Sage.

Gubrium, J. (1988) *Analysing Field Reality*. London: Sage.

Hammersley, M. (1990) *Reading Ethnographic Research. A Critical Guide*. London: Longman.

Hammersley, M. (1992a) On feminist methodology, *Sociology*, 26: 186–206.

Hammersley, M. (1992b) *What's Wrong with Ethnography?* London: Routledge.

Hammersley, M. (1995) Who's afraid of positivism? A comment on Shilling and Abraham, *British Journal of Sociology of Education*, 16(2): 242–7.

Hammersley, M. (2001) On Michael Bassey's Concept of Fuzzy Generalisation, *Oxford Review of Education*, 27(2): 219–25.

Hammersley, M. and Atkinson, P. (1983) *Ethnography. Principles in Practice*, 1st edn. London: Tavistock.

Hammersley, M. and Atkinson, P. (1995) *Ethnography. Principles in Practice*, 2nd edn. London: Routledge.

Hargreaves, D.H. (1967) *Social Relations in a Secondary School*. London: Routledge and Kegan Paul.

Hargreaves, D. (1982) The teaching of art and the art of teaching. Towards an alternative view of aesthetic learning, in M. Hammersley and A. Hargreaves (eds) *Curriculum Practice: Some Sociological Case Studies*. London: Falmer Press.

Hargreaves, D. (1996a) Teaching as a research-based profession: possibilities and prospects. Teacher Training Agency (TTA) Annual Lecture, London.

Hargreaves, D. (1996b) Educational research and evidence-based educational research. A response to critics, *Research Intelligence*, 58: 12–16.

Harrison, B. (1996) Every picture 'tells a story': uses of the visual in sociological research, in E.S. Lyons and J. Busfield (eds) *Methodological Imaginations*. Basingstoke: Macmillan Press for the British Sociological Association.

Herrnstein-Smith, B. (1980) Narrative versions, narrative theories, *Critical Inquiry*, 7(1): 213–36.

Hine, C. (2000) *Virtual Ethnography*. London: Sage.

Hitchcock, G. and Hughes, D. (1995) *Research and the Teacher. A Qualitative Introduction to School-based Research*, 2nd edn. London: Routledge.

Homan, R. (1980) The ethics of covert research, *British Journal of Sociology*, 31: 46–59.

Homan, R. (1982) On the merits of covert research, in M. Bulmer (ed.) *Social Research Ethics*: London: Macmillan.

Homan, R. (1991) *The Ethics of Covert Research*. London: Longman.

Janesick, V.J. (1998) The dance of qualitative research design, in N.K. Denzin and Y.S. Lincoln (eds) *Strategies of Qualitative Inquiry*. London: Sage.

Jayaratne, T. (1993) The value of quantitative methodology for feminist research, in M. Hammersley (ed.) *Social Research. Philosophy, Politics and Practice*. London: Sage.

Jeffrey, B. and Woods, P. (1996) Creating atmosphere and tone in primary classrooms, in R. Chawla-Duggan and C. Pole (eds) *Reshaping Education in the 1990s. Perspectives on Primary Schooling*. London: Falmer Press.

Kelle, U. (1995) *Qualitative Computing: Using Software for Qualitative Data Analysis*. Aldershot: Avebury.

Kitzinger, J. (1994) The methodology of focus groups: the importance of inter-action between research participants, *Sociology of Health and Illness*, 16(1): 103–21.

Klein, G. (2000) Improving Inspection for Equality, *Improving Schools*, 3(2): 38–43.

Lacey, C. (1970) *Hightown Grammar*. Manchester: Manchester University Press.

Lather, P. (1991) *Getting Smart: Feminist Research and Pedagogy With/in the Postmodern*. London: Routledge.

Lee, R. (ed.) (1995) *Information Technology for the Social Scientist*. London: UCL Press.

Lee, R. (2000) *Unobtrusive Methods in Social Research*. Buckingham: Open University Press.

Levitas, R. (1996) Fiddling while Britain burns? The measurement of unemployment, in R. Levitas and W. Guy (eds) *Interpreting Official Statistics*. London: Routledge.

Lofland, J. (1971) *Analysing Social Settings*. Belmont: Wadsworth.

Lofland, J. (1974) Analysing qualitative data: first person accounts, *Urban Life and Culture*, 3(3): 307–9.

Luff, D. (1999) Dialogue across the divides: 'moments of rapport' and power in feminist research with anti-feminist women, *Sociology*, 33: 687–704.

McKinney, J.C. (1966) *Constructive Typology and Social Theory*. New York: Appleton-Century-Crofts.

MacNaughton, G., Rolfe, S.A. and Siraj-Blatchford, I. (eds) (2001) *Doing Early Childhood Research. International Perspectives on Theory and Practice*. Buckingham: Open University Press.

Malinowski, B. (1922) *Argonauts of the Western Pacific*. London: RKP.

Malinowski, B. (1935) *Coral Gardens and their Magic, Volume 2*. London: Allen and Unwin.

Malinowski, B. (1967) *A Diary in the Strict Sense of the Term*. London: Routledge.

Mandelbaum, D.G. (1982) The study of life history, in R.G. Burgess (ed.) *Field Research: A Sourcebook and Field Manual*. London: Allen and Unwin.

Marsh, C. (1982) *The Survey Method: The Contribution of Surveys to Sociological Explanation*. London: George Allen and Unwin.

Marshall, B. (1998) *The Oxford Dictionary of Sociology*. Oxford: Oxford University Press.

Mason, J. (1996) *Qualitative Researching*. London: Sage.

Matza, D. (1969) *Becoming Deviant*. Englewood Cliffs, NJ: Prentice Hall.

May, T. (1993) *Social Research. Issues, Methods, and Process*. Buckingham: Open University Press.

Mead, M. (1963) Anthropology and the camera, in W.J. Morgan (ed.) *The Encyclopaedia of Photography, Vol.1*. New York: Greystone Press.

Measor, L. and Sikes, P. (1991) Visiting lives: ethics and methodology in life history, in I. Goodson (ed.) *Studying Teachers' Lives*. London: Routledge.

Miles, M.B. and Huberman, A.M. (1994) *Qualitative Data Analysis. An Expanded Sourcebook*, 2nd edn. London: Sage.

Mills, C.W. (1959) *The Sociological Imagination*. Harmondsworth: Penguin.

Mizen, P., Pole, C. and Bolton, A. (1999) *Work, Labour and Economic Life in Late Childhood*. ESRC Final Report, Award No. L129251035. Coventry: University of Warwick.

Morgan, D. (1988) *Focus Groups as Qualitative Research*. Newbury Park, CA: Sage.

Morgan, D. (ed.) (1993) *Successful Focus Groups*. Newbury Park, CA: Sage.

Morrison, M. (1990) *School-focused INSET: A Case Study of Salford LEA*, CEDAR Reports 2. Coventry: University of Warwick.

Morrison, M. (1995) Teaching to time: supply teachers' lives and work. PhD thesis, University of Warwick.

Morrison, M. (1996a) A Curriculum for food. Places left at the Curriculum table?, *Curriculum Journal*, 7(1): 51–73.

Morrison, M. (1996b) Cross-cultural perspectives on eating: a hidden curriculum for food, in R. Chawla-Duggan and C. Pole (eds) *Reshaping Education in the 1990s: Perspectives on Primary Schooling*. London: Falmer Press.

Morrison, M. (1999) Researching public libraries and ethnic diversity: some black and white issues, in G. Walford and A. Massey (eds) *Studies in Educational Ethnography, vol. 2*. London: JAI Press.

Morrison, M. (2002) What do we mean by educational research? in M. Coleman and A. Briggs (eds) *Research Methods in Educational Leadership and Management*. London: Paul Chapman Publishing.

Morrison, M. and Benn, J. (2000) Educating eaters: cross-cultural approaches to food and eating in English and Danish schools, in C. Pole and R.G. Burgess (eds) *Cross-Cultural Case Study*. New York: Elsevier Science, for JAI Press.

Morrison, M. and Galloway, S. (1996) Researching moving targets: using diaries to explore supply teachers' lives, in E.S. Lyons and J. Busfield (eds) *Methodological Imaginations*. Basingstoke: Macmillan Press for the BSA.

Morrison, M. and Osler, A. (2002) Blame it on the methodology: research into race equality and school inspection. Paper presented to the Annual Conference of the British Sociological Association, University of Leicester, March.

Morrison, M. and Scott, D. (1994) *Libraries for Learning. Approaches to Book Resources in the Primary School*, Library and Information Report 97. London: British Library.

Morrison, M. and Watling, R. (2002) Building bridges and walking the high wire: developing education for citizenship in Northern Ireland. Paper presented at the Collaborative Action Research Network Conference, Northern Ireland, University of Ulster, Derry, November.

Murcott, A. (ed.) (1998) *The Nation's Diet: The Social Science of Food Choice*. London: Longman.

Musello, C. (1979) Family Photographs, in J. Wagner (ed.) *Images of Information*. Beverley Hills: Sage.

Nespor, J. (1997) *Tangled-Up in School: Politics, Space, Bodies, and Signs in the Educational Process*. Mahwah, NJ: Lawrence Erlbaum.

Oakley, A. (1981) Interviewing women: a contradiction in terms, in H. Roberts (ed.) *Doing Feminist Research*. London: Routledge and Kegan Paul.

Oates, C. (2000) The use of focus groups in social science research, in D. Burton (ed.) *Research Training for Social Scientists*. London: Sage.

O'Connell-Davidson, J. and Layder, D. (1994) *Methods, Sex and Madness*. London: Routledge.

O'Kane C. (2000) The development of participatory techniques: facilitating children's views about decisions which affect them, in P. Christensen and A. James (eds) *Research with Children. Perspectives and Practice*. London: Falmer Press.

Osler, A. and Morrison, M. (2000) *Inspecting Schools for Race Equality: OFSTED's Strengths and Weaknesses*. Stoke-on-Trent: Trentham Books for the Commission for Racial Equality.

Ozga, J. (2000) *Policy Research in Educational Settings: Contested Terrain*. Buckingham: Open University Press.

Palmer, V.M. (1928) *Field Studies in Sociology. A Student's Manual*. Chicago, IL: University of Chicago Press.

Parlett, M. and Hamilton, D. (1972) *Evaluation as Illumination: A New Approach to Illuminative Programmes* (Occasional Paper 9). Edinburgh: Centre for Research in the Educational Sciences.

Pink, S. (2001) *Doing Visual Ethnography*. London: Sage.

Plummer, K. (2001) *The Documents of Life 2. An Invitation to Critical Humanism*. London: Sage.

Pole, C. (1991) *Records of Achievement in Warwickshire. Herbert Marshall School. A Case Study*, CEDAR Report. Coventry: University of Warwick.

Pole, C. (1998) *Life Histories of Black Teachers: Giving Voice*, ESRC end of award report. Report No. R#to#to#to221688. Swindon: ESRC.

Pole, C. (1999) Black teachers giving voice: choosing and experiencing education, *Teacher Development*, 3(3): 131–328.

Pole, C. (2001) Black teachers: curriculum and career, *The Curriculum Journal*, 12(3).

Pole, C. and Lampard, R. (2002) *Practical Social Investigation. Qualitative and Quantitative Methods in Social Research*. Harlow: Pearson Education for Prentice Hall.

Pole, C., Bolton, A. and Mizen, P. (1999) Realizing children's agency in research: partners and participants? *International Journal of Research Methodology*, 2: 39–54.

Powney, J. and Watts, M.D. (1987) *Interviewing in Educational Research*. London: Routledge and Kegan Paul.

Pring, R. (2000) *Philosophy of Educational Research*. London: Continuum.

Prosser, J. (ed.) (1998) *Image-based Research*. London: Falmer Press.

Ramazanoglu, C. (1992) On Feminist methodology. Male reason v. female empowerment, *Sociology*, 26: 207–12.

Reckless, W. (1933) *Vice in Chicago*. Chicago: University of Chicago Press.

Redfield, R. (1955) *The Little Community*. Chicago: University of Chicago Press.

Reiner, R. (1996) The case of the missing crimes, in R. Levitas and W. Guy (eds) *Interpreting Official Statistics*. London: Routledge.

Reinharz, S. (1992) *Feminist Methods in Social Research*. New York: Oxford University Press.

Richards, T. and Richards, L. (1994) From filing cabinet to computer, in A. Bryman and R.G. Burgess (eds) *Analysing Qualitative Data*. London: Routledge.

Richards, T. and Richards, L. (1998) Using computers in qualitative research, in N. Denzin and Y. Lincoln (eds) *Strategies of Qualitative Inquiry*. London: Sage.

Richardson, L. (1990) Narrative and Sociology, *Journal of Contemporary Ethnography*, 19: 116–35.

Richardson, L. (1995) Writing stories. Co-authoring *The Sea Monster*, a writing story, *Qualitative Inquiry*, 1.

Richardson, L (1997) *Fields of Play: Constructing an Academic Life*. New Brunswick: Rutgers University Press.

Richardson, L. (2000) Writing: a method of enquiry, in N. Denzin and Y. Lincoln (eds) *Handbook of Qualitative Research*, 2nd edn. Thousand Oaks, CA: Sage.

Richardson, L. and Lockridge, E. (1998) Fiction and ethnography. A conversation, *Qualitative Inquiry*, 4.

Roach, P. and Morrison, M. (1998) *Public Libraries, Ethnic Diversity and Citizenship*. London: British Library Board.

Roberts, H. (ed.) (1981) *Doing Feminist Research*. London: Routledge and Kegan Paul.

Rudd, P. *et al.*, (2002) *Long-Term External Evaluation of the Beacon Schools Initiative 2001–2002*. Slough: NFER.

Sammons, P. (1989) Ethical issues and statistical work, in R.G. Burgess (ed.) *The Ethics of Educational Research*. London: Falmer.

Scheurich, J. (1997) *Research Methods in the Postmodern*. London: Falmer Press.

Schockley Lee, S. and Lee, K.W. (1998) Unmasking the white knight: a Gramscian image of Principal Haines. A paper presented at the Collaborative Action Research Network Conference, Anglia Polytechnic University, Chelmsford, October.

Schratz, M. and Steiner-Loffler, U. (1997) Pupils using photographs in school self-evaluation, in J. Prosser (ed.) *Image-based Research*. London: Falmer Press.

Schwartz, H. and Jacobs, J. (1979) *Qualitative Sociology. A Method to the Madness*. New York: Free Press.

Scott, D. (2000) *Realism and Educational Research*. London: Routledge Falmer.

Scott, J. (1990): *A Matter of Record*. Cambridge: Polity.

Seale, C. (1999) *The Quality of Qualitative Research*. London: Sage.

Shaw, C. (1930) *The Jack-Roller: A Delinquent Boy's Own Story*. Chicago: University of Chicago Press.

Shipley, P. and Moir, D. (2001) Editorial, in P. Shipley and D. Moir (eds) *Ethics in Practice in the 21st Century*. Proceedings of the Interdisciplinary Conference of the Society for the Furtherance of Critical Philosophy. Eynsham Hall, Oxford, October 1999. Oxford: Society for the Furtherance of Critical Philosophy.

Shipman, M. (1981) Parvenu evaluation, in D. Smetherham (ed.) *Practising Evaluation*. Driffield: Nafferton Books.

Silverman, D. (1997) *Qualitative Research: Theory, Method and Practice*. London: Sage.

Silverman, D. (2001) *Interpreting Qualitative Data. Methods for Analysing Talk, Texts, and Interaction*, 2nd edn. London: Sage.

Simons, H. (1995) The politics and ethics of educational research in England: contemporary issues, *British Educational Research Journal*, 21(4): 435–49.

Skilbeck, M. (1983) Lawrence Stenhouse: research methodology, *British Educational Research Journal*, 9(1): 11–20.

Sklair, L. (1999) Globalisation, in S. Taylor (ed.) *Sociology: Issues and Debates*. London: Macmillan.

Slee, R., Weiner, G. with Tomlinson, S. (eds) (1998) Introduction: school effectiveness for whom? *School Effectiveness for Whom? Challenges to the School Effectiveness and School Improvement Movements*. London: Falmer.

Smith, D.E. (1987) *The Everyday World as Problematic: A Feminist Sociology*. Boston: Northeastern University Press.

Sprokkereef, A., Lakin, E., Pole, C. and Burgess, R.G. (1995) The data, the team, the ethnograph, in R.G. Burgess (ed.) *Computing in Qualitative Research*, Studies in Qualitative Methodology, Volume 5. Greenwich: JAI Press.

Stake, R. (1978) The case study in social inquiry, *Educational Researcher*, 7 February: 5–8.

Stewart, D.W. and Shamdasani, P.N. (1990) *Focus Groups. Theory and Practice*. Newbury Park, Ca: Sage.

Strauss, A. (1987) *Qualitative Analysis for Social Scientists*. Cambridge: Cambridge University Press.

Strauss, A. and Corbin, J. (1990) *Basics of Qualitative Research: Grounded Theory Procedures and Techniques*. London: Sage.

Strauss A. and Corbin J. (eds) (1997) *Grounded Theory in Practice*. London: Sage.

Stroh, M. (2000a) Computers and qualitative analysis: to use or not to use . . .? in D. Burton (ed.) *Research Training for Social Scientists*. London: Sage.

Stroh, M. (2000b) Using NUD*IST version 4: a hands-on lesson, in D. Burton (ed.) *Research Training for Social Scientists*. London: Sage.

Stronach. I. and Maclure, M. (1997) *Educational Research Undone. The Postmodern Embrace*. Buckingham: Open University Press.

Sutton, R. (1992) Feelings about a Disneyland visit: photography and reconstruction of bygone emotions, *Journal of Management Inquiry*, 1: 278–87.

Tesch, R. (1990) *Qualitative Research. Analysis Types and Software Tools*. New York: Falmer Press.

Thrasher, F. (1927) *The Gang*. Chicago: University of Chicago Press.

Tooley, J. (1997) On school choice and social class: a response to Ball, Bowe, and Gewirtz, *British Journal of the Sociology of Education*, 18(2): 217–31.

Tooley, J. with Darby, D.J. (1998) *Educational Research. A Critique*. London: Ofsted.

Troyna, B. (1994) Blind faith? Empowerment and educational research, *International Studies in the Sociology of Education*, 4(1): 3–24.

Tyler, S.A. (1987) *The Unspeakable: Discourse, Dialogue, and Rhetoric in the Postmodern World*. Madison: University of Wisconsin Press.

Van Maanen, J. (1988) *Tales of the Field: On Writing Ethnography*. Chicago: University of Chicago Press.

Walker, R. (1981) Getting involved in curriculum research: a personal history, in M. Lawn and L. Barton (eds) *Rethinking Curriculum Studies*. London: Croom Helm.

Ward-Schofield, J. (1993) Increasing the generalizability of qualitative research, in M. Hammersley (ed.) *Social Research. Philosophy, Politics and Practice*. London: Sage.

Warren, A. (1988) Gender Issues in Field Research. Newbury Park, Ca: Sage.

Watling, R. (2001) Practical media work and the curriculum of the future, *Curriculum Journal*, 12(2): 207–24.

Watling, R. (2002a) Visual ethnography: research workshop. Materials prepared for the Doctoral Research Methods Training Programme, School of Education, University of Leicester.

Watling, R. (2002b) The analysis of qualitative data, in M. Coleman and A. Briggs (eds) *Research Methods in Educational Leadership and Management*. London: Paul Chapman Publishing.

Watling, R., Cotton, T., Hignett, C. and Moore, A. (2000) Critical reflection by correspondence: perspectives on a junior school media, mathematics and the environment workshop, *Educational Action Research*, 8(3): 419–34.

Webb, E., Campbell, D. *et al.* (1966) *Unobtrusive Measures: Nonreactive Measures in the Social Sciences*. Chicago: Rand McNally.

Weber, M. (1949) *The Methodology of the Social Sciences*. New York: Free Press.

Wirth, L. (1928) *The Ghetto*. Chicago: University of Chicago Press.

Wolcott, H. (1981) Confessions of a 'trained' observer, in T.S. Popkewitz and B.R. Tabachnick (eds) *The Study of Schooling*. New York: Praeger.

Wolcott, H. (1990) *Writing Up Qualitative Research*. Newbury Park, Ca: Sage.

Wolcott, H. (1995) *The Art of Fieldwork*. Walnut Creek, CA: Alta Mira Press.

Woods, P. (1985) New songs played skilfully: creativity and technique in writing up qualitative research, in R.G. Burgess (ed.) *Issues in Educational Research*. Lewes: Falmer.

Woods, P. (1990a) *The Happiest Days? How Pupils Cope with School*. Lewes: Falmer Press.

Woods, P. (1990b) *Teacher Skills and Strategies*. London: Falmer Press.

Woods, P. (1993) *Critical Events in Teaching and Learning*. London: Falmer Press.

Woods, P. (1999) *Successful Writing for Qualitative Researchers*. London: Routledge.

Yin, R.K. (1994) *Case Study Research: Design and Methods*, 2nd edn. Thousand Oaks, Ca: Sage.

Zorbaugh, H. (1926) *The Gold Coast and the Slum*. Chicago: University of Chicago Press.

Index

LIFE HISTORY RESEARCH IN EDUCATIONAL SETTINGS
LEARNING FROM LIVES

Ivor Goodson and Pat Sikes

It has long been recognized that life history method has a great deal to offer to those engaged in social research. Indeed, right from the start of the twentieth century, eminent sociologists such as W.I. Thomas, C. Wright Mills and Hubert Blumer have suggested that it is the best, the perfect, approach for studying any aspect of social life. In recent years, life history has become increasingly popular with researchers investigating educational topics of all kinds, including: teachers' perceptions and experiences of different areas of their lives and careers; curriculum and subject development; pedagogical practice; and managerial concerns. *Life History Research in Educational Settings* sets out to explore and consider the various reasons for this popularity and makes the case that the approach has a major and unique contribution to make to understandings of schools, schooling and educational experience, however characterized. The book draws extensively on examples of life history research in order to illustrate theoretical, methodological, ethical and practical issues.

Contents

144pp   0 335 20713 8 (Paperback)   0 335 20714 6 (Hardback)